AMERICAN STEAM LOCOMOTIVE

Brian Solomon

MBI

This edition first published in 1998 by MBI, an imprint of MBI Publishing Company, Galtier Plaza, Suite 200, 380 Jackson Street, St. Paul, MN 55101-3885 USA

MBI titles are also available at discounts in bulk quantity for industrial or sales-promotional use. For details write to Special Sales Manager at MBI Publishing Company, Galtier Plaza, Suite 200, 380 Jackson Street, St. Paul, MN 55101-3885 USA.

Library of Congress Cataloging-in-Publication Data

Solomon, Brian
    American steam locomotive / Brian
    Solomon
      p. cm.
    Includes index.
    ISBN 0-7603-0336-3 (hardback : alk. paper)
    1. Steam locomotives--United States
    I. Title.
    TJ603.2.S65 1998
    625.26'1'0973--dc21   97-52219

On the front cover: On a frigid July 6, 1996, Duluth & Northern Minnesota No. 14, a Baldwin-built Mikado, backs out of the station in Duluth for its run to Two Harbors. The 2-8-2 Mikado was one of the most popular steam locomotives in the twentieth century. More than 14,000 of the type were built in the United States after 1900.

On the frontis piece: Northern Pacific No. 328 drive wheels glint in the morning sun. This locomotive is operated by the Minnesota Transportation Museum, and is one of several 4-6-0 Ten-Wheelers serviceable in the 1990s.

On the back cover:
Top: Nickel Plate Road Berkshire No. 765 at Buffalo, New York in 1989. The Lima 2-8-4 Berkshire was one of the most significant evolutionary developments in steam locomotive technology during the twentieth century. It was also one of the last types built by commercial locomotives in the United States.

Bottom: Sleek looking streamlined steam locomotives, while relatively few in number compared to the vast hordes of utilitarian workhorses, were at the forefront of public attention. The Milwaukee Road's *Hiawatha,* seen here approaching St. Paul Minnesota, was among those used to haul the most deluxe, premiere passenger trains. Streamlined styles were varied and distinctive and conveyed speed, comfort, and style. The early designs were originally intended to improve the locomotive's performance while later streamlining merely promoted the illusion of speed. *Jay Williams collection*

All photos by the author unless credited otherwise

Edited by Lee Klancher
Designed by Katie Sonmor

Printed in Hong Kong

CONTENTS

ACKNOWLEDGMENTS

In researching and preparing the text and photographs for this book, I received considerable help from many knowledgeable individuals. Their assistance was indispensable and I am extremely grateful for their enthusiastic participation. Robert A. Buck of Tucker's Hobbies was especially helpful with proofreading and insight on the Boston & Albany. His collection of black and white prints has added a level of breadth to the book that could not have been obtained elsewhere. John P. Hankey lent invaluable historical perspective, factual information, and the generous use of his photography collection. John's insightful tours of the B&O have provided me a greater understanding of early industrial America than any text I have ever read. My father, Richard Jay Solomon, had more to do with the inspiration and writing of the text than anyone else. In addition to bringing me to see steam locomotives when I was very young and photographing the passing of the steam age, he volunteered to review the text. Ed King, a noted author himself, graciously offered his perspective on the steam locomotive and helped check for technical gaffes. George C. Corey also provided technical support and lent his collection of outstanding steam locomotive action photos. George had the privilege of observing and photographing many of the locomotives illustrated in this story. Lee Klancher, editor of the project, has been very helpful in offering his perspective along the way.

Tracking down photographs can be tedious, and John Gruber of *Vintage Rails* made this task much easier. His son Dick Gruber was also extremely helpful in directing my efforts. Dick's commitment and involvement in railway preservation is admirable. Like his father he is a volunteer at Mid Continent and lends a helpful hand wherever one is needed. Without people like Dick, there would not be active steam locomotives today.

I am also indebted to the many people whose actions made this book possible: Harry Vallas for technical perspective and English usage; Dean Sauvola for the steam locomotive diagram; Doug Moore for photographic support; Paul Hammond, Jay Slinde, and Ed Truslow of the Boone & Scenic Valley; Steve Bogan and Staci M. Roy of the Valley Railroad; Stan Searing of the Mid-Continent Railway Museum; Ed Williams of the Ellicott City B&O Railroad Station Museum; Steve Butler of the Kettle Moraine Railway; Clark Johnson and Nona Hill of High Iron Travel; Ellen Halteman of the California State Railroad Museum Library; Hans Halberstadt, James Speaker, Steve Solombrino, Jay Williams, Mike Del Vecchio, Don Marson, Brian L. Jennison, Jamie Schmid, Mel Patrick, Mike Gardner, Tom S. Hoover, Tom A. Hoover, and Mike Schafer of Andover Junction Publications; Robert W. Jones of Pine Tree Press; and my brother Séan Solomon.

Brian Solomon

INTRODUCTION
THE STEAM LOCOMOTIVE IN AMERICA

A lonesome steam whistle echoing up the valley is one of the most captivating sounds in American history. Billowing clouds of steam and smoke, steam locomotives were a sight to behold in the days when these behemoths reigned. Few machines have matched the steam locomotive's awe-inspiring power. These romantic images, cherished symbols of speed and strength, inspired an American love affair with steam engines.

Beyond all of the romance and nostalgia, steam engines were practical and powerful machines built to satisfy our nation's need to grow. The steam locomotive played a crucial role in the rapid emergence of the United States as a world power. With steam locomotives, railroads enabled Americans to cross the Appalachians and Rockies and settle the West; take coal from the ground to the furnace; bring crops and livestock to market; and do so faster and cheaper than ever before. The railroad allowed the unprecedented rapid growth of the United States—never had a continent been tamed and settled so quickly.

Urban centers on the East Coast that had suffered from inadequate transportation, such as Baltimore and Boston, thrived with the coming of the railroad. The building of lines like the Baltimore & Ohio was heralded with great celebration. Steam whistles were welcomed in small towns and villages across the country as the sounds of commerce. From Bellows Falls, Vermont, to Sacramento, California, the steam locomotive ushered in prosperity.

A mere 40 years passed from the introduction of the earliest practical steam locomotive in the United States to the completion of the first transcontinental railroad. At Promontory, Utah, on May 10, 1869, two steam locomotives were brought pilot to pilot, symbolizing the unity of the nation, an event announced by telegraph to cities and towns all over America. People celebrated wildly, and parades heralded the joining of rails. By the end of the century, railroads and steam locomotives had conquered virtually every corner of the nation: from the top of New Hampshire's Mount Washington to California's Pacific shore; from the woods of the Pacific Northwest to the swamps of Florida.

In most nations, railroads merely connected existing cities and towns; but entire regions grew up around the railroads in the United States. Towns bypassed by the railroads did not prosper, while towns that two railroads passed through became major centers. Little podunks like Hornell, New York; Altoona, Pennsylvania; Roanoke, Virginia; North Platte, Nebraska, and a host of others thrived and grew when the railroad came to town and set up shops and yards. Many towns owe their entire existence to the railroad.

As the railroads grew in importance, so did the United States as a world power. The perfection of the steam locomotive into a powerful, heavy freight hauler and fast passenger carrier had profound effects on the nation's population and industrial distribution. Commuting via train made it possible for home and work to be separated by miles rather than blocks. Factories could bring in supplies from all across the land, and major cities were not exclusively dependent on slow water transportation, often incapacitated in frozen winter months.

The railroad practically invented the patterns and methods for modern business. Railroads were the first big businesses and the men who ran or financed them, such as Cornelius Vanderbilt, Leland Stanford, Jay Gould, and J. P. Morgan, became fabulously wealthy. They wielded awesome power and lived like European nobility. In his day, J. P. Morgan, railroad financier, was considered one of the most powerful individuals in the world.

From the early wood burners with bonnet stacks to modern sleek, streamlined speedsters of the 1930s and 1940s, there was no mistaking American locomotives with those from any other place. These distinctly American machines grew to be the largest, most powerful locomotives on the planet.

Yet, one hundred years after they came to dominate American transportation, steam locomotives were replaced by more efficient types of motive power. The diesel-electric replaced the steam locomotive as the prime mover on North American railroads in less than a generation. This change was reflective of an even greater transportation revolution. The disappearance of the steam locomotive symbolized fundamental changes in industrial America.

While the loss of the steam locomotive was not the loss of the railroad, during three decades of the steam locomotive's decline, the American railroad drifted out of the limelight into the shadows. The steam locomotive evolved from a symbol of power and mobility to that of a nostalgic anachronism; simultaneously, the railroad lost its primacy. As the railroads switched from steam to diesel-electric power between 1925 and 1955, Americans switched from riding trains to driving cars and flying in airplanes. So today, while railroads continue to haul freight and, to a very limited extent, passengers with diesel-electric locomotives, there are far fewer trains. The majority of Americans are no longer directly reliant on the rails for transportation. An era has ended.

Nevertheless, steam locomotives invoke nostalgia for earlier times. Perhaps no other machine in the history of technology is better remembered or had a more distinct image.

1

STEAM PIONEERS

In a world where change is constant and rapid, it is difficult for us to fully appreciate how long it took for the steam locomotive to be developed. Nearly 100 years passed from the construction of the first stationary steam engine to the first successful steam locomotive in 1804. Another 20 years passed before the first common carrier steam railroad was built. Early rail lines were strictly used for mines and quarries.

In addition to the technological challenge of creating this new machine, the steam locomotive faced social barriers. Many people living in the early nineteenth century considered the concept of a mechanically powered conveyance absurd and impractical. Even after the steam locomotive was demonstrated as a viable alternative to the horse, those who were threatened socially or economically by steam railroads discouraged their progress.

Despite the tremendous challenges they faced, railroad pioneers prevailed. Once proven, the steam locomotive quickly changed the world.

The locomotive developed in a parallel rather than linear fashion. At approximately the same time, British and American inventors built steam carriages independent of one another. In both cases these designs were refined by many individuals and resulted in distinctively European and American steam locomotive designs. While the early British technology ultimately prevailed in America, its adaptation to American conditions produced a different locomotive evolution.

NEWCOMEN'S ENGINE

As with much of early American history, the story of the American steam locomotive begins, not in America, but in England. In 1705, Thomas Newcomen, a Cornish blacksmith born in 1663, assembled the first operating stationary steam engine. Newcomen perfected

---

Matthias Baldwin built his first steam locomotive in 1832, and by 1950 his company had built an estimated 80,000 steam locomotives. The builder's plate on this Denver & Rio Grande Western Mikado indicates it is the 58,585 locomotive completed by Baldwin. The company went on to build electric and diesel-electric locomotives; it finally ceased production in 1956.

The replica of Peter Cooper's locomotive, a diminutive machine now known as the *Tom Thumb,* rolls past the Ellicott City, Maryland, depot. Built in 1831 it is the oldest railroad station in the United States. Peter Cooper's engine was built in 1830 to show the directors of the Baltimore & Ohio that practical steam locomotives could be built domestically.

Peter Cooper publicly demonstrated his diminutive locomotive on August 28, 1830. It successfully hauled 13 tons at 4 miles per hour and reached speeds in excess of 15 miles per hour. On November 9, 1996, Ed Williams, director of the Ellicott City B&O Railroad Station Museum, assumes the role of Peter Cooper by posing with a 1927 replica of the locomotive. The original locomotive weighed only 1 ton, while this replica weighs roughly 7 tons.

Thomas Savery's suction engine and successfully built a steam-actuated pump by applying low pressure (about 10psi) steam to a piston in a sealed cylinder. This type of primitive engine was first used to remove water from flooded mines. Although a revolutionary pump, the engine employed an awkward, inefficient design with a single cylinder. Steam acted on the piston in only one direction—air actually moved the piston when the steam departed the cylinder, creating a vacuum. The action of the engine raised a beam that pumped water, and a counter weight was used to push the piston back to the top of the cylinder. This ponderously slow engine operated only four or five strokes per minute.

After introducing the engine, Newcomen improved the design. He found that injecting water into the cylinder enhanced the engine's performance, as did a network of ropes to open and shut the valves, which allowed steam in and out of the cylinder.

Others improved upon the Newcomen engine. While inefficient compared to later engines, the Newcomen engine provided a more economical solution to pumping water than either previous mechanical pumps or animal power. Seventy-five years after its introduction, more than 100 stationary steam pumps were working in Great Britain. These large, simple engines varied in output from 15 to 150 horsepower.

James Watt, a Scottish instrument maker working at Glasgow University, began experimenting with a Newcomen engine about 1763. During a 20-year period, he studied the mathematical relationship between heat and power and made several significant improvements to the steam engine. In 1769, he moved the steam condensing process from the cylinder to a separate chamber, thereby reducing the heat (power) loss and greatly improving the engine's thermal efficiency.

A more significant development came in 1781 when Watt built a double-acting, reciprocating steam engine. By sealing the cylinder and using valves to direct steam alternately to either side of the piston—thus pushing it back and forth—Watt harnessed steam power with much greater effect. In 1784, he further improved on his double-acting engine by converting the reciprocating motion to rotary motion using a beam attached to a set of revolving gears (known descriptively as "sun and planet wheels"). Watt's interest in the steam engine was not simply academic; he entered a business partnership with industrialist Matthew Boulton to build steam engines, and the two profited greatly from Watt's work.

THE FIRST STEAM LOCOMOTIVES

In 1769, while Watt was refining the Newcomen engine in Britain, Nicholas Joseph Cugnot built two steam carriages in France, today sometimes referred to as the first "steam locomotives." While these curious steam conveyances appear to be the first of their kind, they did not run on tracks and had virtually nothing to do with subsequent locomotive development. Cugnot's "steam carriages" were clumsy, three-wheeled contraptions designed to haul heavy artillery. Serious design flaws, coupled with unfavorable attitudes, resulted in very brief careers for these steam carriages. The disproportionately large boiler located ahead of a single front wheel made steering the carriages a precarious and difficult task. Despite the boiler's weight, it was incapable of

The *James I* was one of five experimental locomotives entered in the B&O's locomotive trials of 1831 in Baltimore. It is a good example of an early American attempt at building an inexpensive, lightweight, and comparatively powerful locomotive. In the early days of American railroading, most locomotives were imported from England. The B&O's trials were an effort to promote American locomotive building. This full-size model was built in 1893 for the Colombian Exposition. *John P. Hankey collection*

providing sufficient steam to maintain constant pressure; as a result the carriage was forced to stop frequently to gather steam. One of the carriages was preserved and can be seen at the Musée de Transports in Paris.

While Watt's contributions to the stationary steam engine were crucial to its development, he actively discouraged work on steam locomotives. Watt was distrustful of high pressure steam engines (those above 75 to 100 psi). His engines and Newcomen's operated at only very low pressures, and he viewed work on a steam locomotive as a waste of time. Despite Watt's prejudices, his assistant William Murdock went ahead and constructed an operating model locomotive using a diminutive 0.75-inch cylinder in 1784. When Watt and Boulton discovered Murdock's miniature experiment, they successfully discouraged him from further work on steam-powered vehicles.

The Americans took an early interest in steam power, though they were less successful than their British contemporaries. In part this was a result of inadequate industrial development and financial resources. In the late eighteenth century, several people adapted steam engines for marine purposes in the United States. One, an obscure inventor named John Fitch, experimented with steam technology in the 1780s or 1790s and built a variety of steam-powered contrivances including a working model of a locomotive with flanged wheels on tracks, the first known of its kind. While Fitch had visionary foresight and proposed constructing a full-sized locomotive to haul wagons over the mountains, he was unable to persuade his peers of the viability of his ideas, and his invention did not immediately lead to further locomotive development. While Fitch is often deprived of the credit he deserves as the first to build a steam locomotive to operate on rails, Fitch did inspire others to pursue steam technology. Many incorrectly credit Cornishman Richard Trevithick with the honor of the first railway locomotive. Nevertheless, Trevithick's locomotives, not Fitch's, are the direct technological ancestors of most later successful steam locomotive designs.

THE PEN-Y-DARRAN ENGINE

In 1797, at the age of 26, Trevithick built and tested a model double-acting stationary steam engine featuring a cylinder 1.5 inches in diameter and a 3.5-inch stroke, using the "dangerous" high pressure steam that had given Watt anxiety. Despite its dangers, Trevithick successfully harnessed high pressure steam and patented an engine. He moved from stationary engines to steam carriages and then, in 1803, he constructed his first locomotive designed to run on rails. It was this four- or five-ton machine—known for the Pen-y-Darran Iron Works in Wales and first operated on February 13, 1804—that often receives credit as the first locomotive on tracks. It operated at the relatively slow speed of four miles per hour. This distinctive locomotive had one cylinder with very unusual dimension—8x54 inches—and a large flywheel. The long stroke and flywheel are the trademark of this early attempt.

The *Pen-y-Darran* was distinctly different from the more familiar locomotives that descended from it: its piston did not directly turn the drive wheels but used a series of gears. Direct linkage of piston and drivers would come much later, in the 1820s. To generate sufficient power, Trevithick employed a return flue boiler that operated at about 50 psi—five times the pressure of Watt's engines. This boiler type employed an exhaust steam jet to produce a draft in the firebox, and thus a hotter fire. The result was more available steam than that produced in earlier designs.

With this locomotive, Trevithick also demonstrated that smooth wheels running on smooth rails had sufficient adhesion to haul a load up a grade. The locomotive was capable of hauling 25 tons, a remarkable feat for the time. Trevithick and the owners of the Pen-y-Darran Works had hoped this radical application of a steam engine would prove more economical than contemporary animal power. However, as with many subsequent early locomotives, this pioneer proved too heavy for its tracks. The laying of rails had long preceded the steam locomotive; many British industries, such as quarries and iron works, built tram railways of wooden tracks topped with iron straps to reduce wear. These simple railways enabled horses to haul greater loads by reducing friction. The tracks at the Pen-y-Darran Works were typical. They were lightly built and easily damaged by a four-ton locomotive, which broke the rails and pushed the track out of gauge.

In 1805, Trevithick constructed a second locomotive known as the Gateshead engine for use in Christopher Blackett's Wylam Colliery. While the *Pen-y-Darran* locomotive ran with flangeless wheels on flanged tracks, the Gateshead engine featured flanged wheels and ran on flangeless track, which evolved to be the normal arrangement for railways. This new design was not successful on the crude wooden tracks employed at the Wylam Colliery, and

The Baltimore & Ohio bought a fleet of vertical boiler 0-4-0 Grasshopper type locomotives in the 1830s. This one was built as the *John Hancock* by Gillingham & Winans in 1836, and it remained in service on the B&O until the 1890s. In 1927 it was rebuilt with a steel boiler and renamed *Thomas Jefferson* for B&O's Fair of the Iron Horse—a celebration of 100 years of American railroading. *John P. Hankey collection*

the locomotive was quickly redeployed by management as a stationary engine.

In 1808, Trevithick brought his third (and last) locomotive called *Catch-me-who-can* to London where he demonstrated it on a circular track by hauling wagons filled with curious riders at 12 miles per hour. This locomotive featured a more progressive design: the single cylinder and flywheel design of the first two efforts was abandoned, and the new engine employed two cylinders instead. This was also probably the first time a steam locomotive was used to transport people. Until that time tram railways had been used exclusively for hauling goods.

PUFFING BILLY

Over the next decade inventors experimented with locomotive designs. The brilliant George Stephenson was the most significant innovator. Born on June 9, 1781, in Wylam (near Newcastle-on-Tyne in England), George Stephenson spent his early years around collieries and mills where he learned the ways of Newcomen's stationary engines. In addition Stephenson observed the pioneer works of Trevithick and others, including John Blenkinsop and William Hedley. Hedley's locomotive *Puffing Billy*, constructed for the Wylam Colliery in 1813, had the greatest influence on Stephenson, inspiring him to build a better locomotive by improving the design.

Hedley had employed a return flue boiler similar to Trevithick's to provide steam for two large 9x36-inch vertical cylinders. The pistons pushed upward to beams suspended above the boiler, while vertical rods connected the beams to a network of gears that transmitted power from the engine to the drive wheels. While the *Puffing Billy*'s initial performance suffered because of its excessive weight (a problem rectified in 1815 by adding two sets of unpowered wheels for a more even weight distribution), it proved a successful locomotive and remained in service until 1862. It is preserved at the Science Museum in London and is one of the oldest existing locomotives.

BLUCHER

By contrast, Stephenson's first locomotive, completed in 1814, was less successful. He named it *Blucher* to honor Gebhard Leberecht von Blücher, a Prussian field marshal popular in England for heroic action in the decisive battle of Waterloo. Stephenson's attempts to improve on Hedley's design resulted in a more complex and less efficient machine that did not perform well. But Stephenson continued to refine his locomotive design, and within ten years he was the foremost locomotive builder in Britain and the world.

THE FIRST STEAM RAILWAY

The first common carrier (or public) railway, as opposed to a single purpose industrial tram, was the 12-mile Stockton & Darlington. Authorized by an Act of Parliament in 1821, this early railway encountered considerable political resistance, which delayed its construction. When it finally opened in 1825, the management hoped the advantages of rails would increase the load horses could haul (thus bringing economic savings) and provide an improved ride (as compared with traditional stage coaches) for both goods and passengers.

The railway's owners had initially planned to use horses to haul its carriages until George Stephenson successfully persuaded them to employ steam power instead. On September 27, 1825, amidst considerable celebration, George Stephenson operated his *Locomotion* with a train of 34 cars over the railway.

By 1825, Robert Stephenson had joined his father George in the locomotive business. Robert proved exceptionally gifted, making many significant innovations to locomotive design. Despite opposition from naysayers, Luddites, and anti-industrialists, the steam locomotive caught on quickly. By 1828 there were at least 50 locomotives in England.

Significant in the early development of the steam locomotive were the Rainhill locomotive trials, sponsored by the new Liverpool & Manchester Railway in 1829. Four steam locomotives entered the competition. The clear winner was Stephenson's *Rocket*, which attained a top speed of 29 miles per hour—extraordinarily fast for that time. This revolutionary locomotive rendered other designs obsolete. For the first time a locomotive combined the three principle elements later used in nearly all successful locomotives: a multitubular (fire tube) boiler, forced draft from exhaust steam, and direct linkage between the piston and drive wheels. Most earlier designs used a clumsy arrangement of gears.

Angus Sinclair notes in his 1907 book *The Development of the Locomotive Engine* that "When an engineer examines the *Rocket* and compares it with those [locomotives] previously in use, he seldom fails to observe that a leap had been made from complexity to simplicity of design."

There are several notable differences between the *Rocket* and later locomotives. Its drive wheels are located at the front of the locomotive rather than at the rear, and the pistons are located behind the drive wheels rather than in front. In its original configuration, the pistons were positioned at a steep angle to the drive wheels. The locomotive was later modified and the angle of the pistons made more level.

The superiority of the *Rocket*'s design was not universally recognized, and locomotive builders continued to experiment, producing a host of peculiar and mostly unsuccessful designs. Meanwhile, the Stephensons continued to perfect their locomotive design, improving upon the *Rocket* with the Planet type. With the latter, the Stephensons moved the drive wheels to the rear of the locomotive and the cylinders into the smoke box on a level plane with the frame of the locomotive. This was the first type of locomotive to use "outside frames" outside the wheels. Outside frames enjoyed considerable popularity and longevity in Britain. While they were used on some early American locomotives, by the 1840s American builders preferred inside frames and used them almost exclusively thereafter.

RAILROAD VISIONS IN AMERICA

The development and application of steam engines was not exclusive to England; Americans such as John Fitch—also experimented with the new technology. However, a general lack of supporting infrastructure and financial backing, combined with a less progressive attitude toward developing technology, hampered American locomotive development. While Richard Trevithick was perfecting his *Pen-y-Darran* locomotive, Oliver Evans of Philadelphia, Pennsylvania, experimented with steam propulsion. Evans, who was familiar with the Newcomen engine, recognized the value of high-pressure steam and devised his own engine, which operated at between 100 and 150 psi. He successfully installed his stationary engines in grist mills. In 1805, he demonstrated his most significant achievement: a 21-ton dredging scow, powered by one of his engines. This device was remarkable because it also was equipped with wheels for operation on common roads; Evans appropriately named his ingenious amphibious conveyance, *Orukter Amphibolis*. Like John Fitch, Evans believed that steam-powered locomotives could be used to transport goods and people, and Evans proposed the construction of a railroad between Philadelphia and New York. Unfortunately, like Fitch, he was unable to convince his peers, and few people took his ideas seriously.

Fortunately, Evans was not alone in his visionary railroad pursuits. In 1811, Colonel John Stevens, a Revolutionary War veteran who many years earlier had met John Fitch and seen his pioneering steamboat, began publicly advocating steam railroads. John Stevens did not merely preach: in

Philadelphia & Reading's *Rocket* was an inside-connected locomotive built by Braithwaite Milner & Company in 1838. Many early locomotives were "inside-connected," meaning the rods were located between the wheels and usually drove a cranked axle. A typical British import, the *Rocket* was shipped to the United States by sailboat. While it was named in honor of George Stephenson's *Rocket*, it should not be confused with its more famous namesake. *John P. Hankey collection*

The Sandusky was built in 1837 by Thomas Rogers at his Rogers, Ketchum & Grosvenor machine shop in Paterson, New Jersey. It used inside-connected cylinders placed on an incline. This full-sized wooden model was built in 1893 for the Columbian Exposition. *John P. Hankey collection*

Beaver Meadow Railroad's *Hercules* was built by Eastwick & Harrison in 1837. It is believed to be the first locomotive with equalizing beams for the driver springs and the second 4-4-0 built (the first 4-4-0 was built by Campbell in 1836). This model, built in 1893, displays prominent equalizing beams and a Bury boiler lagged with wood and horsehair felt. *John P. Hankey collection*

1815, while America was hooked on canal fever, he obtained a charter to build a railroad in New Jersey. But the allure of canals precluded any further progress for railroads at that time. Canal builders offered a comprehensible transportation solution to the United States' growing internal transportation needs, and politicians and investors were eager to support them. Colonel Stevens' railroad failed to attract serious investors and did not make it past the charter stage.

A true visionary, Stevens was not discouraged and continued to pursue his railroad dream. In 1825, he built an operating experimental "steam wagon," which he ran on his Hoboken, New Jersey, estate. This vehicle propelled itself using a cog and rack and featured a vertical boiler similar to those used on steamboats (which Stevens had also perfected). Ultimately, Stevens' efforts succeeded (and through Stevens, the vision of Fitch and Evans came to pass). His demonstration railroad attracted hundreds of curious visitors and his sons obtained a charter for the Camden & Amboy Railroad across New Jersey. Furthermore, Stevens' locomotive played a role in the development of a truly American line of locomotives.

EARLY AMERICAN RAILROADS

In 1826, Gridley Bryant completed the three-mile-long Granite Railway in Quincy, Massachusetts, to haul stone from a quarry for the Bunker Hill monument. This tram road used horses to pull the cars. While other primitive tram railways had been constructed in the United States, including one using wooden rails on Beacon Hill in Boston in 1795, the Granite Railway must be recognized as America's first railroad.

By the late 1820s several railroads began independently to explore the use of steam locomotives. In 1827, the Delaware & Hudson Canal Company began building a tramway to move coal from its mines to its canal at Honesdale, Pennsylvania. The same year, the Baltimore & Ohio Rail Road was chartered to build a common carrier railroad from Baltimore through the Allegheny Mountains to Wheeling, Virginia (later West Virginia) on the Ohio River. In 1828, the South Carolina Railroad chartered its line from Charleston to Hamburg. The Mohawk & Hudson Railroad was chartered in New York State to build a 16-mile line from

Albany to Schenectady in 1826 but did not begin construction until 1830. Also in 1830, John Stevens' sons, Robert and Edwin, chartered the Camden & Amboy line from New York to Philadelphia.

From the start, the locomotive requirements of American railroads were different from those of British railways, so divergence from British locomotive design began with these early lines. The different track design of American railroads presented one of the most significant considerations in their early development. By 1830, the railways in England exhibited a higher standard of track and roadbed construction. British steam railways preferred solid iron rails, called "fish bellies," designed to carry relatively heavy (7 to 11 ton) rigid-wheelbase locomotives.

In America, track was built to a lighter standard, in part because fledgling railroads had to import iron rails from Britain. A lighter standard of track prevailed. Early lines, with relative small budgets, chose to use cheaper ironclad wooden rails, and to compensate for the lighter track, American railroad pioneers sought innovative solutions to enable the operation of powerful and fast—but light—steam locomotives.

As the American railroads developed, the value of relatively heavy locomotives was demonstrated: larger locomotives were more powerful and hauled more, thus had a distinct economic advantage. Inferior strap-iron rails were gradually replaced with solid iron "T" rails of American design. Another problem leading to the adoption of iron rails was the propensity of the iron strips occasionally to break loose under the weight of a passing train. On rare occasions this caused grisly accidents as the iron straps would curl and thrust up through the floorboards of the passing train, impaling people riding in the coaches. Yet even as American railroads improved their track, the steam locomotive continued to outgrow those tracks. Railroads constantly faced the dilemma of locomotives that were too heavy for their rails.

As they pondered these sorts of questions during the 1820s and 1830s, Americans working for early lines made trips to Britain to investigate railway development and purchase equipment. When the first American railroads were being constructed, domestic firms were not prepared to supply the railroads with rails and locomotives. And even if the industrial elements needed for such items had been in place, many Americans believed that quality railroad supplies had to be imported. The production of railroad materials in the United States took 5 to 10 years to equal that of Britain. In the meantime, early railroads relied on imported British technology.

DELAWARE & HUDSON

In 1828, Horatio Allen, a 27-year old engineer for Delaware & Hudson (D&H) Canal Company, traveled to Britain to study railway technology and acquire iron rails and locomotives for the D&H's proposed line—reported to be the first $1 million construction project in history. He returned with four British locomotives: three from Foster, Rastrick & Company, of Stourbridge, and one from Stephenson. The most famous of these locomotives—and the only one known to have operated on the D&H—was the *Stourbridge Lion*, which arrived in New York on May 13, 1828. It was transported to the D&H tramway at Honesdale, Pennsylvania, and on August 8 Allen operated the locomotive—the first to turn a wheel

on a railroad in the United States (Stevens' experimental locomotive only operated on a circular demonstration track). The *Lion* was a 2-2-0 type with a horizontal boiler on a rigid frame similar to other British locomotives of the day. Like Hedley's *Puffing Billy*, it operated with vertical cylinders and overhead walking beams. The locomotive weighed seven tons—several tons heavier than Allen anticipated. Despite track that had been built for steam locomotives, the *Lion* and its kin proved too heavy for regular railroad operations. Its rigid base, coupled with inadequate suspension, was damaging to the lightly built track. The unfortunate failure of this first American steam railroad had a bright side. It provided the men who operated it, Horatio Allen and John B. Jervis, valuable experience. Both went on to other railroads and had greater success with steam locomotives.

BALTIMORE & OHIO

The Baltimore & Ohio (B&O) started along the same path of locomotive acquisition as the D&H, but soon adopted a diverging route. One year after Allen's trip, two of the B&O's engineers, William G. McNeill and George W. Whistler, also traveled to England to observe and acquire equipment. In 1829 Whistler ordered a Stephenson 0-6-0 locomotive for the B&O. The locomotive was constructed and shipped, but the railroad was denied its first steam locomotive when the ship carrying the engine sunk in the Irish Sea. This unfortunate accident led to one of the most interesting (and frequently misinterpreted) developments of early American locomotive history: that of Peter Cooper and his locomotive.

Shrouded by layers of corporate myth-making and embellishment, an accurate account of Peter Cooper's locomotive business has been elucidated by historian John P. Hankey. The truth turns out to be a good deal more complex and dramatic than the legend.

According to Hankey, Peter Cooper was a successful New York glue maker with investments in the growing port of Baltimore and an interest in mechanics. Following the unsuccessful experience of the Delaware & Hudson with its British built *Stourbridge Lion* and the B&O's bad luck with its not-to-be import, Cooper saw an opportunity to begin a domestic locomotive building endeavor.

Cooper designed an original locomotive, considerably smaller and lighter than British designs, and contracted its construction with local manufacturers in Baltimore. The resulting locomotive featured a very short wheelbase and weighed one ton (compared to the *Stourbridge Lion*'s seven), and was, therefore, better suited to the B&O's relatively tight curvature and light track. To power the locomotive, Cooper designed a multitubular vertical boiler that was conceptually similar to the one used by John Stevens in Hoboken five years earlier. The difference was that Stevens employed a water tube design (water passes through tubes heated by a fire—a popular design for marine applications), and Cooper used fire tubes (the hot gases from the firebox pass through tubes in the water). The firebox was designed to burn anthracite coal with a mechanical blower for draft, and the boiler operated at about 100 psi—roughly twice the pressure of its British counterparts. It featured a single small 3.25x13.5-inch cylinder, which produced an estimated 1.5 horsepower.

The Bury boiler was noted for its oversized hemispherical dome. While comparatively expensive to maintain, it produced ample quantities of steam and was one of the two most popular types of horizontal boilers in the 1830s and 1840s. This locomotive is believed to be Boston & Worcester's *Brookline*. Originally named the *Lion*, it was built by Bury in England in 1835, but was later rebuilt as a 4-2-2. Like many early locomotives, its drivers are inside-connected. *Author collection*

With this prototype Cooper demonstrated to the directors of the B&O that satisfactory locomotives could be built domestically—contrary to prevailing opinion—and their design would be better suited for the railroad's needs. Furthermore, he had both the resources and the know-how necessary to provide the railroad with its motive power needs. After testing on the B&O, Peter Cooper publicly demonstrated his diminutive locomotive on August 28, 1830. It successfully hauled 13 tons at 4 miles per hour, and reached speeds in excess of 15 miles per hour. Many years after Cooper's experiment, his locomotive was compared to a circus figure named *Tom Thumb*. The name stuck, and soon even Cooper began to referring to his diminutive locomotive as the *Tom Thumb*, though he never called it that in the 1830s.

The B&O's directors were impressed. But rather than immediately giving Cooper all of their locomotive business, the company planned a locomotive competition similar to the Rainhill trials of 1829. Five locomotives were entered in the competition, held between January and June 1831. However, Cooper's was not among them. The winning locomotive was the *York*, named for York, Pennsylvania, where the locomotive was constructed. Designed by Phineas Davis, this four-wheel, vertical boiler locomotive was similar to Cooper's, but featured two vertical cylinders.

These cylinders drove vertical main rods that connected to horizontal side rods, which powered the wheels. While the *York* proved the most successful of the five locomotives entered in the trials—one of the others experienced a catastrophic boiler explosion during the trials—it suffered from several design flaws, notably a peculiar but ineffective type of boiler, and was inadequate for regular service.

In September 1831, Cooper proposed building six locomotives of his own design for use on the B&O. The railroad agreed to his proposal, but Cooper failed to deliver his locomotives on the schedule promised. Embarrassed by this failure, he settled with the railroad by selling his locomotive patents to the B&O—a move that resulted in a tangent in American locomotive development.

After Cooper failed to build his locomotives, Phineas Davis adopted Cooper's ideas and improved upon his York design. Aided by Ross Winans, Davis constructed a second locomotive far more successful than the first. This was the *Atlantic* —the first "Grasshopper type"—which employed Cooper's vertical firetube boiler. The *Atlantic* weighed about seven tons and had two vertical cylinders. The Grasshopper design proved reasonably successful, and 20 such locomotives were constructed at B&O's Mount Clare shops. Some operated for more than 60 years and

The *Samson* was an 0-6-0 type built by Timothy Hackworth in England for the General Mining Association in Nova Scotia. It was the first steam locomotive in Canada and ran from the Albion Mines at Stellarton to a loading facility in Picton County, Nova Scotia. Built in 1838, it is a typical British heavy mining locomotive of the period. It is preserved today in Nova Scotia. Note the vertical cylinders and wooden lagging. *John P. Hankey collection*

were finally retired in the 1890s—a very impressive service life. Phineas Davis was killed in an early railroad accident, but Ross Winans went on to develop a line of locomotives incorporating Davis' and Cooper's designs.

SOUTH CAROLINA RAILROAD

As the B&O experimented with Grasshoppers, the South Carolina Railroad also took delivery of American-built locomotives—though of a different design. After his stint on the D&H, Horatio Allen went to work for the South Carolina Railroad as its chief engineer. Based on his experience with locomotives on the D&H, he convinced the railroad's directors to employ steam locomotives. While the directors had considered using horses, the long length of the proposed line made the economic advantages of steam power clear. In January 1830, the railroad committed to steam power—the first common carrier in the United States to do so. (The B&O—the first common carrier, which began construction two years earlier in 1828—had first opted for horse power.)

The South Carolina's first locomotive was designed by E. L. Miller of Charleston, and was constructed at the West Point Foundry in New York City. In 1830, the West Point Foundry was one of the most respected industrial facilities in the United States and had been producing boilers for steamboats for a number of years. It was well suited for the production of locomotives. The locomotive was delivered in the autumn of 1830 and named the *Best Friend of Charleston*. It weighed about 4.5 tons, featured a vertical firetube boiler that burned wood and operated at about 50 psi, and had two 6x16-inch cylinders and four 54-inch drivers in an 0-4-0 configuration. (In the Whyte system of locomotive wheel arrangement desig-

nation, the first number denotes the number of wheels on the lead unpowered truck, the middle set of numbers indicates the number of powered wheels, and the last set of numbers indicates the number of unpowered trailing wheels.) Following minor modifications to its wheels, the locomotive performed successfully in tests during November and December 1830. It produced about 12 horsepower and operated at 20 miles per hour—twice its anticipated speed. On January 15, 1831, the *Best Friend* became the first locomotive to haul a regularly scheduled passenger train.

Allen was so satisfied with the locomotive's performance that he ordered a second Miller designed locomotive from the West Point Foundry. This one, named *West Point* (for the foundry), was in most respects the same as the *Best Friend* except that it featured a horizontal firetube boiler instead of vertical one. Operating early locomotives was hazardous business. In June 1831, shortly before the *West Point* arrived for service, the *Best Friend* was destroyed by a boiler explosion, reportedly caused by an ignorant railroad employee who tied down the safety valve to prevent the locomotive from hissing. The locomotive was later rebuilt as the *Phoenix*, named for the mythical bird that rose from its own ashes to live again.

In 1831, Allen designed an experimental double-ended locomotive with a twin boiler fed from a single firebox. Like the South Carolina Railroad's other early locomotives, this machine was constructed at the West Point Foundry. It was delivered in February 1832 but was not a successful design and did not remain in service long.

This model of Delaware & Hudson's *Stourbridge Lion* was photographed in conjunction with Baltimore & Ohio's 1927 Fair of the Iron Horse. The original *Stourbridge Lion* was built in England and imported to the United States in 1829. It is believed to be the first locomotive to operate in the United States, excluding John Steven's demonstration engine. *John P. Hankey collection*

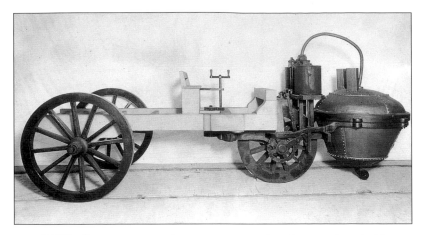

The first steam-powered conveyances were two steam carriages built by Frenchman Nicholas Joseph Cugnot in 1769. They were clumsy, three-wheeled contraptions designed for hauling heavy artillery. One of the carriages was preserved and can be seen at the Musée de Transports in Paris. This replica was built in the 1890s for the Columbian Exposition in Chicago. *John P. Hankey collection*

MOHAWK & HUDSON

In the early 1830s, the state-sponsored Erie Canal dominated transportation through the Empire State. However, the 17-mile long Mohawk & Hudson Railroad was completed in 1831. The Mohawk & Hudson's chief engineer, John B. Jervis (Horatio Allen's former boss on the D&H), ordered two locomotives for the railroad, one locally from the West Point Foundry and one from Stephenson in England. The domestic locomotive, named the *De Witt Clinton* after New York's governor and canal advocate, was ready for service first. On August 9, 1831, it became the first locomotive to operate in New York State and one of the earliest locomotives to haul a train in the United States. The *De Witt Clinton* was similar to the South Carolina's *West Point* as it had a horizontal boiler, 5.5x16-inch cylinders, weighed about 3.5 tons, and featured two 54-inch drivers in a 0-4-0 pattern. While the *West Point* and *Best Friend* were both designed to burn wood, the *De Witt Clinton* was originally intended to burn anthracite coal. However, the locomotive's disproportionately large smoke stack failed to produce a sufficient draft in the firebox. To correct this design flaw, it was soon converted to burn wood. The *De Witt Clinton* suffered from other flaws: it tended to spew hot embers, did not negotiate the railroad's track well, and derailed frequently.

Mohawk & Hudson's Stephenson locomotive, a 7.5-ton 2-2-0 "Planet type," was variously named *Robert Fulton* and *John Bull* (not to be confused with a similar locomotive of the same name that operated on the Camden & Amboy). While it also had minor mechanical flaws, its most serious problem was a combination of great weight and inflexible suspension that caused serious damage to the railroad's lightweight strap iron track. As Jervis did not have the funds to relay the entire line with superior iron "fish belly" rail, (the kind the Planet class was designed to run on), he searched for alternatives. His solution proved to be one of the most significant innovations in American locomotive design of his time.

A steam locomotive is a simple engine that converts fuel into energy, and energy into linear motion. The basic design of the reciprocating steam locomotive was established by the Stephenson *Rocket* in 1829, and while over the years the design was enlarged, refined, and improved upon, the principal arrangement remained essentially the same.

Virtually all reciprocating steam locomotives, from diminutive one-ton teakettles to monstrous articulated machines 118 feet long and weighing 772,000 pounds, follow a basic pattern. The locomotive consists of a boiler, cylinders, and wheels that ride on a frame. The locomotive boiler is made up of a firebox, flues, steam dome, and a smokebox.

Steam is converted to motive power in cylinders in which pistons are forced back and forth with steam pressure. This reciprocal motion is converted to circular motion with a piston rod and crosshead attached to a main rod, which connects to a crankpin on a main wheel. The other driving wheels are linked to the main wheel by means of side rods.

Steam admission and exhaust from the cylinder is controlled by valves operated by valve gear linked to the mechanism, and whose function is under the control of the engineer. Various other apparatus adorn the locomotive that are not required for basic motion but are necessary to its application as a functional railroad locomotive: Brakes to slow it once it is moving; bells, whistles, and lights; and various gadgetry to improve upon the locomotive's operation and thermal efficiency, including feedwater heaters, superheaters, and lubrication devices.

FROM WATER TO STEAM TO POWER

Water is added to the boiler—usually by pump, steam injector, or feedwater heater—and a fire is built inside the firebox, which heats the water and converts it to steam. The steam gathers in the space above the water, usually a steam dome, and is directed by way of a throttle valve through the dry pipe to the cylinders. (In a superheated locomotive the steam is directed through tubes that recirculate the steam through the flues to raise its temperature.)

Within the cylinder assembly are valves that regulate the steam's passage to and from the cylinders. Upon entering the cylinder, the steam expands and acts on the piston, which slides back and forth within the cylinder. The piston transmits force to a piston rod, which drives a crosshead and connects to a main rod. Crosshead guides hold the crosshead vertically in place. The main rods are attached to the main drivers by a crankpin. Side rods transmit the force of the main rods to the remaining driving wheels.

The piston is double acting, meaning steam acts on it in both directions. After steam acts on the piston, it exits the cylinder through the valves and exhaust passages and leaves the locomotive through an exhaust nozzle and the smoke stack. The nozzle/stack arrangement creates a vacuum in the smokebox that draws combustion gasses through the flues, which in turn draws air up through the grates on which the fire rests, allowing faster and more complete combustion. The draft is integral to the efficient operation of the engine; without effective draft, the fire would smolder in the firebox and fail to produce sufficient steam.

Valve gear connects the drive wheels with the valves and synchronizes valve motion. By adjusting the travel of the valves to limit steam input into the cylinder for a smaller portion of the piston stroke, the engineer can use the steam expansively for faster and more economical operation—this is called shortening the cutoff, or hooking up the engine. Hooking up reduces back pressure on the steam exhausting from the cylinder.

With full cutoff the steam acts on the piston through nearly the entire piston stroke; this is most advantageous when starting the locomotive, but inefficient once it is underway.

The travel of the valves is adjusted though use of the reversing lever—also called a Johnson bar. When the lever is brought to the center position, no steam is admitted to the cylinder at all. By bringing the reverse lever past center, the valve travel is reversed relative to the movement of the pistons. This reverses the order that steam enters the cylinders and changes the direction of the locomotive.

The quantity of steam going to the cylinders is regulated by the throttle lever in the cab, which operates the throttle valve. (Traditionally the throttle valve was located within the steam dome, but on most locomotives built after the mid-1920s the throttle valve is located outside the dome.) Once underway, a skillful engineer would choose to regulate the engine's power and speed through manipulation of the reverser, while only making gross adjustments with the throttle. The finesse of this operation eludes many accustomed to the throttle-heavy operation of internal combustion equipment.

Maintaining the level of water in the boiler is crucial to safe and efficient steam locomotive operation. An overfilled boiler will lead to water carryover, a situation where water passes through the throttle into the cylinders. This greatly reduces steam power and wastes energy, while also risking damage to the cylinders. Water cannot be compressed and can damage the heads, pistons, or main rods if it collects in the cylinder.

If the water level drops too low, it will fail to cover the top of the firebox, known as the crown sheet, and may result in burning the firebox. If this situation is left unchecked, the heat of the fire will weaken the metal and cause a crown sheet failure, which can result in a boiler explosion—a catastrophic, exceptionally violent event that usually destroys the locomotive and kills the crew.

The potential risk from boiler explosions resulted in development of safety devices designed to prevent them. To monitor the water level, sight glasses are installed in the cab of the engine to indicate the water level in the boiler. The glasses show the level of boiler water; the lowest point in the glass is well above the top of the crown sheet, giving an added measure of safety. The water glasses can become clogged, leading to a false sense of security among the crew. As a result, the sight glasses must be "blown down" on a regular basis to avoid false high readings. This is accomplished by directing pressurized water through the glass to eliminate mineral build up that may be clogging the glass and obstructing the free flow of water. Boilers are also equipped with safety valves and pressure gauges.

The safety valve is usually a poppet valve held closed by a spring that releases steam from the boiler before it reaches critical pressure, like on a tea kettle. Normally the safety valve is set to lift well below the maximum safe operating pressure (most boilers are tested at three times normal operating pressure). The pressure gauge indicates the pressure inside the boiler. Since the locomotive usually functions most efficiently at the highest safe pressure, it behooves the crew to monitor the pressure gauge and run the engine as close to tolerance as possible. When the safety valve opens, steam goes into the atmosphere without doing any work, which wastes both fuel and water.

The fireman maintains the fire by keeping a sufficient quantity of fuel in the firebox. Bituminous coal is the most common fuel used in American locomotives, and until the advent of the practical mechanical stoker after the turn of the century, the fireman delivered coal from the tender to the firebox with a shovel. The average fireman could shovel about 5,000 pounds of coal an hour, which for many years limited the practical size of firebox construction and thereby locomotive output.

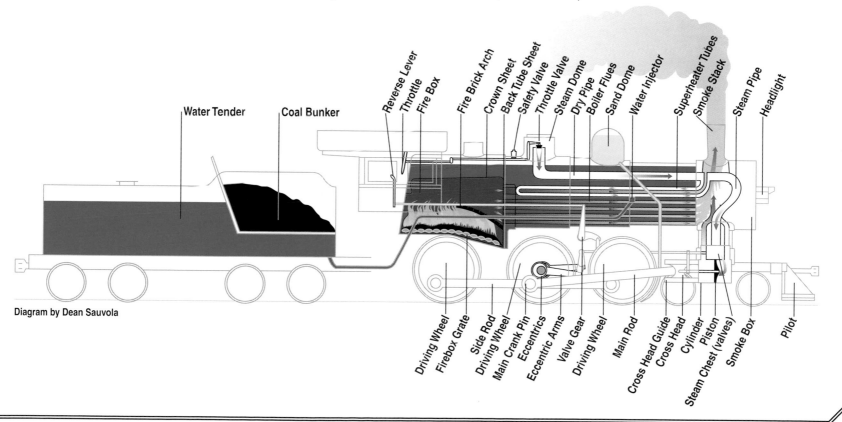

Diagram by Dean Sauvola

To allow for better handling on tight curves and over rough track, Jervis designed a locomotive that featured an unpowered two-axle pivoting guide truck to ride ahead of the drivers. This pivoting truck established a three-point suspension system—the pivot and the two drivers—that was vastly superior to all previous locomotive suspension systems. As with the *De Witt Clinton*, the West Point Foundry constructed Jervis' revolutionary new locomotive. Delivered as the *Experiment* in 1832, this 4-2-0 type locomotive featured an outside frame, 9.5x16-inch cylinders and very large 60-inch drive wheels. The locomotive performed exceptionally well, ran very fast (making speeds in excess of 60 miles per hour), and demonstrated that the guide truck would enable heavier locomotives to run on lightweight American track. By distributing the weight of the locomotive more evenly

The *De Witt Clinton* was built by the West Point Foundry for the Mohawk & Hudson. On August 9, 1831, it became the first locomotive to operate in New York State and was among the first locomotives to operate in the United States. The locomotive pictured here is a replica of the original. Few remnants from the early days of railroading have survived into modern times. *John P. Hankey collection*

Camden & Amboy's *John Bull* is a Stephenson-built Samson type. It arrived in Philadelphia from England in August 1831 and was assembled by Amboy's mechanic Isaac Dripps. The locomotive was modified between 1832 and 1833 to incorporate a "cowcatcher," the first application of this distinctly American device. Although altered, the original *John Bull* seen in this photograph has survived. It is now displayed at the Smithsonian Institution in Washington D.C. *John P. Hankey collection*

On November 9, 1996, the operating replica of Peter Cooper's locomotive rolls along on the original Baltimore & Ohio main line near Ellicott City, Maryland, re-creating the little locomotive's mythic journey from Baltimore in 1830. Peter Cooper spurred a distinctly American branch of locomotive development that ultimately concluded with Winan's Camels in the 1860s.

and guiding it through curves, this innovation limited damage to the track and reduced the likelihood of derailment. This locomotive originally burned anthracite but, in 1833, the railroad converted it to burn wood and renamed it *Brother Jonathan*. Jervis was so pleased with the guide truck, he had the *Robert Fulton* so equipped and ordered a second Stephenson locomotive built to similar dimensions as the *Experiment*. Jervis' pivoting guide truck soon became a standard feature on American locomotives.

CAMDEN & AMBOY

The Camden & Amboy, chartered in February 1830 to run across New Jersey between the Delaware River (opposite Philadelphia) and Raritan Bay (opposite New York City), was the realization of Col. John

Stevens' dream. Robert L. Stevens, John's son, was the railroad's first president and chief mechanical officer.

Aware of the problems with wooden strap iron rails, Robert L. Stevens was determined to use all iron rails, an expensive proposition in 1830. Dissatisfied with the prospect of using "fish belly" iron rails, Stevens designed his own style of wrought iron rail. Although responsible for other innovations, Robert L. Stevens may be best remembered for his invention of the "T" style rail— essentially the same shape of rail (though on a larger scale and made of steel)—in use on railroads today.

Like other pioneers, Robert L. Stevens went to England for locomotives to operate his railroad. He ordered a Stephenson 0-4-0 "Samson" type locomotive, which was delivered to Philadelphia in August 1831; this locomotive was the famous *John Bull* (originally named the *Stevens*).

The *John Bull* required final assembly in the United States, which was accomplished by Stevens' talented mechanic Isaac Dripps. His accomplishment was remarkable because Dripps had never before seen a steam locomotive, although he was familiar with steamboats. For its time, *John Bull* was a large locomotive. Weighing 11 tons, it had a 7-foot long Bury-type boiler (featuring a distinctive "haystack" or "beehive" firebox); its cylinders were 9x20 inches, with 54-inch drive wheels originally set for fivefoot gauge. Steven's foresight in using iron rail enabled the operation of such a large locomotive, yet it initially had difficulty negotiating sharp curves. To compensate for its flaws, Isaac Dripps modified the *John Bull* between 1832 and 1833. It is remembered in its rebuilt form for several reasons: it was one of the first locomotives to feature the ubiquitous cowcatcher and probably the first to carry a tender and use a cab to protect the crew.

Cowcatchers became popular on American locomotives because livestock in the United States often roamed free, whereas in Britain the livestock was contained or the tracks fenced. Dripps added the cowcatcher when he decided the locomotive would handle better if it had a lead truck. He added a set of guide wheels and placed a platform atop them to reduce the chance for derailment when livestock was struck. While the concept behind the cowcatcher caught on, the style that Dripps used did not. Instead, the grill-like triangular appendage, attached to the locomotive frame (rather than riding on its own set of wheels), became the standard form.

BALDWIN

As interest in building railroads grew, so did the need for quality domestically built locomotives. A number of builders soon entered the market, one of the most significant being Mathias W. Baldwin, whose name soon became synonymous with locomotives and railroading.

Baldwin began as a watchmaker, as did several other early locomotive builders including Phineas Davis, but he soon turned his interests to industry. Prior to 1830 Baldwin had constructed a small stationary steam engine, though this was not the main thrust of his business. In 1831, Charles Wilson Peale, operator of a Philadelphia museum, asked Baldwin to design and construct a small operating steam locomotive for display. This model proved popular and, as a result, the directors of the Philadelphia, Germantown &

Norristown Railroad commissioned Baldwin's first commercial locomotive project. Before beginning his work, it is believed Baldwin went to inspect two Stephenson locomotives: the Camden & Amboy's 0-4-0 Samson type, *John Bull*, then being assembled nearby in Bordentown, New Jersey, and a 2-2-0 Planet type on the Newcastle & Frenchtown.

Baldwin's resulting locomotive, named *Old Ironsides* (possibly for Oliver Wendel Holmes' 1830 poem), was a near duplicate of the Stephenson Planet type. It weighed 5 tons, featured an outside frame, a 7-foot long horizontal boiler, 9.5x18-inch cylinders, and a single pair of 54-inch driving wheels. Baldwin tested the locomotive in November 1832

type of locomotive was well suited to American track and sufficiently powerful for both passenger and freight trains of the period.

Baldwin was not as much an inventor as an innovator. Although he resisted radical new locomotive types and cannot be credited with much originality, he perfected existing designs and built reliable locomotives. Baldwin engines were noted for good performance and ease of maintenance. Among Baldwin's contributions to 1830s locomotive technology were the introduction of a superior pipe joiner that allowed for safe boiler operation in excess of 100 psi and innovations with parts standardization on his locomotives. Baldwin's success as a locomotive builder carried on long after his death in 1866. By 1950, his company, the Baldwin Locomotive Works, had produced about 80,000 steam locomotives.

By 1833 railroads were rapidly changing the nature of transportation in America. The number of railroad companies and the miles of track operated began to skyrocket. Meanwhile, a host of builders further refined the American locomotive. In 1836 Philadelphia locomotive builder Henry R. Campbell patented and constructed a 4-4-0 locomotive for the Philadelphia, Germantown & Norristown. This significant locomotive— the first of the *American* type wheel arrangement—used two pairs of coupled drivers and provided significantly greater tractive effort than the 4-2-0. However it and other early 4-4-0 types suffered from a number of design flaws, mostly relating to poor suspension, that precluded the new type from immediate acceptance by the railroad industry. In 1837 Joseph Harrison, of locomotive builder Eastwick and Harrison, improved upon the 4-4-0's suspension by introducing an equalization lever. This innovation allowed the 4-4-0 type to enjoy Jervis' three-point suspension. In its improved form, the *American* type was vastly superior to the 4-2-0, and despite resistance from Baldwin it quickly became the new general service locomotive. By the early 1840s the 4-4-0 was the dominant type of new locomotive in American service, and the 4-2-0 type faded into obscurity. Some 4-2-0s were rebuilt into 4-4-0s. The 4-4-0 design was refined over the following decade, and it was produced in great numbers by many builders, including Baldwin (who purchased Campbell's original patents).

By 1840, the railroad had grown from a technological curiosity to an accepted and needed form of transportation, while the American locomotive had assumed an established form notably different from that used in England. The 4-4-0 was the primary general service locomotive into the 1880s and remained in production on a limited basis nearly to the end of the steam era. Today it is without question the most identifiable type of locomotive. Other types have long since come and gone, but the 4-4-0 was the standard locomotive in the formative years of the railroad. It is this design that children of all ages will identify as a steam engine.

and experienced some initial difficulties. Once he worked the bugs out, however, it performed reasonably well. Subsequent Baldwin locomotives were based on Jervis' successful 4-2-0 *Experiment*.

For about 10 years the 4-2-0 type reigned as the standard American locomotive, largely because of Baldwin's promotion of the concept. This

2

THE FORMATIVE YEARS

The noontime sun bakes the sand and sagebrush of the remote central Nevada desert. Vast barren plains stretch between jagged brown mountains jutting into the horizon. The only sign of humanity is a lone steam train on a maiden voyage of epic importance. Leading the train is a shiny, colorfully painted Victorian gem: Central Pacific's *Jupiter*. Like most locomotives of the 1860s, it is a 4-4-0, a wheel arrangement known as the American type. It is one of thousands of similar locomotives used to haul trains around the United States. Like most locomotives of the time, it is a wood burner and is maintained handsomely by its attentive crew, who make sure its brass is polished, its rods are clean, and its boiler plate sparkles in the spring sun.

The Civil War has ended and the United States is on the verge of another historic event. *Jupiter* is headed east from California to Promontory, Utah, where a gala celebration is planned to mark the completion of the nation's first transcontinental railroad. There, *Jupiter*, representing the Central Pacific, will be photographed pilot-to-pilot with a similar locomotive, Union Pacific No. 119, another wood-burning 4-4-0, making these machines world famous locomotives.

More than 125 years later, long after larger, more efficient machines have replaced it as a prime mover, *Jupiter* still represents the classic American locomotive. For more than 30 years, *Jupiter* was in many respects the typical American locomotive. And it was this type of engine that made the United States a much smaller place. The hammering of the Golden Spike at Promontory drove that point home to all Americans, because the travel time from coast to coast had been effectively reduced from weeks to just a few days!

The American locomotive assumed its basic technological form by 1840, but it did not assume its distinctive American appearance until after 1850. During the 1840s, locomotives were not uniformly adorned with cabs, head lamps, pilots (often called cowcatchers), whistles, and bells, but by

---

Baldwin builders plate on a 2-6-0 Mogul type built in 1883 for the Tehuantepec & Interoceanic Railroad. This locomotive later operated on the Duluth & Northern Minnesota and is now displayed in Two Harbors, Minnesota.

Central Pacific's *Jupiter* met pilot to pilot with Union Pacific 119 at Promontory, Utah, on May 10, 1869, marking the completion of the Transcontinental Railroad, one of the most remembered events in railroad history. *Jupiter* was a 4-4-0 American type, typical of the ornate, brightly decorated locomotives of the period. This replica is seen at the Golden Spike National Historic Site at Promontory, Utah, one day before the 125th anniversary of the historic event. *Kyle K. Wyatt*

The Winans Camels, built by Ross Winans, were the last in the line of a branch of locomotive development begun by Peter Cooper. This full-sized wooden model, built in 1893 for the Columbian Exposition in Chicago, is one of the first Winans Camels, a short furnace type built in 1848. It was intended to burn soft coal. The extra pipe on the stack is to collect cinders. *John P. Hankey collection*

the early 1850s this equipment had become standard. Despite the growing predominance of the 4-4-0 in the 1840s, builders continued to experiment with a variety of unorthodox machines, the vast majority of which were failures with no lasting influence on future designs other than to preclude their duplication. However, by the early 1850s, American locomotive design was firmly established, and during the following decades there were few changes to the basic pattern of the locomotive, although a number of radical improvements were made. Several new wheel arrangements were introduced, and the locomotive was refined and greatly enlarged.

TRENDS IN DEVELOPMENT

Some innovations during this period are clearly the work of one individual, but often several people came up with similar ideas at about the same time. This can make the developmental history of the locomotive appear confusing. Furthermore, even when innovative designs demonstrated a clear superiority over earlier practice, they were rarely adopted universally. While this is partly attributable to poor communication between locomotive builders and railroaders, it is probably more a function of highly individualistic practices in the industry at that time. Locomotive building in the nineteenth century was an empirical craft not

an exact science, and it was difficult to demonstrate clearly the superiority of one design over another. Railroading has always been a conservative industry—the proven is usually preferred over the experimental. Also, catering to local economies and to strong personalities of individual railroaders was as important in the design of an engine as technological superiority. So just producing a locomotive with greater efficiency did not guarantee its acceptance. As a result, inferior, obsolete designs were often built for years after better machines could have supplanted them.

In addition, many new designs failed; the development of the steam locomotive has had a fair share of freaks, curiosities, and bizarre, ineffective hybrids. Most of these are not worth mentioning except to illustrate their inherent flaws or to demonstrate extreme aberrations of railroad technology. At the same time, some seemingly practical innovations, which may have resulted in better engines, were never adopted by the industry. Therefore, tracing the linear development of the steam locomotive can be difficult and muddled. For every state-of-the-art machine that was built, another example can be found of a tired design that remained in production to satisfy traditionalists.

The best understanding of locomotive development comes from following general trends in the industry, while noting specific innovations and landmark locomotives.

THE AMERICAN LOCOMOTIVE IN THE 1850S

Railroads in America experienced unequaled growth during the decade prior to the Civil War. Total track miles more than tripled, going from just 9,000 miles in 1850 to more than 30,000 miles in 1860. While railroads were being built all over the world, the impact of the railroad on

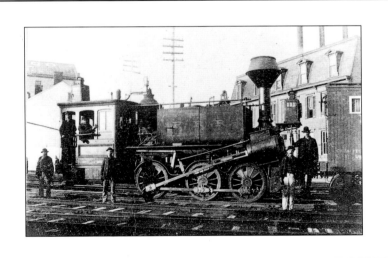

Pennsylvania Railroad 0-6-0T is a flexible-beam locomotive built by Baldwin in 1863. Locomotives with a long, rigid wheelbase were hard on cheaply built tracks. Baldwin designed the flexible-beam locomotive to provide high adhesion by placing the full weight of the locomotive on the drivers. The truck design allowed two of the three driving axles to move laterally while remaining parallel, which enabled the locomotive to negotiate tight curvature and poor track with ease. *Author collection*

C umberland Valley Railroad's *Pioneer*, a 2-2-2T built by Seth
Wilmarth of Boston in 1851, features a single pair of 54-inch driving
wheels. Seen here at B&O's Fair of the Iron Horse at Halethorpe,
Maryland, in 1927, the locomotive was later donated to the Smithsonian
Institution by the Pennsylvania Railroad, successor to the CVRR. Today the
Pioneer is exhibited at the National Museum of American History in
Washington, D. C. *John P. Hankey collection*

the United States is unparalleled. The growth of railroads in America was
equal to that of the entire rest of the world. Even Britain, where both the
railway and steam locomotive were born, could claim only a mere 6,400
rail miles in 1857. This rapid pace of railroad construction was possible
because American companies built lightweight lines, using cheap con
struction, rather than more substantial rights-of-way. They planned to
improve their physical plant using future profits, but in the meantime
these lightweight tracks necessitated light, nimble locomotives.

In these early years, locomotive manufacture required few special metal-
working tools or skills, and there was nothing so specialized that any competent
heavy machine shop could not handle. Many firms already engaged in machine
shop work found they could easily add a line of railway locomotives to their cat-
alog. Once the basic pattern for the American locomotive was established,
dozens of manufacturers took up locomotive construction. Some remained in
business for many years, such as Baldwin, which constructed locomotives for
more than a century, while others such as Covington Locomotive Works of
Covington, Kentucky, had an exceptionally brief tenure in the business.

INSIDE VERSUS OUTSIDE CONNECTION

By the 1850s, the American locomotive assumed its modern arrangement with inside frames (those located between the wheels) and cylinders
located outside the frames and connected to the drive wheels by outside

drive rods. These locomotives are "outside connected." Some early
American-built locomotives inspired by British practice used outside
frames (beyond the wheels) and had cylinders located just below the
smokebox and between the frames. In this arrangement, cylinders powered
a crank axle. Locomotives with this arrangement are known as "inside connected," because the cylinder connections are between the wheels.

A few early outside connected 4-4-0s operated with drive rods connecting the cross head to the *second* set of drivers; however, by the 1850s
this arrangement had been abandoned in favor of the drive rods connecting the *first* set of drivers. There were advantages to inside connected
engines. They had fewer problems with drive wheel oscillation because the
rods were connected to the cranked axle. However, since most of the critical moving components were located between the drivers, making them
difficult to reach, maintenance was far more cumbersome than on outside
connected locomotives. Easy access to the rods, crossheads, and other reciprocating gear was one of the principle reasons why American lines preferred outside connected locomotives. British railways were not as affected
by difficult maintenance because they had inspection pits at frequent, regular intervals along their lines, where they could work on inside gear with
less difficulty. American lines shunned the expense of building such elaborate maintenance facilities, preferring to do maintenance on level ground.
Eventually the difficulties associated with outside connected oscillating drivers were solved with improved driving wheel counterbalances.

BOILERS

The vertical boiler favored by several American builders, most
notably Ross Winans, was not used after 1841, and thereafter nearly all
locomotives used horizontal firetube boilers. During the 1830s and 1840s,
American builders favored two different types of horizontal boilers, both
of British design: Stephenson, and Bury types.

The Stephenson boiler, designed by the Stephenson Works, was char-
acterized by a more or less even diameter and slightly swelled region
around the firebox crown. This type was popular because it was relatively
easy to build and featured a comparably large firebox grate. The Bury boiler, designed by Edward Bury, was noted for its oversized hemispherical
dome. Its ample steam capacity made it desirable, but it suffered from a
small firebox grate and was more expensive to manufacture and maintain
than the Stephenson type. For a time the Bury boiler was popular with several large American builders, including Baldwin, Norris, and Rogers,
while the Stephenson boiler was popular with the New England builders.
The Bury was advantageous for railroads that used poor water because its
ample steam capacity handled foaming well. Attempts to enlarge these
early boiler designs failed, and a better boiler was needed.

In 1850 the Rogers Locomotive Works built a locomotive called the
Madison, which employed a new boiler design. Known as the Wagon Top,
this ingenious boiler combined the best features of both Stephenson and
Bury, and ultimately supplanted both to become the most successful boiler type in the United States. It featured a relatively large grate area, provided ample steam, and was easy to manufacture. However, it suffered

In the 1850s to 1870s locomotives were colorful, ornately decorated, and highly polished machines. Eureka & Palisade's No. 4, the *Eureka*, is a real gem, and typical of the style of that period. It is a wood-burning three-foot gauge American type built by Baldwin in 1875. Note the liberal use of polished metal and elaborate striping. Today the *Eureka* is privately owned. In September 1995 it ran a series of trips on the Durango & Silverton. *Kyle K. Wyatt*

from weak joints between the firebox and steam dome and required numerous stay bolts (long bolts used to support firebox sheets) and crown stays (rods and angle bars used to hold the firebox together) to provide the required strength.

Initially boilers were constructed of iron plates riveted together. In his book *A History of the American Locomotive*, John White notes that riveted steel boilers were introduced as early as the mid-1850s, but it took nearly 40 years for steel to fully supplant iron as the primary boiler material. The great cost of steel combined with its brittle qualities discouraged boiler makers from using it. Only as cheaper steel and more malleable alloys became available did steel construction take precedence over iron.

ALL THE BELLS AND WHISTLES

The phrase "all the bells and whistles" undoubtedly comes from those locomotive trappings that were not necessary for basic operation. In the early days train speeds were limited, and trains usually operated only during the daytime, so most early locomotives were not equipped with either headlights or cabs. But by the mid-1850s, railroads were operating trains day and night, year round, and in all sorts of weather, necessitating both headlights and protective cabs. By this time bells and whistles had also been universally adopted as warning devices, and a variation of the cowcatcher—originally adopted by Isaac Dripps for the John Bull—had become an identifying icon of the American engine. This "nonessential equipment" gave the American locomotive its distinctive character.

The steam locomotive whistle is perhaps its most endearing attribute. In the nineteenth century, locomotives were equipped with identifying whistles, and up until the end of steam, each railroad had distinctly different sounding whistles. The less romantic bleating of a diesel horn just isn't the same. Had some other warning device come to dominate the railroad industry, we might not have images of a lonesome whistle heralding the locomotive's arrival.

WOOD BURNERS

In the beginning, several railroads tried burning anthracite (hard coal) but generally found that wood was a more practical and economical fuel. John White explains that wood was abundant, inexpensive, easy to handle, and burned well, whereas anthracite was difficult to mine, expensive, and hard to kindle in a small firebox. So, with a few exceptions, American railroads burned wood in their first three decades. One drawback of wood-burning engines was their propensity to spew showers of sparks and burning embers from their stacks. Burning sparks were bad for business: they damaged equipment and merchandise, injured employees and passengers, and threatened buildings and the countryside along the right-of-way. As a result, a number of elaborate smokestack designs were developed to prevent sparks from leaving the locomotive.

The draft on the firebox caused by cylinder exhaust is key to successful steam locomotive design, and an effective smokestack must not interfere with this process or the engine's efficiency will suffer. One of the most popular and successful designs was the bonnet stack, which employed a conical matrix and screens to trap and contain sparks while allowing for free passage of gases from the cylinders and boiler. This large, inverted cone became a signature of woodburners from the period.

KING COAL

In the 1850s, new coal mines developed as railroads expanded into the interior of the country. These new mines, located primarily in central and western Pennsylvania, western Maryland, Virginia, and southern Illinois, produced softer bituminous coal that was cheaper to mine and easier to burn than anthracite; as a result, it was better suited to railroad locomotive fireboxes. The abundance of bituminous coal resulted in relatively low prices, which, coupled with a gradual rise in timber costs, resulted in a shift away from wood and toward coal as the primary fuel for locomotives. The railroads in the coal-serving regions were usually the first to make the conversion, spurred by the proximity of the fuel and links to the coal industry. Railroads far from the coal fields, such as those in northern New England and in the deep south, where timber was particularly abundant, were more reluctant to make the switch and converted much later. As coal became dominant, some railroads purchased coal mines to ensure their uninterrupted supply of the fuel, just as railroads had purchased forests in earlier years. By the 1890s, roughly 90 percent of American railroads were burning coal, although some obscure lines hung onto wood into the twentieth century.

The conversion from wood to coal fundamentally changed the locomotive and contributed to the enormous growth of American locomotives between the end of the Civil War and the turn of the century. Coal has a much higher BTU content than wood, and a fireman could provide a great deal more fuel to the firebox with coal than he could with wood. The result was more powerful locomotives.

Anticipating major changes in firebox construction, locomotive builders developed a number of radical firebox designs to accommodate these changes. John White indicates that these designs were largely ineffective and unnecessary. With a few minor modifications, the basic firebox design of the period intended for wood burning turned out to be well suited for bituminous coal. However, the anthracite burning locomotive required a broad, shallow firebox that accommodated a substantially larger grate to allow the slower-burning coal proper combustion.

One of the first effective changes made to the firebox to facilitate coal usage was the fire brick arch, which was independently introduced by both George S. Griggs of the Boston & Providence, and Matthew Baird of Baldwin. The fire brick is a row of bricks mounted on arch tubes inside

Baltimore & Ohio's Mt. Clare Shops built this 4-6-0 Ten Wheeler in 1863. It features a bonnet smokestack, wooden cowcatcher pilot, and a large kerosene headlight. The Ten Wheeler was the second most popular type in the mid-1800s, after the American type. Today this locomotive is displayed at the Baltimore & Ohio Railroad Museum in Baltimore.

The Advent of the Double-Ended Steam Locomotive

American locomotive manufacturer William Mason of Taunton, Massachusetts, was a creative designer and a progressive builder who always looked for ways to improve his locomotive business. In the late 1860s, he was inspired by the British Fairlie type, a small articulated locomotive design that combined locomotive and tender on one frame. He decided to adapt the Fairlie to American rails, and in 1869, built a relatively large, articulated double-ended locomotive with two boilers sharing a common firebox and two complete sets of running gear in an 0-6-6-0 wheel arrangement for the Central Pacific. Its name "Janus" was apt, because Janus was the Roman god of doorways (or gateways) and is often depicted with a two-faced head; he is associated with coming and going. (The first month of the year, January, is also named for him.)

In May of 1869, the Central Pacific and Union Pacific had joined rails at Promontory, Utah, completing the first transcontinental railroad, so perhaps Janus was also intended to be symbolic of that historic union.

However, Central Pacific rejected the curious Janus locomotive, and Mason was forced to search for another buyer. It was tested by several Eastern lines, including the Boston & Albany, and in 1871 Mason sold it to the Lehigh Valley. Angus Sinclair notes in *The Development of the Locomotive Engine* that "[Janus] did good work as a pusher, and was popular with the engineers, but it never was duplicated." It was scrapped in 1877.

Despite the efforts of Mason and others such as Horatio Allen, who had designed an experimental double-ender in 1831, the double-ended steam locomotive never achieved widespread popularity in the United States. But double-enders of a more conservative design than Janus found limited application in suburban passenger service on several railroads, the Boston & Albany among them. Much later, the double-ended design was almost universally adopted for electric locomotives and some diesel-electric locomotives. In other countries, double-ended steam locomotives were employed with considerable success.

In 1869, William Mason built a double-ended articulated locomotive for the Central Pacific named *Janus*. CP rejected the engine, and it eventually went to work for the Lehigh Valley. The double-ended steam locomotive had a long history in the United States, beginning with the *South Carolina* in 1832. Despite the efforts of William Mason and others, the idea never really caught on. *Author collection*

The 4-4-0 was the most popular type in North America, with more than 25,000 built. It was also one of the longest lived. This American type was built by the Canadian Pacific shops in September 1887 and remained in service on the CP until the early 1960s when it was used on lightweight branch lines. *Richard Jay Solomon*

the firebox at an angle above the grate to act as a partial barrier between the grates and the firetubes. This forces hot gases from the fire to take a longer, less direct path to the firetubes, ensuring more complete combustion. It results in more efficient coal use and a cleaner burning engine (and also allows the firebox to absorb more heat).

Prior to the introduction of coal fuel, copper was a primary material in firebox construction. John White explains that while copper fireboxes were more expensive than those made from wrought iron, they were more durable. However the corrosive nature of bituminous coal caused copper to deteriorate rapidly, prompting the use of wrought iron, and later, steel fireboxes and boiler tubes.

Coal-burning locomotives produced fewer sparks, and while they still needed a smoke stack, did not require the elaborate bonnet stacks that wood burning engines used. George S. Griggs pioneered the diamond style smoke stack for coal locomotives; essentially a modified version of the

bonnet stack but with a very different appearance. Later designers placed spark-arresting devices in the smokebox ahead of the boiler, eliminating the need for elaborate smoke stacks.

VICTORIAN MACHINES

The period from 1850 to the early 1890s was indisputably the most colorful era for American locomotives. The railroads decorated their engines in the ornate, eclectic style of the Victorian era. Boiler jackets were made from highly polished Russian iron, which could be made in a variety of metallic hues including blues and greens. The wheels were tastefully painted with bright colors: red, turquoise, and occasionally yellow. The cabs were finished with fine woods, arched windows, and decorated with elaborate patterns and gilded trim. Headlights and bells were supported by decorative cast iron platforms with complex patterns of gingerbread curls. The sides of the headlights, front of the engines, tenders, and panels on the cab were sometimes decorated with detailed paintings depicting the American landscape, wildlife, or portraits of significant personalities. Locomotives exhibited a liberal use of polished brass; the bells, steam domes, sand domes, cylinder heads and lagging, whistles, and cab controls would all glow with a yellow shine. While the use of paint was usually restrained, the overall effect was stunning.

No two locomotives were alike. Each had individual character and was the pride and responsibility of the crew who operated it. (During this period a crew was nearly always assigned a specific locomotive.)

Locomotives were often identified by names in lieu of numbers. Inspiration for locomotive names varied widely. Some engines took their persona from war heroes, such as Baltimore & Ohio's *Thomas Jefferson* and *Andrew Jackson*; others bore the name of the railroad's president or important officials or carried the name of principal points along the lines. More than one locomotive was named in honor of the country it served, thus several locomotives were named *America*. State names were popular too: there was Philadelphia & Reading's *Illinois*, and *Pennsylvania*, and Atlantic & St. Lawrence's *State of Maine*. Biblical and mythological sources were drawn upon, as were names from the animal kingdom: the Central Pacific operated several varieties of fox, including *Silver Fox* and *Gray Fox*.

As the railroads grew and their locomotive rosters swelled, colorful, ornately decorated locomotives gradually gave way to more Spartan utilitarian machines. Ultimately, practicality and financial concerns won over aesthetics. Rising locomotive construction costs and the burning of bituminous coal, which produced great quantities of black soot and grime, contributed to a trend toward plainness in locomotive decor. By the 1890s, locomotives were almost entirely devoid of eclectic frivolity, usually painted black, featured minimal amounts of brass, and were identified by numbers rather than names. Those that retained names were solely for symbolic purposes and not for operational identification.

WHEEL ARRANGEMENTS AND LOCOMOTIVE APPLICATIONS

While the 4-4-0 was the dominant type between 1850 and 1880, it was not used exclusively. Other wheel arrangements were used for specific applications. During the 1840s, 0-6-0 and 0-8-0 types had been developed for heavy freight service in graded territory. High adhesion was achieved by placing the full weight of the locomotive on the drivers. This arrangement sacrificed the locomotive's ability to track through curves, which greatly limited its speed. However, since heavy freight trains rarely operated at more than 10 miles per hour, tracking problems were less of a concern back then.

Some of the first 0-8-0s were built by Winans for the Western Railroad of Massachusetts. They were essentially enlarged versions of his Crab-type 0-4-0s and employed a vertical boiler and horizontally mounted 14.25x24-inch cylinders, which turned cranks that powered a geared drive. Four sets of relatively small drive wheels evenly distributed the locomotive's 22.5 tons, an exceptionally heavy engine for the time. Western ultimately operated seven of these locomotives, which were nicknamed "Mud Diggers" because they stirred up the crude dirt ballast of the period: four were built by Winans

The railroad helped shaped the growth of the United States and by the 1880s it was an established, accepted part of the American landscape. Steam locomotives could be found in all parts of the country and were relied on for basic transportation. On a stormy November evening a steam train rolls across the cornfields toward the depot in Strasburg, Pennsylvania.

and three by Baldwin under contract. Winans built a number of similar locomotives, albeit with horizontal boilers, for the Baltimore & Ohio.

Winans went on to design a more successful 0-8-0 that employed a more conventional cylinder linkage. White states that this type was the first mass-produced coal-burning engine that required an abnormally large firebox (23.5 square feet). To accommodate the firebox Winans located the engineer's cab above the boiler, giving the locomotive a unique humpbacked appearance. The odd-looking engines came to be known as "Winans' Camels." They typically weighed about 27 tons and featured 19x22-inch cylinders. The Winans' Camel, although a highly unorthodox locomotive, was a reasonably successful design, despite flaws stemming from a weak connection between the firebox and boiler. Winans built at least 200 Camels between 1848 and 1860 and some worked until the 1890s.

Matthias Baldwin had a novel approach toward heavy freight locomotive design. He recognized both the problems associated with rigid six-coupled locomotives and the need for greater tractive effort supplied by these locomotives. While some lines could accommodate a long rigid wheelbase, others could not. Locomotives with such a design were hard on lightly built American tracks. Yet, many of these lightly built lines had a need for high adhesion engines. Baldwin's solution was the flexible-beam locomotive: a locomotive that provided high adhesion with the full weight of the locomotive on the drivers, yet could negotiate tight curvature and poor track. It featured a truck design that allowed two of the three driving axles to move laterally while remaining parallel.

The first flexible-beam locomotive was built in 1842 and proved to be a very successful design. Originally only 0-6-0s were offered, but later 0-8-0s were also built. According to John White, Baldwin built 930 flexible-beam locomotives between 1842 and 1866, although they had fallen out of favor after other locomotive types were developed in the mid-1850s.

TEN-WHEELERS

In the late 1840s, the 4-4-0-type was enlarged and adapted into a 4-6-0-type. Before the Civil War, the 4-4-0 was commonly known as an Eight Wheeler, and its larger cousin the 4-6-0 became known as a Ten Wheeler. While the 4-4-0 later became known as the American type, the 4-6-0 held on to its original name and never gained a more colorful moniker.

The 4-4-0 American type was the standard locomotive during the formative years of American railroading. It was built by dozens of different builders and used in all kinds of service. Here Boston & Maine 4-4-0 No. 346, the *Reliance*, an 1879 product of the Hinkley Works in Boston, pauses for its portrait with a three-car passenger train on a tall steel trestle. *Author collection*

William Mason built locomotives at Taunton, Massachusetts, and was among the most inventive and innovative builders of his time. This locomotive, built in 1874 and named for its builder, was a "Bogie Engine," which rode on an articulated truck and used Walschaerts outside valve gear—the first known application of this later popular type of gear in the United States. *Author collection*

It is not clear who built the first 4-6-0, but Norris' *Chesapeake*, built for the Philadelphia & Reading, appears to be one of the first. The additional set of driving wheels made the 4-6-0 an ideal high-adhesion freight locomotive, and it was initially used primarily in heavy freight service. In the 1860s, the type gained popularity as a passenger locomotive, and by the 1870s it was beginning to overtake the 4-4-0 as the standard general-service engine. It became one of the most widely built locomotive types of the nineteenth century, and it remained popular as a branch line locomotive into the early twentieth century. In the 1890s, high-drivered 4-6-0s were used as fast passenger locomotives. In the 1920s, years after the type had been supplanted by larger, more powerful locomotives on most railroads, the Pennsylvania Railroad refined and adapted the 4-6-0 for suburban commuter service. Roughly 17,000 4-6-0s were built, and in the nineteenth century it was second only to the American type in popularity.

MOGULS

Six-coupled locomotives with a pivoting two-wheeled pony truck in a 2-6-0 configuration were introduced about 1860. (Locomotives with this wheel arrangement in a rigid configuration had been built in the 1850s but, because they did not feature pivoting front wheels, are generally not considered true 2-6-0s.) This type became known as the Mogul, probably in reference to the Indian Moghul Emperors, because the engines were comparatively large and powerful. White points out that the name Mogul was once used in reference to any large locomotive, and the specific reference to 2-6-0s may stem from a locomotive called the *Mogul* built in 1866 by the Taunton Works for the Central Railroad of New Jersey. By the 1870s, the term Mogul was established to mean a 2-6-0.

The New England builders were notoriously slow to adopt new designs. Even after outside connected locomotives had become standard elsewhere in the United States, some New England builders continued to construct inside connected locomotives. This 4-4-0 was built in 1851 or 1852 by the Amoskeag Manufacturing Company of Manchester, New Hampshire. Photographs of inside connected locomotives such as this one are very rare. *Author collection*

Early Mogul types suffered from inadequate suspension that resulted in frequent derailments. As with other early locomotives this was as much a function of poor track as a flaw in locomotive design. The suspension was vastly improved in the late 1860s when the superintendent of the Rogers Locomotive works, William S. Hudson, designed an equalizing radial truck that gave the Mogul type three-point suspension, putting the locomotive on par with the 4-4-0. This was the technological equivalent of Jervis' lead truck on the 4-2-0 and Harrison's equalizing lever on the 4-4-0, inventions that permitted large-scale application of those designs. The key to Hudson's equalizing truck is a centerpin bolster, which held it in place yet permitted lateral wheel movement.

Moguls were originally intended for heavy freight service, and often used in situations where 4-4-0s could not provide sufficient power or adhesion, such as steeply graded territory and "fast" freight service on level track. Among the first proponents of the Mogul type were broad gauge lines: the Erie Railroad and Louisville & Nashville, which operated unusually heavy freight trains over relatively steep grades. The Erie was known for its "big engines" and had been an early supporter of the Ten-Wheeler. In the mid-1870s, the Baltimore & Ohio used Moguls for passenger service on its mountainous "West End" between Cumberland, Maryland, and Grafton, West Virginia. In the twentieth century, some railroads, such as the Boston & Maine, employed Moguls in light suburban passenger service, by which time much larger machines were hauling freight.

In the mid-1870s, the Mogul's ascension as the premier American freight locomotive was cut short by the development and widespread acceptance of a larger, more capable machine: the 2-8-0. Still, some 11,000 Moguls were built for service in North America, and the locomotive remained in general production until well after the turn of the century.

THE CONSOLIDATION

The 2-8-0 type was developed to move heavy trains at reasonable speeds, especially on grades. The advent of the practical two-wheel leading truck used on the Mogul type naturally led to the development of the 2-8-0. As with other wheel arrangements, the 2-8-0 has more than one "first" application. John White credits a first of the type to the Pennsylvania Railroad, which rebuilt a Baldwin flexible-beam locomotive to a 2-8-0 configuration in 1864 or 1865. However he allows Alexander Mitchell the glory of designing the first "true" 2-8-0.

Mitchell was the master mechanic of the Lehigh and Mahanoy Railroad, an anthracite coal hauler in eastern Pennsylvania. He needed a locomotive that could haul heavy coal trains of 200 to 300 tons up the line's steeply graded routes at reasonable speed. While 0-8-0s could move heavy trains, they were slow, ponderous machines not suited for moving faster than a crawl. Mitchell was aiming to design a more agile machine. In 1865, he drew up plans for a 2-8-0 type, which used a radial two-wheel pony truck to help negotiate curves, and after some negotiating with Baldwin, finally convinced the veteran builder to construct his prototype. (Baldwin's conservatism did not lend itself to enthusiastic support of

Boston, Clinton & Fitchburg's No. 21, the *F.B. Fay,* leads a train at Walpole, Massachusetts, in about 1880. New England railroads often bought locomotives locally. This locomotive was built by Hinkley in Boston in 1872 and features 60-inch drivers and 16x24-inch cylinders. Note that it is a woodburner and uses link and pin couplers. Within two decades most locomotives would be coal burners with automatic "knuckle" couplers. *Author collection*

Mitchell's new type.) As the locomotive was being built, Mitchell's Lehigh and Mahanoy was merged (or "consolidated") with the ever-growing Lehigh Valley Railroad. The locomotive was named the *Consolidation* in recognition of this corporate union. The name stuck, and the 2-8-0 has since become known as the Consolidation-type.

This first Consolidation had an unusually large 25-square-foot firebox grate, which was necessary to burn anthracite. The locomotive had 48.5 inch drivers, 20x24-inch cylinders, and weighed 75,160 pounds without fuel and water. Many long wheelbase locomotives, including the Mogul and Consolidation types, employed "blind" or flangeless wheels on its middle drivers to facilitate negotiation of tight curvature. The guiding wheels of the pony truck and front and rear driving wheels were sufficient to keep the locomotive on the track.

The Lehigh Valley management was pleased with both the new engine and Mitchell, who became the master mechanic of the railroad's new Mahanoy Division. The Consolidation type, however, did not attain popularity for nearly another decade. In 1875 the Pennsylvania Railroad adopted the Consolidation as one of its "standard types," and other railroads began taking notice of the 2-8-0. Soon the Consolidation became the standard American workhorse, and railroads were ordering thousands of them. By 1900, roughly 9,000 2-8-0s had been built, the type remained in continuous production for 50 years, and ultimately some 23,000 Consolidations were constructed for domestic service. An additional 10,000 were built for use in other countries. Narrow gauge lines adapted the 2-8-0, and it was a particularly

Wilson Eddy of the Western Railroad of Massachusetts (later part of the Boston & Albany) built distinctive 4-4-0s. Eddy was a strong proponent of the straight boiler and disliked the steam dome. His locomotives were noted for their good performance and known on the railroad as Eddy Clocks. Boston & Albany No. 217, a typical Eddy Clock, poses with its crew at Palmer, Massachusetts. One of Eddy's 4-4-0s is preserved at the Museum of Transport in St. Louis, Missouri. *Robert A. Buck collection*

popular type for the steeply graded three-foot gauge lines in the West where high-adhesion locomotives were a must. Most standard gauge Consolidations used 57-inch drivers until about the turn of the century when 63-inch drivers became more common.

By World War I, the Consolidation could be found all over the country and in every type of freight service. It was the most common locomotive type used in the twentieth century and was employed in great numbers everywhere.

NEW ENGLAND BUILDERS SET PRECEDENT

In the 1850s, New England was one of the most active and innovative regions of industrial development in the United States, and a great many firms in the region were engaged in the construction of locomotives. Some had great success and others none at all, but designs from New England had considerable influence in the refinement of the American locomotive.

WILSON EDDY

Wilson Eddy, master mechanic of Western Railroad of Massachusetts (which became part of the Boston & Albany after a merger with the Boston & Worcester in 1867), designed and built exceptionally high-quality locomotives that set standards for the rest of the industry. His first locomotive was a high-drivered 4-2-2, designed in 1849 and built in 1851, named the *Addison Gilmore* after the railroad's president. It was intended for fast passenger service and had several dis-

tinguishing features. Its firebox grate was abnormally large for a wood burner of the period, 11.13 square feet as opposed to just 8 feet for the average woodburning passenger locomotive, which gave the engine more than ample heating surface. This feature alone was progressive because locomotives of that era were notorious for their lack of steaming capacity. Its single pair of 81-inch driving wheels was also abnormally large for the 1850s. Typical passenger locomotives of that time would have had drive wheels of only 60 to 70 inches. Huge driving wheels were not unique to Eddy's machine. A number of British locomotives featured enormous drivers, and the 6-2-0 Crampton types on the Camden & Amboy in New Jersey featured gargantuan 96-inch drivers. However, its most significant features were level outside-connected 15.4x26-inch cylinders riding over the front truck, a departure from the angled cylinders found on most locomotives at that time. In fact, the *Addison Gilmore* is believed to be the first American locomotive to feature this level cylinder configuration. By the end of the decade this was the prevailing method of arranging cylinders on American locomotives and remained so for the next 100 years.

Although his first machine was a 4-2-2, this type did not provide adequate adhesion, and most of Eddy's subsequent locomotives were 4-4-0s. He was a supporter of this traditional type and stood by it even into the late 1870s, when other locomotive types were demonstrating superior performance. His 4-4-0s were universally known as "Eddy Clocks" for their handsome proportions, exceptional reliability, and ease of maintenance.

Eddy employed some peculiar practices that bucked trends in the industry. His locomotives did not use the standard Wagon top boiler, instead they employed the straight boiler. This boiler type was a cylinder of uniform diameter that did not feature a steam dome but instead used a steam pipe to direct steam to the cylinders. It was a more stable boiler design but had less steaming capacity. By the 1880s his 4-4-0s, while admired, were notably antiquated. Still they had an undeniable influence on American locomotive design.

WILLIAM MASON

William Mason, a successful textile manufacturer in Taunton, Massachusetts, entered the locomotive business in 1852. The railroad boom was going full swing, and there was a large demand for locomotives. While established builders such as Baldwin and Norris claimed a fair percentage of the new locomotive market, there was still room for newcomers like Mason. In a relatively short time, Mason had earned the respect of the railroads and his peers by producing high-quality, innovative machines. Unlike Baldwin who discouraged new designs, Mason encouraged them and had a lasting effect on the industry. He embraced a number of concepts that resulted in better, more efficient locomotives.

He is most often credited with improving American locomotive aesthetics by building balanced, well-proportioned engines that established a pleasing standard that greatly influenced other builders. Many simply copied his basic designs and did little more than enlarge upon his basic plan. Like Eddy, Mason built locomotives with level outside

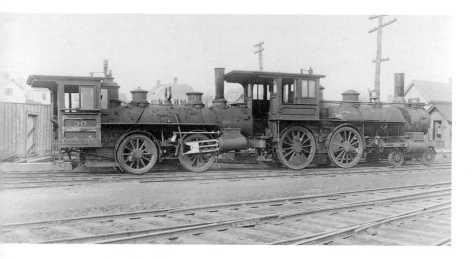

After locomotives had reached the end of their useful life, they were often placed in storage awaiting sale or scrapping. Between 1880 and 1900 the average size of new locomotives grew dramatically, rendering many older engines obsolete by comparison. The New York & New England dead line at Norwood contains two forlorn machines. The 4-4-0 on the right was built by the Rhode Island Locomotive Works in 1873. *Author collection*

Central Vermont No. 84, the *E. H. Baker*, poses at the roundhouse in White River Junction, Vermont. An 1883 product of the Rhode Island Locomotive Works in Providence, this engine is a typical New England–built 4-4-0 of the period. *Author collection*

Worcester & Nashua No. 7, the *Geo. T. Rice*, was built by the Taunton Locomotive Works in Taunton, Massachusetts, in 1864. Note the ornate woodwork and eclectic windows on the cab and the intricate designs on the headlight and tender. By the 1890s colorful machines such as this gave way to more spartan, drab locomotives. *Author collection*

cylinders. Rather than placing the cylinders above the front truck as Eddy did, Mason spread the lead truck wheels and placed the cylinders between them.

In the 1860s and 1870s, Mason promoted several unusual but progressive locomotive designs. His double-ended *Janus* was a unique application of the British Fairlie type (see sidebar). He also developed a "Bogie" engine that cleverly placed drive wheels in a pivoting truck, enabling the locomotive to negotiate sharp curves. Mason employed outside valve gear design by a Belgian, Egide Walschaerts, on his Bogie engines, rather than the traditional types of inside valve gear commonly in use at the time. (Inside valve gear, such as Stephenson's, operates between the drive wheels of the locomotive and usually takes its motion from cam-actuated eccentrics riding on the driving axle. Outside valve gear rides outside the driving wheels and may take motion from eccentrics attached to the ends of the main crankpins.) Mason is credited as the first American to use Walschaerts' valve gear, and he applied it to a number of his locomotives. He was harshly criticized for this practice, even though Walschaerts' gear was widely used overseas.

In a basic textbook written at the turn of the century, *The Development of the Locomotive Engine*, Angus Sinclair states "[w]e do not know of any subject that excites so much interest among the rank and file of railroad mechanical men as valve motions." He continues to write that Mason's critics felt that the Walschaerts gear had too many joints and that its pins suffered from unusually rapid wear. So while Mason's application of Walschaerts did not directly influence future designs, his use of the gear proved visionary and well ahead of its time. After the turn of the century, many years after Mason ceased production, Walschaerts' outside valve gear became widely accepted and eventually supplanted inside valve gears on most locomotives.

THE LOCOMOTIVE GROWS

"THE TREND OF LOCOMOTIVE BUILDING IN 1907 IS TOWARDS ENORMOUSLY HEAVY ENGINES [THOSE WEIGHING 200-TONS]." —ANGUS SINCLAIR, *THE DEVELOPMENT OF THE LOCOMOTIVE ENGINE*.

Amidst a cloud of steam, the morning *Express* rolled into the depot and its locomotive caught the attention of virtually everyone in earshot. While locomotives had been gradually getting larger and larger over the years, this engine was really *BIG*. It was one of the new Baldwin Vauclain compounds of an Atlantic wheel arrangement. Its drivers were seven feet tall, and its firebox was so big it needed a set of trailing wheels just to support it. While locomotives of all varieties attracted the attention of boys, this newcomer attracted grown men. Its huge drivers, compound cylinders, large firebox, and enormous boiler loomed large over the platform. Surely this was the biggest passenger locomotive anyone had ever seen. It could handle heavier trains and run faster than any locomotive that had come here before.

The engineer ignored the crowd around his engine, anxious for the departure signal so he could get back up to speed on the high iron. It was there that his engine was most impressive. Later it was heard that the *Express* had hit a speed of more than 100 miles per hour on the flats east of town!

Until the mid-1880s the size of the American locomotive had grown relatively slowly and had remained in proportion with those in the rest of the industrialized world. By the 1890s, however, critical changes in American railroad technology made the operation of significantly faster and heavier trains possible. These changes, coincident with a great expansion of railroad traffic, spurred the growth of the American locomotive. So, by the early twentieth century, the American engine had become much larger and more powerful than those used in the rest of the world.

A builders plate for a Pennsylvania Railroad 4-4-2 Atlantic type now numbered 7002. With its large firebox and tall drivers, the Atlantic was designed for fast passenger service. The original PRR Atlantic E2 No. 7002 is reported to have set the world speed record by attaining the remarkable speed of 127 miles per hour—an achievement that is in question because of the timing methods used. This PRR E2 Atlantic, preserved at the Railroad Museum of Pennsylvania, was renumbered in its honor.

Duluth & Northern Minnesota Railway No. 14 rolls along north of Duluth, Minnesota. This locomotive is a typical Mikado type built by Baldwin in 1913. Baldwin built 2-8-2s for Japan in 1897, and the type came to be associated with Japan about the time Gilbert & Sullivan's opera *The Mikado* was popular.

Size Comparison

According to John White, a typical 4-4-0 American locomotive in 1855 weighed about 50,000 pounds (not including tender), had a 14-square foot firebox grate, a boiler that operated at 110 psi, and produced an estimated 7,000-pound tractive effort. By the mid-1870s locomotives were only nominally larger and slightly more powerful. A 4-4-0 weighed 64,000 pounds and produced 10,500-pound tractive effort. The firebox grate had grown to 15 square feet, less than a 10 percent increase in 20 years.

By 1900, the typical locomotive was a 4-6-0 that weighed 165,500 pounds—more than three times the weight of a typical locomotive in 1855—and produced nearly four times as much tractive effort. The grate area and boiler pressure had doubled. However, the really explosive growth occurred over the next 40 years. By the beginning of World War II, some locomotives were nearly 15 times heavier than those in 1855, and nearly 5 times heavier than those in 1900. The Union Pacific 4-8-8-4 Big Boy articulated locomotives were among the heaviest reciprocating engines ever built. While atypical of late era steam power because of their extreme dimensions, the Big Boys provided a good illustration of the sheer size and power that the American locomotive had attained. They weighed 772,000 pounds, had a 150.5 square foot firebox grate, operated at 300 psi boiler pressure, and could deliver 135,400-pound tractive effort—almost 20 times that of the typical 4-4-0 in 1855. No locomotive outside the United States would ever approach the magnitude of a Big Boy's specs.

Why Build a Better Engine?

The small size of early fireboxes was the principal limiting factor in locomotive output. Attempts to build more powerful engines in the nineteenth century without dramatically increasing the size of the firebox usually resulted in failure. Traditionally, the firebox was located between the locomotive frames, over the rear driving wheel axles, restricting its size. The firebox could be made marginally longer, but it could not be made substantially wider. A locomotive burning bituminous coal rarely had grates larger than 15 square feet. Yet these relatively small machines satisfied most railroad needs in the first 50 years of railroading. There was little need for extremely powerful locomotives because weak track structure, primitive braking systems, imprecise train dispatching, and a lack of fail-safe, line-side signaling precluded the operation of either very fast or exceptionally heavy trains. Also, clumsy link-and-pin couplers and flimsy wooden car frames limited practical train lengths. Heavy, powerful locomotives could damage both the railroad's right-of-way and its relatively fragile rolling stock. The advent of several innovative technologies permitted the development of gigantic locomotives, including coal as fuel, steel rails, the automatic air brake, automatic coupler, steel framed rolling stock, automatic signaling, and a number of mechanical innovations in locomotive technology.

WESTINGHOUSE AIR BRAKE

One of the first significant improvements to railroad operation was the perfection of the air brake by George Westinghouse in 1869. Prior to the development of the air brake, trains were stopped by a combination of reversing the locomotive and manual hand brakes. Trains would usually have several brakemen who, on a whistle signal from the engineer, would apply or release brakes by literally jumping from car to car to turn the brake wheels. This system was inefficient, slow, and dangerous. Operating heavy trains on grades was particularly hazardous, and runaway trains were not uncommon. Pity the poor brakeman who had to ride the top of a freight car on a freezing winter night while descending a steep mountain pass. The slightest wrong move could be fatal, and many brakemen lost their lives.

Westinghouse's first air-brake system—known as the straight air brake—used a steam-powered pump on the locomotive to compress air into a pressurized reservoir. Sealed rubber hoses, called a brake pipe, connected the engine and cars. The flow of air was controlled by the engineer who could remotely set brakes throughout the train by releasing the air

The 1890s brought a push toward larger, faster, and more powerful locomotives. This rare action photograph, taken between 1895 and 1900, shows Philadelphia & Reading No. 385 sprinting between Jersey City and Philadelphia. It is an unusual 4-2-2 type Baldwin-built Vauclain compound. Note the two sets of cylinders and the Camelback configuration. Trailing wheels allowed for a larger firebox, and while it was a fast locomotive, it could only effectively haul four or five cars. *John P. Hankey collection*

Frisco 4-8-2 Mountain No. 1522 rolls along at Sargeant, Missouri, on July 19, 1994. The first Mountain types were built for passenger service on the Chesapeake & Ohio in 1911. Later the type became popular in the United States as a dual service locomotive. The type was a logical enlargement of both the primarily passenger 4-6-2 Pacific type and the primarily freight 2-8-2 Mikado. *Brian Jennison*

S team locomotives used lots of water, and as a result water tanks were spotted at strategic locations along the line, usually at engine houses and important stations. On a cold February 18, 1996, Saginaw Timber Company No. 2 takes on water at North Freedom, Wisconsin. This locomotive is a 2-8-2 Mikado. The 2-8-2 became a popular freight locomotive following the turn of the century.

from the reservoir into the brake pipe. The air would act on pistons within cylinders on each car, which, acting through a system of rods and levers called "brake rigging," pressed the brake shoes against the train wheels. This system was a big improvement over the traditional method of braking, but it had several inherent flaws. As the air pressure built from the front to the rear, the front train cars slowed before those at the rear. This resulted in rough handling as the rear cars bunched up. The system's biggest defect was that it was not fail-safe: a loss in air pressure would cause the brakes to release.

In 1871, Westinghouse introduced an improved version called the automatic air brake. The principles behind this system were similar to the first,

but with a few important modifications. An air reservoir, brake cylinder, and a control valve were located on each car. The control valve was called a triple valve in the early days because it had three functions: charging the car's reservoir, applying the brakes by putting air from the reservoir into the cylinder, and releasing the brakes by exhausting the air from the cylinder to the atmosphere. After charging the train's brake system with air at the proper pressure (usually 75 pounds for freight, 100 pounds for passenger), the engineer applied the brakes by letting air out of the brake pipe; the strength of the brake application was proportional to the amount of air let out. The control valve on the car would respond to changes in the pressure in the train line, applying and releasing the brakes at the engineer's command. The advan-

An integral part of a steam locomotive is the valve gear, which allows the engineer to control the power and direction of the engine. As locomotives became larger, there was less room for inside valve gears between the drivers. As a result, outside valve gears became popular. Walschaerts and Baker were the two most popular types of outside valve gears. This is an example of a Baker valve gear on Strasburg No. 475, a former Norfolk & Western 4-8-0 Twelve Wheeler.

Two of the best known icons of American railroading, the steam locomotive and the caboose, are both obsolete remnants of an earlier era. The steam locomotive was supplanted by the diesel-electric, while the caboose riding on the end of a freight train was replaced by an electronic box with a flashing light. Northern Pacific Ten Wheeler No. 328 hauls a caboose around the wye at Dresser, Wisconsin.

CAMELBACKS

The coal hauling railroads in eastern Pennsylvania, collectively known as the Anthracite Roads, had access to ample supplies of cheap anthracite slack called culm, but did not have an efficient means to burn it. Conventional locomotive fireboxes were not well suited to slow-burning anthracite, and attempts to burn this fuel had not met with much success.

In 1877, the general manager of the Philadelphia & Reading, John E. Wootten, solved this problem by developing a shallow wide firebox that could provide adequate grate area to allow complete combustion of the slow burning slack. Because his firebox had 2.5 times more grate area than the typical steam locomotive of the period, it was too big to ride between the locomotive frames—where the firebox was traditionally located. As a result locomotives were built with the extraordinarily wide Wootten firebox riding *above* the rear driving wheels, rather than between them. Since this arrangement did not provide ample room for the engineer's cab, a separate cab for the engineer was situated ahead of the firebox straddling the boiler, while the fireman rode behind. This made for an awkward and peculiar looking locomotive that came to be descriptively known as a "Camelback," or "Mother Hubbard."

Camelbacks were built by several builders in a variety of wheel arrangements between the late 1870s and the mid-1920s. By World War I, locomotives with Wootten fireboxes were being constructed with a conventional cab and the Camelback arrangement lost favor.

Although curious to watch, and often a favorite among railroad enthusiasts, the Camelback was not a popular design with crews because it was dangerous and unpleasant to operate. The fireman had to ride on a poorly protected platform on the back of the engine, and because he was separated, he could not communicate with the engineer. Furthermore, because the engineer sat directly over the running gear, he was in a very precarious position if the locomotive broke a main rod or side rod. Several fatalities were attributable to this sort of accident.

The Anthracite Roads were the primary users of Camelbacks, and while the type enjoyed limited popularity in the East, they were rarely used elsewhere. The Central Railroad of New Jersey was one of the last to use Camelbacks and ran them until the early 1950s on suburban commuter trains. The Erie Railroad owned the largest of the type, and employed three 0-8-8-0 Mallet Camelbacks in pusher service over Gulf Summit.

The Camelback should not be confused with Ross Winans' Camels. Although the descriptive names sound similar, and the locomotives resemble each other, the two types are not close technological cousins. Where Ross Winans' Camel was the last in a line of locomotives that began with Peter Cooper's engine, the Camelback was an adaptation of the traditional American locomotive to accommodate Wootten's firebox.

---

tages were both faster acting brakes and, more importantly, a fail-safe system: a leak in the line caused the brakes to apply automatically.

It took nearly two decades for the railroads to adopt the automatic air brake, but by 1889 it was in use industrywide. Improvements in braking allowed railroads to operate longer, heavier, and faster trains more safely.

AUTOMATIC SIGNALING, COUPLERS, AND STEEL FRAMES

The high-speed, head-on collision has been one of the most dreaded accidents in railroading. Misread orders or careless operation could result in trains racing at each other at high speed. The results were almost always fatal. While reports of such collisions made spectacular headlines, head-ons were relatively rare. A far more common type of accident was the rear-end collision. It was this type of accident that killed America's most famous locomotive engineer, Illinois Central "hogger" Casey Jones. When passenger trains had heavy traffic, it was not unusual for a second section to operate immediately after the first or for an "advance" section to run just ahead in order to handle the overflow passengers. Often these sections would follow one another closely since both were operating on the same schedule. If the leading section ran into a problem and had to stop suddenly without warning the following train properly, a crash could result. In the days of wooden passenger cars, such wrecks had grisly results.

During the 1890s several companies introduced practical automatic block signaling, which allowed trains operating in the same direction to follow each other safely. These signals operated with a simple electrical track circuit and were strictly for running safely. They did not authorize train movements. By the turn of the century, railroads

with heavy traffic and safety-conscious roads, such as Harriman's Southern Pacific and Union Pacific, were installing automatic block signals along hundreds of miles of main line. These signals were very effective: they increased safety, inspired public confidence in railroad travel, and most importantly, allowed trains to operate much faster with minimal risk of collision.

Automatic couplers were another innovation that greatly improved train operation. The Janney Automatic Coupler (the "knuckle") dated from the 1880s, but was adopted as standard equipment by the Master Car Builders' Association in 1895. This was a significant improvement over link-and-pin couplers and, along with the introduction of steel frames on rolling stock, permitted the operation of longer, heavier trains.

TRAILING TRUCKS AND BIGGER FIREBOXES

After the advent of Stephenson's successful *Rocket* , two significant advances—trailing truck and superheating—facilitated a substantial increase in locomotive power and efficiency.

Longer, heavier, and faster trains needed more powerful locomotives to haul them. The introduction of the trailing truck made bigger fireboxes possible, allowing for more powerful locomotives. Further enlargement of the firebox was made possible through the introduction of mechanical stokers, which could deliver coal faster and more efficiently than a human fireman.

To overcome the restriction of firebox construction between the frames, locomotive builders moved the firebox above the rear drivers, allowing for a wider firebox with more grate area. The first improvement was the Wootten firebox in 1878, designed to accommodate slow-burning anthracite coal (see

A silhouette of Northern Pacific Ten Wheeler No. 328 at Dresser, Wisconsin, as its crew prepares it for its daily run. A steam locomotive can require several hours of preparation before it is ready to operate.

Northern Pacific 4-6-0 No. 328 hauls a passenger excursion across Wisconsin Central's gargantuan St. Croix River Bridge, which straddles the Minnesota-Wisconsin state line. The Ten Wheeler was first used in the 1840s, gained in popularity in the 1860s as a passenger locomotive, and continued to be built into the twentieth century as a dual service locomotive, long after other types had been perfected.

On October 20, 1957, Pennsylvania Railroad K4s Pacific No. 612 leads a train to Asbury Park, New Jersey, on the New York & Long Branch. The PRR first refined both the Atlantic and Pacific types; the larger Pacific became known as one of the finest of that type and served as the railroad's standard passenger locomotive for 30 years. *Richard Jay Solomon*

Passing through the cornfields near Strasburg, Pennsylvania, Strasburg Railroad No. 475, a former Norfolk & Western 4-8-0, leads a passenger train in a scene reminiscent of the 1900s. Larger, more powerful locomotives allowed the railroads to get more work done with fewer crews.

Camelback sidebar). The practical application of the Wootten firebox was greatly limited, however, and it was not universally adopted.

At the 1893 Columbian Exhibition in Chicago, Baldwin demonstrated a new type of locomotive designed for high-speed passenger service, featuring a 2-4-2 wheel arrangement. Known as a Columbia, this type never attained much popularity, but it pioneered the use of a trailing truck to carry the weight of the firebox, one of the most significant developments in locomotive technology.

Although rigid trailing trucks had been tried since the very beginning, they had not been used solely to carry the weight of a larger firebox, but to spread the locomotive's weight over another axle not needed for traction. A deep, wide firebox could now be built efficiently, allowing for a substantial increase in both firebox grate and boiler capacity. Several new powerful locomotive designs followed. By increasing the ratio of available boiler steam to cylinder size, high-horsepower locomotives could be built. Most earlier nineteenth century designs suffered from a chronic shortage of steam at higher speeds, so while short bursts of speed were possible, sustained high speed running was not.

Forty years before the introduction of the trailing truck, Wilson Eddy had demonstrated the advantage of high boiler capacity to cylinder size ratio with his *Addison Gilmore*, but the industry had not taken advantage of this innovation. It is difficult to understand why it took the railroad industry so long to accept this basic principle of high speed locomotive design.

Another significant step was the development of the outside bearing trailing trucks. The first trailing trucks allowed only restricted lateral motion, but the outside bearing truck permitted the locomotive to pivot, adding considerable flexibility. The first application of the rear trailing truck was on high speed passenger locomotives. It was nearly a decade before the trailing truck was used on domestic freight locomotives.

Soon after the turn of the century the firebox size reached the endurance limit of the human fireman. Some railroads tried building locomotives with two firebox doors that required two fireman, but this proved expensive and impractical. In 1904, the first practical mechanical

stoker was introduced that conveyed coal to the firebox, relieving the fire-man of physical toil. Within a decade, mechanical stokers had become standard equipment on most new large locomotives.

PHYSICAL PLANT

Gradually the railroads improved their physical plant by strengthening bridges, widening rights-of-way, straightening out sharp curves, and improving overhead clearances. This permitted heavier axle loadings, longer wheelbases, bigger boilers, and therefore larger locomotives. It also widened the disparity between main-line and branch-line railroading. In

1850 there was little difference in the weight and clearance restrictions between main line and branch line, and most locomotives could operate all over a railroad. However, after the turn of the century, there were often extreme differences, and because of branch-line limitations, many of the new heavy locomotives were restricted to main lines.

MECHANICAL INNOVATIONS

As locomotives grew larger and more powerful, a number of other innovations were necessary for efficient operation. Larger locomotives had less room between the drivers for cams, eccentrics, and other parts of the valve gear, and as a result traditional, inside valve gears gave way to outside valve gear such as Walschaerts. Valve gear is a critical part of the locomotive that regulates the passage of steam to the cylinders in order to maximize the efficiency of the engine. It serves a function similar to the transmission in an automobile. Walschaerts was the most popular outside valve gear, but a number of others were introduced to improve the efficiency of the locomotive. Among the most common new outside gears were Baker, Southern, and Young. While Baker and Southern gear were similar to Walschaerts and Stephenson in that they derived valve motion from an eccentric crank located on the end of the crankpin of the main driver, Young derived its motion from the crossheads.

On large powerful locomotives the traditional "Johnson bar" manual reverse lever was no longer sufficient to adjust valve gear (see chapter 2). There are many stories of engineers being injured trying to "hook up" the valves (shortening the steam cutoff to reduce the amount of steam released into the cylinders during the stroke). Adjusting the valve cutoff was crucial to controlling the power of the engine. When starting an engine, a long cutoff was used to obtain maximum power; at speed, a short cutoff was desirable to minimize back pressure caused by exhausted steam exiting the cylinder. Short cutoffs were also used to conserve fuel and water, plus the average boiler capacity would not permit full-stroke running above low speeds (heavy freight locomotives featured relatively large cylinders with long strokes, while fast passenger engines had small cylinders with short strokes). Difficulties in adjusting the valves discouraged efficient operation, so air- or steam-powered reversing cylinders were introduced to make hooking up the valve gears easier and safer. They were first used on large engines, and one of the earliest applications of a power reverser was on the first Mallet compound, Baltimore & Ohio No. 2400 (see chapter 4), in 1904. Like the mechanical stoker, power reverse levers were soon standard equipment, and many older locomotives were rebuilt with them, much to the joy of engineers everywhere.

Between 1905 and 1920 several other advances allowed for a dramatic improvement in the thermal efficiency of the steam locomotive, most notably the successful introduction of superheating. (Superheating is discussed in greater detail in the next chapter.)

ATLANTICS, PACIFICS, PRAIRIES, AND MOUNTAINS

The advent of the trailing truck in the 1890s rendered most existing engine types obsolete. The 4-4-0 American standard, which had been declining in popularity as a general service locomotive, was still being built with large drivers and a short cylinder stroke for high speed passenger service. The trailing truck eventually relegated American to secondary status, although some continued in service nearly to the end of the steam era.

ATLANTICS

In the mid-1890s, fast passenger power was the call of the day. The 2-4-2 Columbia showed that a rear trailing truck and larger firebox could produce plenty of horsepower at high speed, but the type demonstrated poor tracking ability as a result of its two-wheel lead truck and was quick-

Kettle Moraine Railway No. 9, a Baldwin 2-6-2 Prairie type built in 1901, leads an excursion train across a trestle just east of North Lake Wisconsin on a former Milwaukee Road branch line. The Prairie type was introduced as a main-line freight locomotive and was briefly tried as a fast passenger engine. Later it found a niche as a good lightweight branch-line locomotive. The type was popular with logging lines, and this one once worked for the McCloud River Railroad in California.

WHYTE CLASSIFICATION SYSTEM

The most common American method of classifying locomotives is the Whyte System. It was adopted in the early 1900s and replaced a host of less clear classification systems. Whyte's logic was simple. He designated locomotives by the arrangement of their wheels, divided into three locations: leading, driving, and trailing; these are separated by dashes. A zero indicates the absence of wheels in one of these locations. For example, an American type locomotive that has four leading wheels, four driving wheels, and no trailing wheels is designated a 4-4-0; while an Atlantic type, which has four leading wheels, four driving wheels, and two trailing wheels is designated a 4-4-2. Locomotives such as Mallets and Duplexes, with more than one set of drivers and running gear, count each grouping of drivers separately. "Old Maud," Baltimore & Ohio's pioneer Mallet type with two sets of six driving wheels, but no leading or trailing wheels is designated a 0-6-6-0. Locomotives without tenders, such as Forneys, that have built-in tanks are designated with a "T" following the wheel counts. A typical Forney type would be designated 0-4-4T.

In addition to the Whyte classification, most standard wheel arrangements have names. Early names were descriptive, such as the "Ten Wheeler." Later names often represented the railroad that first used the wheel arrangement. The Atlantic Coast Line was first to employ the Atlantic type. Several arrangements have more than one name. The 4-8-4, which is generally known as a Northern type, is also known by a host of other names, almost as many as the number of railroads that operated this type.

Types used in America are as follows:

Wheel Arrangement	Classification	Whyte Name
<ooOO	4-4-0	American
<oOOo	2-4-2	Columbia
<ooOOo	4-4-2	Atlantic
<oOOO	2-6-0	Mogul
<oOOOo	2-6-2	Prairie
<ooOOO	4-6-0	Ten Wheeler
<ooOOOo	4-6-2	Pacific
<ooOOOoo	4-6-4	Hudson
<oOOOO	2-8-0	Consolidation
<oOOOOo	2-8-2	Mikado
<oOOOOoo	2-8-4	Berkshire
<ooOOOO	4-8-0	Mastodon or Twelve Wheeler
<ooOOOOo	4-8-2	Mountain
<ooOOOOoo	4-8-4	Northern
<oOOOOO	2-10-0	Decapod
<oOOOOOo	2-10-2	Santa Fe
<oOOOOOoo	2-10-4	Texas
<ooOOOOO	4-10-0	SP El Gobernador
<ooOOOOOo	4-10-2	Southern Pacific
<ooOOOOOOo	4-12-2	Union Pacific
<OOO OOO	0-6-6-0	Mallet
<oOOO OOOo	2-6-6-2	Mallet
<oOOO OOOoo	2-6-6-4	Mallet
<oOOOO OOOOo	2-8-8-2	Mallet
<oOOO OOOooo	2-6-6-6	Allegheny
<oOOOO OOOOoo	2-8-8-4	Yellowstone
<ooOO OOoo	4-4-4-4	Pennsylvania Duplex
<oooOO OOooo	6-4-4-6	Pennsylvania Duplex
<ooOOO OOoo	4-6-4-4	Pennsylvania Duplex
<ooOO OOOoo	4-4-6-4	Pennsylvania Duplex
<ooOOO OOOoo	4-6-6-4	Challenger
<ooOOOO OOOOoo	4-8-8-4	Big Boy

ly supplanted by the 4-4-2. The 4-4-2 was first built for the Atlantic Coast Line in 1894 and so came to be known as the Atlantic type. It combined the best attributes of the American and the Columbia and quickly proved to be an outstanding high speed passenger locomotive. For about 10 years it was the most popular type of new passenger locomotive. However as trains grew heavier and longer it was supplanted by the more powerful 4-6-2 Pacific type.

The Atlantic was primarily a passenger machine designed for high speed. One report indicates a Pennsylvania Railroad Atlantic attained the phenomenal speed of 127 miles per hour. However, the Atlantic was not well suited to other tasks and was a particularly poor freight hauler because of its tall driving wheels and relatively low tractive effort. It was not widely built after 1910.

After the Pacific became the predominant form of new American passenger power, the Pennsylvania Railroad, which consistently bucked trends set by the rest of the industry, developed and refined the Atlantic into a super passenger locomotive and the PRR's class E6s Atlantic was probably the best of the breed (the "s" is not plural, but indicates the locomotive is equipped with superheaters). It was a tribute to the PRR's excellent engineering and to the railroad's exceptionally high standards. Because the PRR maintained its track structure and bridges to allow heavier axle loadings, it was able build a heavier, more powerful Atlantic type. PRR was not, however, the last railroad to embrace the type; Milwaukee Road revived the Atlantic in the mid-1930s when it ordered four high-speed 4-4-2 streamliners with 84-inch drivers that regularly hauled passenger trains faster than 100 miles per hour.

PRAIRIES AND PACIFICS

The weight of passenger trains grew rapidly after the turn of the century. Growing passenger traffic resulted in longer trains and larger and heavier passenger cars, especially because the switch from wooden to all steel cars resulted in a 50 to 75 percent increase in weight per car. Traditional wooden cars were dangerous; during collisions they would splinter and burn, killing and maiming many passengers. When trains

Valley Railroad No. 40, an Alco-built Mikado, leads a passenger excursion north of Essex, Connecticut, amidst brilliant fall foliage. The 2-8-2 Mikado was one of the most popular types of steam locomotives built in the twentieth century.

crashed at high speed, or hit head-on, wooden cars would telescope—the impact of the collision would push the body of one car into that of another. This type of wreck was unusually deadly. Eventually, the federal government banned wooden cars from interstate operations.

To haul heavier trains, the railroads needed locomotives with greater power, both for starting and when moving. This meant a locomotive with greater tractive effort and higher horsepower. Four-coupled passenger locomotives did not provide sufficient adhesion, and six-coupled 4-6-0 Ten Wheelers did not have sufficient firebox capacity to maintain high speeds with heavy consists. The 2-6-2 Prairie type—introduced as the first domestic freight locomotive with a trailing truck—was briefly tried by some railroads as a fast passenger engine. However, as with the 2-4-2 Columbia, its two wheel lead truck did not provide sufficient tracking ability, and the locomotives did not perform well in fast service. They tended to "nose" from side to side at high speed. As a result, they were quickly removed from premier assignments and were not ordered in large numbers. (The 2-6-2 found a niche as dual-service branch line locomotive and was also popular with logging lines for its relatively low axle loadings.)

The 4-6-2 proved a better solution. Its six-coupled drivers provided high tractive effort, it had a large firebox for adequate steam capacity, and it featured a four-wheel leading truck to maintain stability at speed. The type was first used in the United States in 1903 by the Missouri Pacific, and as a result is known as the Pacific (a name that nicely complemented the 4-4-2 Atlantic). The Pacific was an excellent locomotive; it rode well and provided outstanding pulling power on level track as well as on grades and so could easily maintain fast passenger schedules with long trains. By 1907, the Pacific had become the standard American passenger locomotive. For many lines, the Pacific served satisfactorily for more than 40 years, until finally displaced by the diesel electric in the 1940s and 1950s.

The Pacific was refined by many American lines. One of the greatest of the Pacifics was Pennsylvania Railroad's famous K4s, essentially an enlargement of Pennsy's very successful E6s Atlantic. The PRR built 425 K4s Pacifics between 1914 and 1928 and used them to haul its passenger trains as late as 1957. Another excellent example of the type was Southern Railway's class Ps4. Developed relatively late, these were the last new passenger steam locomotives the railroad would ever buy. When other lines were looking at more advanced locomotives, Southern was content to operate its Pacifics.

MOUNTAINS

While the Pacific performed admirably in passenger service in most situations, in 1910 Chesapeake & Ohio found that it still needed to double-head heavy passenger trains operating over the Allegheny Mountains. To combat this problem it designed a new type of engine that essentially

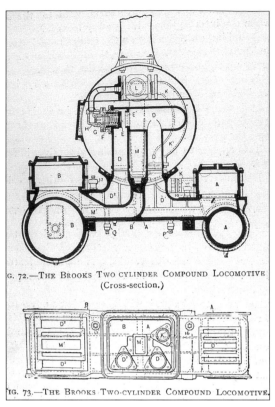

FIG. 72.—THE BROOKS TWO CYLINDER COMPOUND LOCOMOTIVE
(Cross-section.)

FIG. 73.—THE BROOKS TWO-CYLINDER COMPOUND LOCOMOTIVE.

A diagram of a Brooks two-cylinder cross compound locomotive. The high-pressure cylinder on the left exhausts into the low-pressure cylinder on the right. The cross-compound was one of the more popular nonarticulated compound types. *Locomotive Mechanism and Engineering*

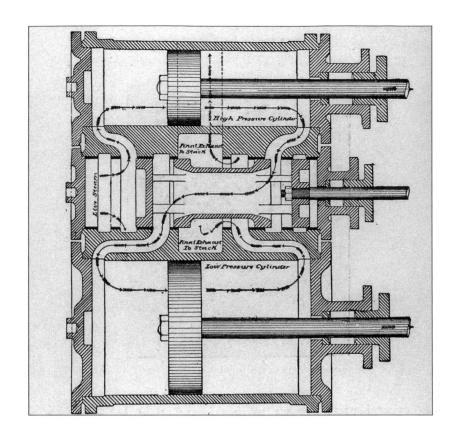

B aldwin's Samuel Vauclain designed a balanced compound with both high- and low-pressure cylinders on each side of the locomotive. This diagram is a cross-section of the cylinder assembly on one side of the locomotive. The smaller, high-pressure cylinder exhausts into the larger, low-pressure cylinder. *Locomotive Mechanism and Engineering*

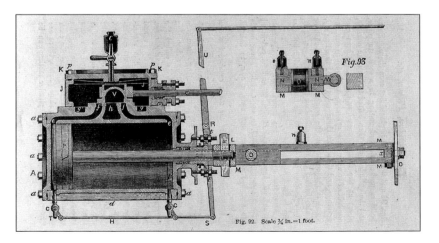

C utaway view of a steam locomotive cylinder and valve assembly. This is an older arrangement using a slide valve (labeled "v"). The valve regulates the passage of steam to and from the cylinder. All steam locomotives use double-acting cylinders—steam acts on each side of the piston alternately. Steam enters and exits the cylinder through passages labeled "f" and steam is exhausted from the cylinder assembly through passage "h." *Locomotive Mechanism and Engineering*

combined the best qualities of the low-drivered 2-8-2 Mikado being used in freight service (discussed below) and the high-drivered 4-6-2 Pacific used in passenger service. What it came up with was a 4-8-2 with 62-inch drivers, slightly larger than those on Mikados but not quite as tall as those on the Pacifics. The first 4-8-2s were delivered in 1911, and they were exactly what C&O was hoping for. The railroad designated them Mountains, presumably after the Alleghenies.

The Mountain was slow to catch on. Most railroads were satisfied with their Pacifics and Mikados and did not see an immediate need for larger passenger power. Eventually the advantages of the 4-8-2 were recognized, and some 2,400 were built, making them only one-third as popular as the Pacific, but more numerous than either the Atlantic or Prairie types. Mountains were well suited for freight service, particularly the fast freight service that was becoming popular at the time of World War I. While better designs superseded the Mountain in the mid-1920s, some railroads continued to order them until the end of steam. The Rutland took delivery of six Mountains in 1946, after World War II. New York Central was particularly fond of the 4-8-2—although it called them Mohawks after the river its Water Level Route followed—and refined the type to an exceptionally powerful passenger hauler.

MIKADO: THE TWENTIETH CENTURY WORKHORSE

If one were to have witnessed a typical American freight train in the second quarter of the twentieth century, chances are it would have been hauled by a 2-8-2. Why? Because, by the 1920s, the 2-8-2 was *the* most popular type of new steam locomotive in the United States. It was a solid, well-balanced locomotive designed for freight service, and it came with an unorthodox name: Mikado. If it sounds Japanese, that's because it is! Mikado is an archaic name for the Japanese emperor.

In the 1860s, Lehigh Valley rebuilt a pair of 2-10-0 types into 2-8-2s. However these were freaks and not replicated, yet as with much of locomotive history they need to be mentioned because they were the first of the type. In the early 1890s, Baldwin began building 2-8-2s for export, selling them first to Mexico and then, more prominently, to Japan in 1897. Japan had just recently restored its emperor to power, and more to the point, Gilbert & Sullivan's comic opera, *The Mikado*, had recently achieved widespread popularity. Because the 2-8-2 was associated with Japan, it became known as the Mikado type, although at the time the locomotive was not yet in general use in the United States. Throughout most of their career, 2-8-2s were frequently referred to as just "Mikes," although during World War II strong anti-Japanese sentiment caused some railroads to rename them the MacArthur type, in honor of the popular American general. After the war the name reverted to Mikado. It should be no surprise that the Mikado type was particularly popular in Japan, and many were in regular service there into the 1970s.

The first true American Mikados were diminutive Baldwins built for the Bismarck, Washburn & Great Falls Railway in 1903. Nearby giant Northern Pacific took notice, and in 1905, placed the first large American order for 2-8-2s with Alco's Brooks Works. At the time these were big locomotives intended for heavy freight service: they featured 44 foot firebox grates, 24x30-inch cylinders, 63-inch drivers, operated with a boiler pressure of 200 pounds psi generating 46,600 pounds tractive effort. They met their task exceptionally well and over the next two years NP acquired 160 Mikados for freight service. These fine locomotives are generally considered to be the best of traditional saturated steam locomotive development. Northern Pacific was extremely satisfied with the type. A number remained in service for nearly 50 years, right up to the end of the steam era, although by that time many had been modified with modern appliances such as superheaters, and some had been converted from coal to oil burners.

The Mikado quickly became a popular type because of its flexibility, relatively low axle loadings and power. Between 1910 and about 1930 it remained the most popular type of new steam locomotive and replaced the 2-8-0 as the standard American freight locomotive. Although more advanced locomotives eventually supplanted the Mikado in heavy mainline freight service, the type is among the longest-lived designs built in the twentieth century. They were in production domestically as late as 1949, and overseas until the late 1980s. Alfred Bruce estimates approximately 9,000 Mikados were built for domestic service, and another 5,000 were built for export. It was the most popular type to feature the two-wheel trailing truck. In the United States, there were more Mikados built than all Mountain, Berkshire, Santa Fe, Texas, and Northern types combined.

USRA Supports the Mike

The United States Railroad Administration (USRA), which controlled the railroads during World War I and set standard designs for locomotive production, preferred the Mikado. Of the 12 standard designs it offered, two were Mikados, and more USRA Mikados were built than all other USRA designed locomotives. Both USRA Mikes featured 63-inch drivers. The USRA "light" Mikado had 26x30-inch cylinders, weighed 292,000 pounds, and delivered 54,700 pounds tractive effort, while the USRA "heavy" Mikado had 27x32-inch cylinders, weighed 320,000 pounds, and delivered 60,000 pounds tractive effort.

The great popularity of the type meant that by the 1920s one was probably more likely to find a Mikado in general freight service than any other type of locomotive, save perhaps a 2-8-0 Consolidation. Until the diesel era, Mikados were the American railroad's workhorse. They could be found on main lines and branch lines alike. They were also one of the most popular designs for narrow gauge lines. Diminutive 2-8-2s operated all over Colorado on the three-foot gauge tracks, and on lines like Pennsylvania's coal hauling East Broad Top too. Some of the large eastern railroads owned more Mikados than many smaller railroads owned locomotives.

Pennsylvania Railroad Standard Mikes

The Pennsylvania Railroad adopted the Mike in 1914, much later than other railroads. But once it did, it built them in quantity based on a standard design. Between 1914 and 1919 it took delivery of 574 virtually identical Class L1s Mikados (the small "s" indicates the locomotive was superheated). Some were built by the railroad's proficient Juniata Shops in Altoona, while others were products of either Lima or Pennsy's favorite supplier, Baldwin. As was usually the case with Mikes, Pennsy intended to use them as replacements for aging 2-8-0 Consolidations in freight service. The L1s Mikados weighed in at 320,700 pounds, with 27x30-inch cylinders, 62-inch drivers, boiler pressure of 205 psi, and a firebox with a 70 square foot grate that often required healthy firemen to keep it satisfied. The L1s produced 61,465 pounds of tractive effort, a significant increase over railroad's H10s Consolidation. This was an excellent example of Pennsy's commitment to standardization among classes, because the L1s type shared many common parts with Pennsy's exemplary K4s Pacific including the firebox—PRR's typical, boxy Belpaire.

New York Central probably had the largest fleet of Mikados. It operated 1,387, and it also owned one the most impressive examples of the type. In 1922 it took delivery of a super Mikado, No. 8000 from Lima, a locomotive that ultimately led to the design of the first Lima Super Power, the 2-8-4 Berkshire.

Today the Mikado is one of the most popular types used at tourist railroads and museums, and it is among the most common type found overseas. Hundreds of 2-8-2s are still working in daily service in China.

Compounds

In a simple steam engine, after the steam expands in the cylinder it is exhausted into the atmosphere. This wastes expansive power left in the steam. To take advantage of the remaining power in the exhausted steam, a variation called the compound engine was developed. The compound engine improves upon the thermal efficiency by double expansion of the steam through the use of high-pressure and low-pressure cylinders; the low-pressure cylinders use the steam exhausted from the high-pressure cylinders. In a typical nineteenth century compound engine, steam enters the high-pressure cylinder at roughly 170 psi, expands, and is then exhausted into the low-pressure cylinder at roughly 80 psi where it expands again and exhausts into atmosphere at approximately 5 psi.

The compound or double expansion engine is a much more efficient device than a simple steam engine; it uses less steam to perform the same work and therefore burns less fuel and uses less water. A properly functioning compound locomotive may consume up to 20 percent less fuel and 50 percent less water than an equivalent simple locomotive, which made it very attractive to railroads like the Santa Fe that had difficulty procuring water in the deserts of the Southwest. However, a compound is a more complicated machine, with more moving parts and steam connections. It requires more lubrication and maintenance than a simple engine, and unless it functions properly, will not result in improved efficiency.

The first known compound steam engine was developed in England by Jonathan Hornblower in 1781. While the concept was not taken seriously at that time, it was revived in 1804 by Arthur Woolf who refined and perfected the compound engine. In 1814, he built a compound pump engine intended for commercial use. Trevithick's high-pressure engines, which were just becoming available, were far less complicated to maintain and therefore achieved greater success. The compound engine was revived again in the 1840s and was first applied to an American locomotive in the 1860s when the Shepard Iron Works in Buffalo, New York, built a tandem compound (see description below) from an earlier locomotive. Little is known of this engine, but it was not very successful and did not directly affect future development of the compound locomotive in America. The first serious American interest in compound locomotives began in the 1880s, when railroads were looking for ways to improve fuel efficiency and boost locomotive performance. A half dozen compound arrangements gained popularity.

AMERICAN COMPOUND LOCOMOTIVES

One of the earliest systems was the three-cylinder compound, first developed in the late 1870s. There were two varieties, one where a single high-pressure cylinder between the frames exhausted into two conventionally located low-pressure cylinders; the other used the opposite arrangement—two outside high-pressure cylinders exhausted into a single inside low-pressure cylinder. In both systems the center cylinder powered a cranked axle, with the three crankpins located 120 degrees apart. This system attained some popularity in Europe but was not widely used in the United States.

The tandem compound mentioned above employed a four-cylinder arrangement, two on each side of the locomotive, where the high-pressure cylinder and low-pressure cylinder are mounted end to end (normally the high pressure is ahead of the low pressure). Both high- and low-pressure pistons drive a common rod. A Boston & Albany locomotive was equipped with this arrangement about 1883, but the first truly successful application of the tandem compound did not occur until the 1890s.

One of the first successful double expansion applications was the cross compound, which was developed in Germany in 1887. In this two-cylinder arrangement, a high-pressure cylinder on one side of the locomotive exhausts into a low-pressure cylinder on the other. Although the cross-compound locomotive had a distinctly unbalanced appearance, it worked reasonably well. In 1889 Albert J. Pitkin of the Schenectady Locomotive Works refined the cross compound for American use, and it was one of the more widely accepted compound designs. It was promoted by Schenectady, Richmond, and then by Alco after the turn of the century.

The most popular type of nonarticulated, double-expansion locomotive in the United States was the Vauclain compound, designed by Samuel Vauclain of Baldwin in 1889. This four-cylinder system employed two sets of cylinders on each side of the engine. The high-pressure and low-pressure cylinders were located directly above one another on each side of the engine. The high- and low-pressure pistons drove separate rods but were connected by a common crosshead. Vauclain compounding on passenger locomotives with high drivers had the low-pressure cylinders below; low-drivered engines had the high-pressure cylinders below to accommodate tight clearances. One of the advantages of Baldwin's Vauclain compound was that it could be easily applied to existing locomotives. (Vauclain went on to become the president of Baldwin.)

Another popular European double-expansion locomotive that was tested in the United States but not widely adopted was the bal-

Builders photo of a Union Pacific 4-6-0 Vauclain compound clearly shows the high- and low-pressure cylinders connected to a common crosshead. With 79-inch driving wheels and the compound cylinder arrangement, this locomotive was designed specifically to haul long passenger trains with great fuel and water economy. It would have been considered a very large passenger locomotive in May 1900, when it was built. *Author collection*

In the 1920s, Samuel Vauclain, by then Baldwin's president, devised the "Prosperity Special" as a new locomotive promotion gimmick. Here 25 brand-new Southern Pacific 2-10-2 Santa Fe types are coupled together as a special train for their delivery run from Baldwin's Eddystone shops (near Philadelphia, Pennsylvania) to the Southern Pacific. The words Prosperity Special written on a placard can be seen on each locomotive. *Author collection*

The 4-6-2 Pacific type was the standard passenger locomotive on many North American railroads during the first half of the twentieth century. Many Pacifics displayed a spartan, utilitarian appearance, while others were dressed up for their passenger duties. Chicago Great Western No. 916 was built in 1903, and later rebuilt and painted red to match the cars of the *Red Bird*. Note the detailed striping on the wheels, cab, and tender. *Author collection*

The Pennsylvania Railroad adopted the Pacific type later than some railroads. However, once it settled on the Pacific it perfected the type. Developed in 1914, the K4s Pacific was an outstanding machine and the backbone of the railroad's passenger fleet for more than three decades. A K4s, such as 5449 seen here, could easily haul a 12-car passenger train unassisted. *Author collection*

Canadian Pacific No. 29, a Class A-1e 4-4-0 type built in 1887, served the railroad for more than 70 years. It is seen here at Norton, New Brunswick, on August 9, 1956. Although larger and more powerful locomotives had been developed, they required a considerable investment in more substantial track and bridges, and nimble lightweight locomotives were often retained for work on light-branch lines. *George C. Corey*

anced compound, designed in France by Alfred G. DeGlehn. This type of locomotive employed four cylinders in a similar arrangement to the three-cylinder compounds. Two high-pressure cylinders inside the locomotive powered crank axles and exhausted into outside low-pressure cylinders that powered external rods connected to crankpins. One of the drawbacks of this system was increased maintenance costs incurred by the interior cylinders. It was felt that the maintenance costs of these engines negated any potential savings from increased efficiency.

The most popular type of compound in the United States was the articulated Mallet type, which was introduced in 1904 just as the nonarticulated double-expansion locomotive was falling out of favor (the Mallet type is discussed at length in chapter four). Nonarticulated compound locomotives attained their greatest popularity in the 1890s, but quickly lost favor when railroads realized that savings achieved through double expansion were often lost in the shop because of increased maintenance costs. Furthermore, when railroads failed to keep the complex compound types in perfect running order, they did not run well.

Alfred Bruce indicates that at the end of 1904 roughly 6 percent of American steam locomotives were of a compound design, representing nearly 2,900 locomotives. One of the most popular types for compounding was the 2-8-0 Consolidation. Of the 11,398 2-8-0s in service at the end of 1904, 764 were four-cylinder compounds, and 376 were two-cylinder compounds. The next most popular wheel arrangement for compounding was the 4-6-0 Ten Wheeler. There were 9,232 4-6-0s; of these 502 were four-cylinder compounds and another 280 were two-cylinder compounds.

Most compounds employed an intercepting valve, which allowed the engineer to use high-pressure steam in all cylinders, thus turning the compound into a simple engine; this was useful in starting heavy trains. In addition to fuel economy, compounds had an added advantage in heavy freight service.

By 1910, the nonarticulated compound was fading from interest. Many compound locomotives had been converted to simple operation to lower repair costs. The nonarticulated compound was finally killed by the advent of superheating. Superheating effectively achieved the same efficiency as compounding but used less complicated machinery (requiring less maintenance). Where compound locomotives had achieved a limited popularity, superheated locomotives were adopted universally. Compounding was briefly revived in the 1920s when several railroads, most notably the Delaware & Hudson, built a few experimental high-pressure compound locomotives. The D&H constructed four engines, the last one in the early 1930s. This was a very high-pressure triple-expansion locomotive, the only such locomotive known in North America. While the engine performed well, it was never duplicated.

Great Northern Railway Class K-1, 4-4-2 No. 1705, leads nine steel passenger cars. The locomotive was one of 10 balanced compounds built by Baldwin for GN in 1906—the only Atlantics owned by the railroad. The locomotive has an unusual configuration: inside high-pressure cylinders were coupled to the first pair of drivers, while the outside high-pressure cylinders were coupled to the rear pair of drivers. Like many Great Northern locomotives, this Atlantic features a Belpaire boiler. *Author collection*

4

ARTICULATED LOCOMOTIVES

"This type of 'double' engine was especially suited to our far West where trains were long, the roadways were winding and heavy grades were unavoidable. In 1906 we [Baldwin] went after Jim Hill's [the renowned owner of the Great Northern Railway] Mallet business, I proposed selling him five monster Mallets. Each was to be carried on six pairs of driving wheels, three front and three back, with a two wheeled truck on front and rear. Each engine was to weigh about 350,000 pounds. A 175-ton locomotive was then something to talk about.

"When I spoke of five Mallets to the Great Northern genius he hedged.

" 'I might try one out,' he dryly said.

" 'We can't sell you just one big Mallet,' I demurred. 'If we sold you one it would be passed from one division master mechanic to another, each one glad to get rid of it. You know the average railroader will shy at novelties. You should buy five Mallets for service on the Cascade Mountains at Skyskomish where the grade is 2.2 percent and short curves are combined with tunnels and plenty of snowsheds.'

" 'What if I find them of no use to me?' he asked bluntly.

" 'You can send them right back to us,' I promised.

" 'All right,' he answered. 'Build five for me. We'll try them.'

"We filled the order. The Mallets were so satisfactory that we made many more for the Jim Hill system."—*Baldwin President, Samuel M. Vauclain's anecdote of his early Mallet experience from his autobiography* Steaming Up!

MALLETS

The St. Louis Exposition of 1904 was one of those great public events in the history of locomotive development. In many respects it was the early twentieth century equivalent of the

---

Articulated locomotives with two complete sets of running gear became popular after 1904. Early articulated locomotives were built as Mallet Compounds, later the simple articulated locomotive, such as Union Pacific's 4-6-6-4 Challenger No. 3985 seen here, replaced the Mallet as the the dominant articulated type.

On a humid August 1, 1958, at Blue Ridge, Virginia, Norfolk & Western Mallet No. 2152, one of the railroad's famous Y6s, shoves on the rear of a heavy eastbound coal train. A six-car local freight powered by N&W Y6a No. 2160 is overtaking the slow-moving coal train on the adjacent track. The N&W continued to embrace the Mallet Compound long after most other American railroads had abandoned the design. *Richard Jay Solomon*

The Northern Pacific bought a small fleet of 2-8-8-4 simple articulated locomotives called Yellowstones, and for many years they were the largest locomotives in the world. Initially used on the heavily graded line between Glendive, Montana, and Mandan, North Dakota, they were later transferred west. These engines were intensely disliked by crews because one 2-8-8-4 replaced two 2-8-2s, thus reducing the need for engineers and firemen. A single Yellowstone handles a manifest freight in the North Dakota Badlands near Medora. *Otto C. Perry,* Denver Public Library Western History Department

Rainhill trials of 1829. The Fair was a celebration of the Louisiana Purchase Centennial and highlighted technological innovation. A number of new locomotive designs were built specifically for exhibit at the fair, several of which would never be duplicated.

Of all the locomotives displayed, one engine attracted the most attention: Baltimore & Ohio number 2400, a monster of unparalleled proportion and peculiar design. It weighed a tremendous 167 tons, featured *six* pairs of 56-inch drivers, and was 80 feet long! Its most outstanding characteristic, however, was its unorthodox design; it was an articulated compound with two complete sets of running gear. The rear set was the conventional high-pressure variety, while the front set were exceptionally large low-pressure cylinders powered by exhaust steam from the rear set. The rear drivers and cylinders were attached to the boiler in the traditional fashion, while the front portion of the engine was hinged to the rear frame but not rigidly attached to the boiler, allowing the long engine needed flexibility in tight curves.

It was the sort of machine that both novice and professional noticed immediately. Spectators at St. Louis were taken aback. No one had ever seen such a locomotive, and skeptics immediately doubted its practicality. In the 100 years since Trevithick had first demonstrated an operating locomotive, many bizarre designs had come and gone. So, surely this contraption was a freak? It wasn't, it was a viable, practical locomotive that would have lasting effect on subsequent steam locomotive development.

Baltimore & Ohio 2400 was the inspiration of the railroad's president, Leonor F. Loree, and the work of B&O's brilliant mechanical officer, James Muhlfeld. Although radical in the eyes of American railroaders, the concept behind the articulated compound locomotive was not new. It is credited to Anatole Mallet (the "T" is silent and his name is correctly pronounced as Mallay), a French-Swiss man who first designed diminutive articulated compounds in 1874 for narrow gauge lines in the Alps. Articulated compounds are frequently referred to as Mallet Compounds or simply as Mallets (the French pronunciation is often lost on many American railroaders whose reference to the articulated locomotives sounds like the description of common hammer).

An irony in the Mallet's American application was that Anatole Mallet saw his engine as strictly a mountain branch-line machine, and never intended it for heavy main-line service. Also, just as the type was attracting attention in the United States, it was falling out of favor in Europe. Loree had heard of the miniature Mallets running in Europe and hoped the design could be adapted to work on the B&O's rugged mountain grades. The advantage of a vastly more powerful locomotive under the control of one man was purely economical. It would result in a great savings by allowing the railroad to run longer trains with fewer locomotives and fewer crews.

In 1903 and 1904 Alco built the 2400 for the B&O, completing it just in time for the St. Louis Expo. It gained the nickname "Old Maud" after a popular cartoon mule of the era. Following the Expo, the 0-6-6-0 Mallet entered service on the B&O and quickly quieted its skeptics with its successful performance running on one of the railroad's toughest lines.

OLD MAUD TACKLES SAND PATCH

The B&O mainline is relatively level between Cherry Run, West Virginia, and Cumberland, Maryland. West of Cumberland the line splits. The original line to the Ohio River crosses the Alleghenies by way of a series of steep mountain grades via Grafton, West Virginia, while the Chicago line heads northwest through the Cumberland Narrows and into Pennsylvania toward Pittsburgh. Sand Patch grade begins near Hyndman Tower. Just north of the Maryland-

Pennsylvania state line the railroad winds its way along Wills Creek toward the summit of the Alleghenies at Sand Patch, near Meyersdale. A long tunnel just east of the mountain summit made the grade more difficult for heavy trains. The west slope of Sand Patch was not as grueling as the east but still could present a serious challenge to heavy eastbound trains. To expedite train movements over the grades west of Cumberland, B&O regularly assigned helpers to heavy trains. It was here that Old Maud demonstrated its merit. In tests, Old Maud could

The Virginian operated some of the largest Mallets ever built, enormous 2-10-10-2s with low-pressure cylinders 4 feet in diameter. These locomotives had tremendous pulling power and could deliver 176,600 pounds tractive effort, the highest of any reciprocating steam locomotive ever built. Virginian 801 crosses the Norfolk & Western in Norfolk, Virginia, on August 7, 1932. *Otto C. Perry,* Denver Public Library Western History Department

march up Sand Patch with a 2,000 ton freight as easily as two of B&O's heavy 2-8-0 Consolidations. This feat was particularly remarkable because the Mallet climbed the hill using 30 percent less coal than pairs of 2-8-0s.

Old Maud was well engineered and well built. The rapid acceptance and popularity of the Mallet type in the United States can be attributed to Muhlfeld's and Alco's careful attention to detail. Had Old Maud stalled repeatedly on Sand Patch in her early days the skeptics would have had their day and B&O may have dropped the Mallet concept before it was proven. However, the concept *was* valid, and its execution was proven from the onset. This first Mallet remained in service on the B&O for 30 years. The Mallet design was refined and approximately 2,400 locomotives of this design, using a variety of wheel arrangements, were built for service on U.S. rails over a 45-year period.

As an 0-6-6-0, Old Maud was intended primarily as a pusher engine and was not intended to work on the head end of trains, thus the obvious lack of front guide wheels. However the promise of the first Mallet soon led to the development of road engines using its design.

MALLETS FOR THE MOUNTAINS

Just after the turn of the century, James J. Hill's Great Northern improved its treacherous crossing of Washington's Cascade Mountains by constructing the first Cascade Tunnel (during a route improvement in the 1920s GN constructed a much longer tunnel of the same name near the original bore), which reduced GN's ruling grade from an impossible 4 percent, to a more reasonable, yet still steep, 2.2 percent.

To suit GN's needs, Baldwin designed a modified Mallet type and delivered five 2-6-6-2s to the Great Northern for road service in 1906. In addition to being the first Mallets intended to lead main-line freights, they were also the first Mallets to employ the boxy Belpaire firebox, a standard feature on most new GN locomotives. Great Northern, like the Pennsylvania Railroad, preferred this type of firebox over the radial-stay design in general use in the United States at the time. The 2-6-6-2 proved successful, and by 1908 GN had taken delivery of an additional 45 Mallets.

Climbing toward Soldier Summit, having just passed Castle Gate, Utah, two Rio Grande 2-8-8-2 Mallets shove on the rear of a heavy 57-car train. Castle Gate, located a few miles west of Helper Utah, was one of the most famous landmarks along the old Rio Grande. Unfortunately, half of the famous gate was deliberately destroyed to make room for a highway. *Otto C. Perry,* Denver Public Library Western History Department

The popularity of the Mallet type spread rapidly and was well established by 1909, only five years after its introduction. Ultimately the Mallet would prove the most practical and popular compound design, and the only type of compound to survive until the end of steam. While Mallets were built in a number of wheel arrangements, including 0-8-8-0, 2-8-8-0, 2-6-8-0, 2-4-4-2, and even 2-10-10-2, the two most popular arrangements, which accounted for the majority of Mallet types in the United States, were the 2-6-6-2 and 2-8-8-2 types, representing 1,300 locomotives and 625 locomotives respectively.

The Santa Fe, an ardent supporter of the compound steam locomotive, embraced the Mallet Compound with unbridled enthusiasm. Where many railroads used Mallets in slow, heavy freight service, Santa Fe tried them in high-speed passenger service. This Baldwin 2-6-6-2 Mallet built in 1910 featured 69-inch drivers and was intended for passenger service. *Author collection*

The 2-6-6-2 was generally assigned to heavy drag service—slow speed freight trains often carrying a single commodity such as coal or iron ore. As a result they employed small driving wheels, usually just 56 inches in diameter, and rarely operated faster than 20 miles per hour. While these speeds may seem ponderously slow, few freight trains operated much faster than that until after World War I, so the Mallet's speed was not a concern.

The 2-8-8-2 type was originally developed in 1909 by Baldwin for Southern Pacific service on Donner Pass in the California Sierra,

Santa Fe's passenger Mallets were relatively short-lived and as a result rarely photographed. Noted western railroad photographer Otto C. Perry caught Atchison, Topeka & Santa Fe No. 1179 under steam in Albuquerque, New Mexico, in October 1920. Although some of Santa Fe's Mallets had jointed boilers—an experiment in flexibility that failed—this locomotive featured a rigid boiler. *Otto C. Perry,* Denver Public Library Western History Department

Union Pacific operated 25 Big Boys, which were 4-8-8-4s built by Alco in 1941 and 1944. These were among the largest locomotives ever built and weighed 772,000 pounds, just a few tons less than C&O's 2-6-6-6 Alleghenies. On September 11, 1958, a Big Boy hauls 110 cars over Sherman Hill near Dale, Wyoming. *Otto C. Perry,* Denver Public Library Western History Department

but it quickly caught on for other applications. Many 2-8-8-2s weighed little more than 2-6-6-2s of the same period and were not used to obtain substantially more power but to reduce axle loadings by distributing the weight of the engine over more driving wheels.

SANTA FE'S MALLET MONSTERS, FREAKS AND EXPERIMENTS

Not all Mallets were intended for slow speeds or freight service, and while ponderous 2-6-6-2s were the dominant type, a number of curious and sometimes exotic Mallet types rolled on U.S. rails. The Santa Fe, which had been an ardent supporter of compound locomotives, employed the Mallet type with great enthusiasm. When most lines were acquiring Mallets for slow freight service, Santa Fe ordered several high speed 2-6-6-2 passenger Mallets from Baldwin. It also experimented with flexible boilers and a number of unorthodox wheel arrangements, including innovative 4-4-6-2s, in an effort to achieve greater performance. The railroad tried two different arrangements of flexible boilers in an effort to improve the Mallet's vertical and lateral flexibility when negotiating curves. The first type employed ball and socket connections. When this proved flawed, the railroad tried an accordion-like joint using 60 riveted steel rings.

Neither arrangement was successful, and all Santa Fe's flexible-boilered locomotives were eventually separated and rebuilt as conventional, nonarticulated simple engines.

In 1911 Santa Fe pushed the limit of the Mallet design in another direction by assembling 10 2-10-10-2 types in its shops using existing parts from existing 2-10-2s and new driving gear and boiler sections provided by Baldwin. At the time these were the largest locomotives in the world, and featured 28 and 38x32-inch cylinders, 57-inch drivers, weighed 616,000 pounds (nearly twice that of B&O's Old Maud), and delivered 111,600 pounds of tractive effort. These engines were also failures and were rebuilt into conventional 2-10-2s. Santa Fe's imagination did not end with these curiosities, but seriously contemplated even more bizarre machines,

Summit near Susquehanna, Pennsylvania. In all respects these locomotives were truly monstrous. They had six 36x32-inch cylinders; two sets of which rode below the boiler, and the third set below the tender. (The middle cylinders worked on high-pressure steam directly from the boiler; the right cylinder exhausted into the front engine and the left cylinder exhausted into the rear engine. Thus the triplex was a variation of the double expansion engine and *not* a triple expansion engine.) The engine weighed an incredible 853,050 pounds (more than 42 times the weight of Camden & Amboy's *John Bull* —which was considered heavy for its day) and rode on 63-inch wheels. Its boiler operated at 210 psi, and the locomotive could produce an unheard of 160,000 pound starting tractive effort, making the Erie 2-8-8-8-2s the most powerful locomotives in the world up until that time. The downfall of the triplex was its poor performance and complex equipment. Despite its size, the boiler failed to produce enough steam to power the engine for any length of time—the six large cylinders required an enormous amount of steam—and it was nearly impossible for the engineer to balance the power of the triplex's three engines. Furthermore as the fuel and water were exhausted, the weight on the rear set of drivers dropped, resulting in a serious loss in adhesion that could cause it to slip. The rear cylinders exhausted steam through a stack on the tender, and this created problems with the firebox draft (required for a normal rate of combustion). Lastly, the sheer complexity of the machine resulted in excessive maintenance.

Although the Erie triplex failed to perform adequately, in 1916 the Virginian ordered a single, slightly modified triplex from Baldwin featuring a 2-8-8-8-4 wheel arrangement. While not as massive as the Erie machines, the Virginian engine, classed XA, suffered from the same basic design flaws and was even less successful. None of the triplexes was in service long, and all were converted to less complicated engines within a few years.

While the triplex experiment was an interesting failure, in 1918 the Virginian acquired another group of Mallet behemoths of a different design for the 2 percent grade from Elmore, West Virginia, up to Clark's Gap. These were 10 2-10-10-2s built by Alco, which were significantly larger than the unsuccessful Santa Fe engines of the same wheel arrangement. Ultimately they were more successful than either their Western predecessors or the triplex disasters. Though the Virginian's clearances were capable of accommodating the gargantuan Mallets, they had to be transported from Alco in several pieces because the connecting railroads were not capable of handling them. Their 48x32-inch low-pressure cylinders were the largest ever used on any locomotive in the world; fully assembled the engine weighed 684,000 pounds. They worked at 215 psi boiler pressure and featured 56-inch drivers. They were capable of producing 147,200 pound tractive effort as a compound but could be run as a simple engine to start trains at a phenomenal 176,600 pounds of tractive effort— the highest of any conventional reciprocating steam locomotive ever built. This is so much force that the engine probably would have pulled apart freight cars on most lines, except Virginian's. These big engines served on Clark's Gap mountain until the railroad electrified in the mid-1920s, and then they worked on mine runs and on coal trains between Roanoke and

including a 2-8-8-8-8-2 Quadruplex and a 2-8-8-8-8-8-2 Quintuplex. Eventually sanity prevailed upon Santa Fe's motive power department, and the experiments gave way to more practical locomotives.

ERIE AND VIRGINIAN PUSH THE ENVELOPE

"Uncle John" Santa Fe was not the only road to push the Mallet concept to its limits. The Erie Railroad and later the Virginian both briefly experimented with Mallet types with *three* complete sets of cylinders and running gear called "triplexes." While failures from a technological standpoint, these locomotives are worth mentioning because of their tremendous size and curious application of the Mallet design. In 1914 the Erie took delivery of three 2-8-8-8-2s from Baldwin for service over Gulf

Moving heavy trains over steep mountain grades requires a lot of power. On July 11, 1950, Western Maryland freight WM-1 near Helmstedders Curve is ascending the east slope of the Alleghenies, with Challenger 1208 leading, another Challenger cut into the middle of the train (seen on the far right), and a 2-10-0 Decapod shoving on the rear (out of the picture). *George C. Corey*

Mallet compounds were ideally suited for hauling extremely heavy trains at slow to moderate speeds. On October 11, 1954, two mine runs meet at Georgetown, Ohio. Nickel Plate Road No. 941, leading the loaded train, is a 2-6-6-2 Mallet of United States Railroad Administration design. During World War I, the USRA drew up standard plans for 12 types of locomotives, including two varieties of Mallets. *George C. Corey*

Southern Pacific was happy with its cab-ahead freight Mallets, so in 1911 it ordered 12 2-6-6-2 cab-ahead Mallets, class MM-2, for passenger service. It was soon found that the two-wheel leading truck was not suited for high-speed passenger operation, so the locomotives were rebuilt with four-wheel leading trucks. Eventually the 12 MM-2s were transferred to freight service. Here the class locomotive, No. 4200, is seen with a long string of box cars. *Southern Pacific photo, courtesy of Fred Matthews*

Norfolk for another twenty years. They were capable of moving 17,000-ton coal trains without a pusher, a feat that even today's modern microprocessor-controlled diesel-electric locomotives would be hard pressed to match.

MALLETS SPUR INNOVATION

In addition to its introduction of the articulated compound arrangement, the adaptation of the Mallet design brought about several significant changes to American locomotive design. B&O 2400 established the use of Walschaerts valve gear in the United States. Walschaerts had been around for nearly 60 years but had not attained popularity on American locomotives, although it had been tried on Mason's experimental engines, including the "Bogie" engines in 1876. Prior to the prototype Mallet, most American locomotives used inside valve gear, usually of the Stephenson type. Inside valve gear operates between the frames, while outside valve gear operates outside the drivers. As locomotives grew in size and complexity, there was less and less room for mechanical workings between the frames. Builders resisted the switch to outside gear, but the successful application of Walschaerts on Old Maud set a new precedent; soon outside gear was the norm rather than a curiosity. After Walschaerts' acceptance, other types of outside gear came into vogue, although Walschaerts remained the most popular type.

MALLET EMBRACES SUPERHEATED STEAM

A problem with early Mallet designs that operated on lower boiler working pressures (in the 200-pound range) was that condensation, which occurred as steam, was expanded in the high-pressure cylinders. If enough water was worked into the low-pressure cylinders from this condensation, it could result in knocking out a cylinder head or breaking a piston. To improve upon the Mallet's efficiency a couple of improvements were tried. Some builders (notably Baldwin) used steam reheaters that would circulate the steam exhausting from the high-pressure cylinders either through the smokebox or back through boiler flues before it entered the low pressure cylinders. This boosted the steam temperature and minimized the difficulties associated with condensing steam. A more effective solution was the superheater, which circulated saturated (or "wet") boiler steam through tubes in enlarged boiler flues, raising steam temperature by at least 200 degrees F before it entered the cylinders. Superheated steam does not have greater pressure than saturated steam, but it stores more heat energy in a given volume of steam, thereby increasing its expansive power in the cylinders. This results in greater efficiency as less steam is required to do the same work within the cylinder.

Superheating had been studied since the turn of the century and had been successfully applied to conventional locomotives overseas, but its application on Mallets was among the first for American locomotives.

TOP

Southern Pacific used many of its later cab-forward articulateds in both freight and passenger service. Here an AC-6 4-8-8-2, built by Baldwin in 1930, leads the *Pacific Limited* eastbound through Cisco, California, on its climb toward Donner Pass. The cab-forward design allowed Southern Pacific to use the large articulated locomotives safely on its Donner Pass crossing, which featured many miles of tunnels and snowsheds. *Otto C. Perry,* Denver Public Library Western History Department

ABOVE

The first American application of the articulated Mallet Compound locomotive was an 0-6-6-0 built by Alco for the Baltimore & Ohio in 1904. This locomotive, which came to be known as "Old Maud" after a popular cartoon mule of the period, was first displayed at the 1904 St. Louis Exposition. The locomotive was a resounding success, and several thousand Mallets were built for American railroads. *John P. Hankey collection*

Superheating quickly caught on as a method of dramatically improving the output of conventional locomotives. In 1910, the Schmidt Superheater Company introduced a commercial superheater, and by 1913 virtually all new locomotives were so equipped. One of the most revolutionary improvements since Stephenson's *Rocket*, the superheater dramatically increased steam locomotive efficiency without adding weight.

John White points out that before the advent of superheating all previous increases in locomotive output were dependent on increasing locomotive dimensions. So, while locomotives grew larger and more powerful during the nineteenth century, there was little appreciable gain in thermal efficiency. The weight-to-power ratio had remained essentially the same. Ultimately, the advent of superheating ended the use of most compound locomotives. The nonarticulated compounds, which had largely fallen out of favor by the time the superheater became popular, were the first to go. By the mid-1920s, however, the Mallet compound locomotive design had been largely supplanted by articulated locomotives of a simple design, although some lines, such as Norfolk & Western, continued to use and refine the Mallet compound. Norfolk & Western's Y6 class Mallet were in production until the early 1950s and remained in service until 1960.

CAB FORWARD

Some of the most distinctive American locomotive designs were the articulated steam engines designed specifically to tackle Southern Pacific's rigorous mountain climb through the California Sierra over Donner Pass.

Donner Pass, popularly known as *the* mother of all western mountain grades, is without question one of the toughest stretches of railroad in the United States. Surveyed in the early 1860s by Western railroad pioneer Theodore Judah, the line over the Sierra was built by the Central Pacific as part of the original Transcontinental railroad. Eastward from Roseville, California, the railroad climbs from an elevation of about 125 feet above sea level to just over 7,000 feet at Donner Summit in just under 90 miles. Much of the line battles a continuous 2 percent grade, and in places the grade approaches 2.4 percent.

The westward climb to the summit from Sparks, Nevada (located just east of Reno), while not as severe as the eastward climb, presents a substantial challenge to heavy trains. Although the grade alone represents a formidable climb, what really makes railroad operations tough on Donner is fierce winter weather. The snowfall at Donner Pass is among the heaviest anywhere in North America. One has not experienced winter until one has witnessed the wrath of a heavy Sierra storm. Over the course of a season as many as 700 inches of snow can bury Donner. In "wet" years it is not unusual to find more than 200 inches on the ground at any one time. Winter may begin as early as October and hang on well into May. To combat these extreme conditions, and to allow the railroad to run trains year-round, long snow sheds were constructed to protect the tracks in heavy snowfall territory. At one time there were nearly 40 miles of snowsheds and tunnels protecting the Donner Pass route. It was known colloquially as "railroading in a barn" because nearly the entire railroad from Emigrant Gap to Andover, California, was enclosed, a distance of 30 miles. At Norden, near the summit of the mountain, the railroad maintained an entire village interconnected with the snowsheds covered by passages to facilitate winter operations.

Motive power requirements over Donner had always been demanding. The strenuous operating conditions had spurred the Central Pacific to build 4-8-0 Mastodons, and later experiment with the 4-10-0 *El Gobernador* in the 1880s. (The 4-8-0s were reasonably successful, but the oversized *El Gobernador*, built primarily to satisfy the aspirations of Leland Stanford, the railroad's pretentious president, was a failure.)

By 1909, traffic on Donner was pushing the railroad to capacity and parts of the line were being double-tracked to facilitate greater flexibility. Southern Pacific management had been closely watching development of the Mallet compound. Eastern lines had been using Mallets for several years, and in 1906-1907 the Great Northern had successfully adapted Mallet types for road service over its Cascade Line, which had operating conditions similar to Southern Pacific's line over Donner. Surely this new type of locomotive would be ideal for hauling heavy freight through the California Sierras, so Southern Pacific ordered two oil-burning double-expansion 2-8-8-2s (the first locomotives to employ this wheel arrangement), Class MC-1, for service east out of Roseville. (Southern Pacific's locomotive classification system followed an obvious logic—unlike other lines that classed their locomotives with seemingly random combinations of letters and numbers—MC stood for Mallet Consolidation.) These locomotives produced 85,040 pounds of tractive effort, with 26x30-inch high-pressure cylinders and 40x30-inch low-pressure cylinders. Impressive power indeed. The Mallets showed promise hauling heavy tonnage.

In early trials up on the mountain, crews encountered a severe problem the railroad management had not anticipated. When working upgrade in the sheds and tunnels, great amounts of smoke and gas produced by the big Mallets quickly filled the sheds, obscuring the engineer's view and making it difficult to breathe inside the locomotive. This was hazardous to the crew, and men were unwilling to run the engines over the mountain.

The mighty Southern Pacific was not going to be denied the benefits of improved efficiency because of crew discomfort, so it searched for a solution to the smoke problem. Ultimately, the railroad discovered that by running the Mallets in reverse, smoke was kept in check. So it decided to turn its Mallets around and run them "cab forward." This would have been prohibitively difficult with a coal-fired engine, since the tender would be too far from the firebox, but was reasonable for Southern Pacific's oil-fired Mallets. (The idea for designing a locomotive with its cab forward was not original to the Southern Pacific. Around the turn of the century, a narrow gauge line called the North Pacific Coast, which operated in Marin County—not far from Southern Pacific's corporate headquarters in San Francisco—had converted an aged 4-4-0 to cab-forward operation following a disastrous wreck.) As unorthodox as it seemed, Southern Pacific asked Baldwin to construct a Mallet with the cab in front. This required considerable reconfiguration of traditional equipment. The tender was situated to ride behind the smokebox, and the cab

was arranged to suit the new direction of operation. What was normally the back of the engine facing the tender was now the front. Substantial plating was installed in an effort to provide crew protection in case of collision, large windows provided an unparalleled view of the tracks. Trappings such as the headlight, locomotive bell, number boards, and classification lights were situated on what was now the front of the engine.

On its delivery, the strange-looking machine had more than its fair share of skeptics. Crews were concerned about safety as the plates placed to protect them were small comfort compared to the length and mass of a locomotive boiler that normally rode between them and destiny. It's likely that crews were also unhappy with the Mallets because of the big engine's exceptional pulling power. With these machines, the railroads could haul more tonnage with fewer men, and undoubtedly those potentially displaced by this technological improvement resented it. Eventually the skeptics were quieted as the cab-forward Mallet proved its worth. The novel configuration solved the problems of operating in the snowsheds, and the Mallet's exceptional pulling power pleased railroad management. The cab-forward (also called "cab-ahead" or "cab-in-front"), Class MC-2, had virtually the same specifications as its conventional cab sisters.

PASSENGER SERVICE CAB-FORWARD MALLETS

Southern Pacific was very pleased with its new Mallets in freight service and Santa Fe seemed to have reasonable success running "high-speed" passenger Mallets, so Southern Pacific decided to have cab-forward Mallets built for passenger service. Baldwin delivered 10 2-6-6-2 Class MM-2s (Mallet Mogul) in 1911. These locomotives had larger driving wheels than the freight service MC-2s; 63 inches as opposed to 57 inches, and shorter, wider fireboxes. Their performance was marred by severe tracking difficulties in the California Sierra. To improve the locomotive's stability, a four-wheel leading truck was introduced and the frames strengthened, thus making the MM-2s 4-6-6-2s. While this seemed to solved the tracking problems, the Mallet Moguls were demoted to freight service after a few of years hauling "varnish"—what railroaders called passenger trains (presumably because in the days of wooden equipment, passenger cars were varnished, with or without paint underneath).

MALLETS TOO SLOW

Southern Pacific was generally pleased with its Mallets and ordered two more classes of 2-8-8-2s. By the mid-1920s these ponderous double-expansion engines were up against the same problems as Mallet types around the country. They were proving too slow for the sort of service the railroads were hoping to provide. In the 1920s, the trend was toward fast freight and the

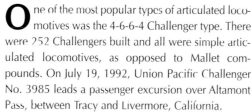

One of the most popular types of articulated loco-motives was the 4-6-6-4 Challenger type. There were 252 Challengers built and all were simple artic-ulated locomotives, as opposed to Mallet com-pounds. On July 19, 1992, Union Pacific Challenger No. 3985 leads a passenger excursion over Altamont Pass, between Tracy and Livermore, California.

On a sunny, clear June 14, 1993, Union Pacific Challenger 3985 leads the *Oregon Trail Special* eastbound up Encina Hill at Quartz, a few miles east of Baker City, Oregon. The Challenger design employed a large flat-bearing surface for its forward engine to pivot upon, which minimized vertical motion and provided a smooth ride at high speeds.

Mallets were capable of only about 10 miles per hour while climbing heavy grades. On the Southern Pacific, newer, single-expansion, nonarticulated engines started to displace the cab-forwards from freight service, and man-agement reevaluated the Mallet's viability. However rather than scrap the cab-forward concept, it was decided to convert the Mallets to single-expan-sion or simple articulateds at Southern Pacific's capable Sacramento Shops. In years past, these shops had designed and constructed a number of loco-motives. The conversion entailed rebuilding and enlarging the boiler for greater steam capacity, casting new, smaller, high-pressure cylinders for the simple engine, and installing new appliances such as superheaters and Worthington feedwater heaters. The conversions were successful, and the simple engines were capable of greater operating speeds and had more than 10 percent greater tractive effort than the old Mallets.

The simple articulated concept was so successful Southern Pacific decid-ed to order some new locomotives of this design, and soon after, it began con-verting the old engines. These new simple articulated locomotives employed four-wheeled leading trucks like the MM-2s and were essentially a modified version of Northern Pacific's Yellowstone type (although they featured a 4-8-8-2 wheel arrangement as a result of the reverse running, rather than the 2-8-8-4 of the NP locomotives). The first new simple articulateds were delivered in 1929, Class AC-4. They had significantly larger fireboxes than the Mallets, larger cylinders than the reconfigured locomotives (24x32 inches as opposed to 22x30 inches on the rebuilt engines), operated at a higher boiler pressure (235 pounds psi versus 210 pounds psi), and featured 63-inch drivers, larger than those on the MC-class Mallets. As a result these new articulateds gener-ated 112,760 pounds tractive effort—substantially more than the converted

Norfolk & Western Class A 2-6-6-4 No. 1218 leads an excursion down 19th Street in Erie, Pennsylvania. Norfolk & Western was one of only a few railroads to build its own steam locomotives in the twentieth century, and 1218 is a 1943 product of the railroad's Roanoke Shops. The N&W A Class were simple articulateds designed for high-speed service They were equipped with roller bearings on all axles; the last five, Nos. 1238-1242, also had roller bearing side and main rods.

MC Mallets. During the course of the next 16 years, Southern Pacific would order eight more classes of cab-forward articulateds and also a single class of 12 Lima 2-8-8-4 articulateds with conventional cab orientation that initially burned coal instead of oil.

The final cab-forwards, Class AC-12, were delivered at the height of World War II in 1943 and 1944, when Southern Pacific's line over Donner Pass was experiencing record traffic levels. More than 100 moves a day were often the norm at Norden, as passenger trains rolled through in multiple sections and heavy freight poured over Donner Pass. The later articulateds were designed for dual service, and during the war they were as likely to haul the *Overland Limited* as a refrigerated boxcar train out of Roseville. The cab-forwards were not relegated just to Donner and found service all over Southern Pacific's Pacific Lines. Southern Pacific classes AC-7 through AC-12 had a semistreamlined appearance in accordance with the styling of the times.

Between 1910 and 1944, Southern Pacific took delivery of 256 cab-forward articulateds (both Mallets and simples), and these were the only locomotives of this type to operate on American soil. While other railroads eyed

the concept, none ever adopted it, and the type remained unique to Southern Pacific—a railroad generally known for its individualistic operations.

Southern Pacific's typical World War II–era operation of a 6,000-ton, 100-car "fruit block" (a solid train of refrigerated cars of California produce) east of Roseville over Donner Pass routinely used four AC class locomotives—representing an estimated 500,000 pounds tractive effort (or more depending on the classes of ACs used)—spread throughout the train. Two ACs would lead the train, the third AC would be "cut in" 60 or 70 cars deep in the train, and the fourth AC "cut in" about 10 cars ahead of the caboose. The train would operate at an average speed of about 15 miles per hour, and if all were running properly, would have made the 140-mile run between Roseville and Sparks within the crew's hours of service (at that time 16 hours on duty). Heavier trains might warrant additional "helpers" at Colfax, 35 miles east of Roseville, and more than 2,000 feet higher! The 30-mile climb eastward from Colfax to Emigrant Gap is particularly brutal. Getting a train over Donner Pass in the days of steam was a show of power not to be soon forgotten.

NORTHERN PACIFIC YELLOWSTONE

In the mid-1920s, the Northern Pacific (NP) was faced with a unique motive power quandary on its Yellowstone Division through the Badlands between Mandan, North Dakota, and Glendive, Montana. The solution was either a new type of locomotive or more radical options. What is so special about the Yellowstone district? While the maximum grade on this line is held to 1.1 percent— generally considered an acceptable railroad grade—the railroad follows a series of summits in a "rock and roll profile" known to railroaders as a "saw tooth."

Elsewhere NPs mainline grade featured long stretches of grueling 2.2 percent grades, notably the crossing of the continental divide at Mullan Pass west of Helena, Montana, and NP's Cascade crossing at Stampede Pass in central Washington State. These grades, although steep, featured continuous, unbroken climbs to a definitive summit, thus were easily conquered by running helpers on heavy freights. But the use of helpers on Yellowstone district was impractical because of the great length of the run and the many short grades. So instead of helpers, NP chose to run shorter trains, limiting most to just 2,000 tons, about half the tonnage permitted on the rest of the mainline. Shorter, more frequent trains required more locomotives and more crews and thus a substantial increase in operating expense.

Traditionally, NP had conserved money by using locally mined coal, rather than importing coal from off-line. The catch was that the local variety, called Rosebud coal, was a sub-bituminous lignite and had a very low BTU content (poor heating value). It took a great deal more Rosebud coal to perform the same work as the higher grade bituminous coal used in most American steam locomotives. Adding to NP's problems was poor water along the line, which produced excessive foaming in locomotive boilers.

Because of the operational difficulties on the Yellowstone Division, the railroad examined relocating the line, an expensive prospect that would bring its own share of challenges. Another option was electrification, which was a popular solution at the time, often proposed as a panacea to troublesome railroad operations. If NP electrified, it could continue to use Rosebud coal. However, like line relocation, electrification was an expensive solution. Instead NP chose to design a new type of steam locomotive.

Working with Alco, NP engineers came up with a simple articulated type that could potentially solve the traffic problems of the Yellowstone district. This new locomotive was based largely on the design of Denver & Rio Grande Western's successful 2-8-8-2, but it featured a greatly enlarged firebox and nominally increased boiler pressure (from 240 psi on the D&RGW locomotive to 250 psi on NP's). To accommodate Rosebud coal, the NP articulated required a firebox 266 inches long and 114 inches wide with 182 inches of grate area (as opposed to the 218x108-inch firebox with a 136.5-inch grate area on the Rio Grande engine).

This gargantuan firebox—the largest ever employed on any steam locomotive—was supported by the rear two drivers on the hind engine and a two axle rear trailing truck—the first application on an American articulated type. The boiler and firebox together require more than 5,000 stay bolts. To publicize the boiler's great size, Alco staged a catered banquet for 12 inside it. While such publicity stunts were not uncommon in the 1920s, this was one event that would not be soon forgotten.

Southern Pacific cab-ahead class AC5 No. 4112 leads an eastbound freight past 16th Street in Oakland, California, in 1952. The Southern Pacific fleet of cab-ahead articulated locomotives was designed for mountain running but could be found on SP routes all over California and Oregon. Many ACs worked off their final miles around the Bay Area, as new Electro-Motive diesels had taken over in the mountains. *Fred Matthews*

Crews found that Mallets were difficult to operate in the Sierra because the cabs tended to fill with smoke, so to take advantage of the Mallet compound (and the later simple articulateds), Southern Pacific turned the locomotives around and put the cab ahead of the boiler. At Roseville, California, on November 30, 1957, Southern Pacific cab-ahead No. 4274 prepares to make one of its last crossings of Donner Pass before its retirement. *Fred Matthews*

At Chemult, Oregon, on August 15, 1949, Great Northern 2-8-8-0 Mallet No. 2019 leads a freight southward toward Bieber, California. This was an M-1 Class locomotive built by Baldwin in 1912, making it somewhat of an antique in 1949. Few railroads were using Mallets in main-line service at this late date, let alone one that was more than 35 years old. Great Northern and Western Pacific used their "Inside Gateway" to compete with Southern Pacific for traffic moving between Oregon and California. *Fred Matthews*

Southern Pacific AC-11 No. 4274 at Sacramento, California. Southern Pacific was the only railroad in the United States to operate cab-ahead articulated locomotives. *Fred Matthews*

Alco delivered the prototype to NP in January 1929. It had two pairs of 26x32-inch cylinders, weighed 717,000 pounds, and produced 140,000 pounds of tractive effort, plus an additional 13,400 pounds of tractive effort with its trailing truck booster. This was one big engine! At the time of its delivery, NP 2-8-8-4 was *the* largest locomotive in the world and it would hold that title for more than a decade. It was named the Yellowstone type, presumably in honor of the Yellowstone River and the division the locomotive was designed to operate on, and possibly too, for Yellowstone National Park, one of NP's largest tourist destinations.

Although big and powerful, the prototypical Yellowstone did not give a flawless performance. It suffered from steam leaks and other minor mechanical problems. Despite these flaws, after a year of testing, the railroad decided the Yellowstone would solve its problems on the troublesome Yellowstone division, and it put up for bid an order for 11 more locomotives. In typical situations, the manufacturer that produced the prototype would expect to win at least a portion of the production order. In this case, Baldwin underbid Alco and won the entire contract. In 1930, Baldwin's Eddystone Plant produced eleven 2-8-8-2s for NP. While slightly heavier and taller than the prototype, these locomotives were built to essentially the same specifications as Alco's original.

When working hard, one of these enormous machines could consume 40,000 pounds of coal per hour. However, in the final assessment

The Virginian Triplex had three complete sets of running gear. This locomotive built in 1916, like three similar locomotives built in 1914 for the Erie Railroad, were unsuccessful attempts at putting more power behind just one throttle. Although built a few years after the Erie Triplexes, the Virginian machine failed to adequately address the design flaws of those earlier engines and has been considered a complete failure. *Baldwin builder photo, Railway & Locomotive Historical Society Collection, California State Railroad Museum*

In June 1945, a Baltimore & Ohio EM-1 Yellowstone hauls a heavy mixed freight eastbound up the Cranberry Grade near Rodemer, West Virginia. B&O's Cranberry Grade between Cumberland, Maryland, and Grafton, West Virginia, is one of the steepest main-line grades east of the Rocky Mountains. *Charles A. Brown, Robert A. Buck collection*

of their service, NP's Class Z-5 Yellowstones are probably better remembered for their statistical superlatives and awesome appearance than their actual performance on the Yellowstone division. Their tenure here was short-lived. The Yellowstones were not welcomed by the men who ran them. Engineers saw the large engines as a threat to their employment. It is likely that their poor attitudes toward the locomotive contributed to the Yellowstones' lackluster performance. Eventually the Yellowstones were placed in helper service on the steeper Rocky Mountain grades to the west, where articulateds had been operating for decades, and the crews had come to accept them. The Yellowstone type, however, was refined and used in greater numbers by several other railroads with considerable success.

at Duluth and Two Harbors. These powerful monsters were capable of singly hauling 19,000-ton ore drags (a tremendously heavy train) and did so with substantially smaller fireboxes—a mere 125 square feet of grate —than NP's original Yellowstones. This was because DM&IR's Yellowstones did not have to accommodate the glorified sod NP called Rosebud coal. Like the 11 NP production 2-8-8-4s, DM&IRs were built by Baldwin.

YELLOWSTONES ON THE B&O

The last of the Yellowstones were built during 1944 and 1945 for Baltimore & Ohio, which had wanted to order diesels but was denied the pleasure by the War Production Board. Compared to NP's massive Z-5s, B&O's EM-1s were small, weighed just 628,700 pounds, and had only 118 square foot firebox grates. Yet they were the largest locomotives ever to operate on the Baltimore & Ohio and provided 115,000 pounds tractive effort.

These 30 locomotives worked the heavily graded lines west of Cumberland, Maryland: the Chicago Line toward Pittsburgh and the old "West End" toward Grafton, West Virginia. The West End is one of the most formidable stretches of main-line grade in the east. It features a series of steep, tortuous grades and is one of the highest main-line crossings of the Alleghenies. It was an important coal route, and the EM-1s were assigned to work east out of Grafton with very heavy trains and would lead both coal drags and "fast freights" alike—although no freight train moves with any great swiftness over the West End. The first climb east of Grafton is the Newburg Grade to Tunnelton. This is just a minor rise compared to the big pull, but most trains would still warrant a pusher. After cresting the grade and dropping down the relatively short Cheat River Grade crossing the famous Tray Run viaduct, to Rowlesburg,

Two Baltimore & Ohio Mallets shove on the rear of a heavy coal train at Amblersburg, West Virginia, on March 20, 1948. Leading this train as it climbs B&O's formidable Cranberry Grade is one of its EM-1 Yellowstones. *Charles A. Brown, Robert A. Buck collection*

During World War II the Baltimore & Ohio, like most American railroads, was in desperate need of more motive power. The railroad wanted Electro-Motive FT diesels, but was denied them by the War Production Board, so it ordered EM-1 Yellowstones instead. Yellowstone 7618 ascends the Cranberry Grade at Amblersburg, West Virginia, on July 14, 1946. *Charles A. Brown, Robert A. Buck collection*

Southern Pacific embraced the 2-8-8-4 and built many locomotives of this type for mountain service in California and Oregon. Most were of Southern Pacific's famous cab-ahead variety and actually featured a 4-8-8-2 wheel arrangement, but 10 locomotives, Class AC9, built by Lima in 1938 followed the more conventional pattern and were the only late-era articulateds on Southern Pacific with conventional cabs. The AC9s were coal burners (unusual on the Southern Pacific, which preferred oil burning locomotives) and were assigned to the tunnel-free Tucumcari Line in central New Mexico. They were handsome locomotives with a semi-streamlined appearance.

In 1943, Duluth, Missabe & Iron Range acquired a fleet of 19 Yellowstones to haul ore from the Minnesota Iron Range to the docks

West Virginia, the real climb begins. East of Rowlesburg begins the Cranberry Grade. This is the sort of climb legends are made of: nine winding miles of a nearly 2.7 percent grueling grade through some of the most scenic terrain in West Virginia. Less than a mile from the top of Cranberry is a sharp curve buffeted by a shear row of distinctive rocks known as Salt Lick. The top of the hill is at Terra Alta, West Virginia. If one stands here and looks west on the B&O, it is like looking down a ramp. A train can be heard working this grade for as long as 45 minutes before it crawls into sight. Watching and listening to an EM-1, with its twin stacks pouring a column of cinders high in the sky as it successfully battled the Cranberry Grade, must have been one of the greatest shows in all railroadom!

On June 11, 1949, EM-1 No. 7619 leads an eastbound Baltimore & Ohio coal train through Tunnelton, West Virginia. Although just easing into a down grade, the big locomotive is still working hard as the bulk of its train is still being hauled up grade through the Kingwood Tunnel and over the summit of B&O's Newburgh Grade. *Bruce Fales, Jay Williams collection*

CHALLENGERS AND BIG BOYS

Until the mid-1930s most articulated locomotives were intended for relatively slow speed service. Instability at high speeds caused primarily by excessive vertical play between the forward and rear engines precluded operating articulated locomotives faster than 40 or 50 miles per hour. In the mid-1930s, Union Pacific and Alco designed a new type of articulated locomotive intended specifically for high-speed service that overcame previous stability problems. It used a 4-6-6-4 wheel arrangement and featured several distinct improvements over earlier articulateds. Its four-wheel lead truck gave the engine added tracking ability, but the most important innovation was a large flat-bearing surface for the forward engine to pivot on. This minimized vertical motion and provided for a much smoother ride at high speed. Precision techniques were used to counterbalance the driving wheels, thus reducing the effect of the reciprocating weights.

The first 4-6-6-4 was delivered in 1936 with 67-inch driving wheels. It was a well-balanced machine, easily capable of 70 miles per hour running. Union Pacific was very pleased with the new engine and designated it the Challenger type. They were used in both freight and passenger service. Because of their short wheelbase, and relatively light axle loadings, the Challengers were capable of operating on most main lines, unlike many earlier articulateds.

The Challenger quickly became the most popular type of simple articulated and was ordered by a number of railroads, including several lines in the Northeast where articulated simple locomotives had traditionally not found much favor. Bruce indicates that 215 Challengers were built. Later Challengers were built with 69- and 70-inch drivers and incorporated a number of modern features such as cast steel engine beds, roller bearings, and balanced disc drivers to improve efficiency.

Norfolk & Western approached the same problem as Union Pacific and Alco, coming up with a slightly different locomotive. N&W's class A articulateds used a 2-6-6-4 wheel arrangement, but possessed many of the same qualities of the Challenger. The As were dual service locomotives capable of operating at 70 miles per hour and Norfolk & Western built 43 of them between 1936 and 1950 at its Roanoke Shops. These were outstanding machines and set records for efficiency and availability.

In 1941, Union Pacific expanded the Challenger into a 4-8-8-4. This was an enormous machine, and among the heaviest reciprocating steam locomotives ever built. It had sixteen 68-inch driving wheels and weighed 772,000 pounds. Appropriately named Big Boy, the type was intended to lift heavy trains over Sherman Hill, west of Cheyenne, Wyoming. The railroad ordered 25 Big Boys and used them until the end of steam. Although they were too big and heavy to operate on most lines and were never ordered by any other railroad, they were among the last big steam engines to operate in the United States and saw service until the late 1950s.

5

SUPERPOWER AND STREAMLINERS

O n a misty autumn morning in 1927, a distinct exhaust note punctuates the otherwise peaceful sounds of the Berkshire Hills in western Massachusetts. A distant westbound freight works upgrade through the rock cuts below Middlefield. The sounds, fading in and out, become gradually louder and more pronounced as the train approaches. It is working the toughest part of the grade, the grueling 1.67 percent between Chester and Becket. Many a train has lost traction and stalled while climbing here, but not today!

A column of steam and smoke appears above the trees, just as the morning sun illuminates the tops of the hills. Deep golden rays of morning sunshine light the fall foliage and exhaust steam. The train crawls through the S-curve below Middlefield Station and crosses an ancient stone arch bridge. Leading this westbound is no ordinary locomotive: it's Boston & Albany No. 1426, a Lima 2-8-4 Berkshire, what the folks at Lima call Superpower. This state-of-the-art modern locomotive incorporates many of the latest developments in steam technology, making it more powerful and more efficient than anything that has ridden these rails before.

As the locomotive passes, a shower of cinders covers the ground. A long string of freight cars follow the engine, grinding upgrade. Twenty minutes after the train has passed the Berkshire, it can still be heard working toward the summit at Washington. Once it crests the top, the Berkshire will pick up speed as it proceeds westward to Selkirk, New York.

These new superpowered locomotives allowed Boston & Albany's parent company, New York Central, to improve freight service. Although the Berkshire slugged it out on the grade, it

A detail view of Southern Pacific's Lima built 4-8-4 Northern No. 4449 displays the locomotives headlight (bottom) and oscillating headlight (top). Of SP's eight classes of 4-8-4s, only its 28 GS-4's and 2 GS-5's were equipped with oscillating headlights, features that improved locomotive visibility, particularly at night.

T he Chesapeake & Ohio remained loyal to steam longer than most other American railroads. It continued to order new steam locomotives into the late 1940s. Its five J-3a Northerns were built by Lima in 1948, making them among the last of the type built in the United States. Norfolk & Western held on to steam even later. C&O J-3a No. 614 picks up its orders at Port Jervis, New York, on June 14, 1997.

could haul more freight over road faster than older engines. Locomotives like this enabled railroads around the nation to speed up their freight services and compete more effectively with the over the road trucks that had been eating into railroad business since the early 1920s.

THE BIRTH OF SUPERPOWER

Traditionally, passenger trains needed to move quickly while freight slowly plodded along. But in 1920, the United States Railway Administration relinquished control of American railroads, and locomotive builders took on a new challenge as the railroads promoted the concept of fast freight.

The traditional slow-moving freight, which ran at an average speed of 10 to 15 miles per hour and took weeks to reach its destination, no longer provided acceptable service. Competition from the new highways mandated better service, and slow moving drags were straining the railroads' capacity. Long, slow freights required more track space, more crews, and more locomotives. If the goods could move over the railroad quicker it would beat the competition, please customers, and relieve some of the strain on railroad resources. So, there was a need for locomotives that could haul heavy tonnage relatively fast. Each of the three major builders came up with solutions to this new motive power requirement with varying degrees of success, but Lima's solution was the clear winner.

In the 1920s, the Lima Locomotive Works was the new kid on the main-line steam locomotives block. Yet, in a relatively short time, it revolutionized the industry. Lima's predecessor companies had been building successful Shay geared locomotives since the 1880s and had only turned to the design and construction of new road locomotives a few years before World War I. Soon the company was selling more conventional steam locomotives than Shays.

In 1916, Lima was purchased by Joel Coffin, who directed the full thrust of the company's efforts toward building main-line steam locomotives. Coffin hired William Woodard as Lima's vice president of engineering. Woodard had worked for both Alco and Baldwin and was one of great geniuses of steam locomotive technology in the twentieth century. His ideas were progressive and practical, and within a short time he was building some of the most efficient steam locomotives in the world.

The New York Central quickly embraced the new builder by placing sizable orders for 2-8-2 Mikado types. Under the direction of Woodard, Lima dramatically improved the performance and efficiency of the Mikado type by refining its design and successfully integrating several recent advances, including feedwater heaters, automatic stokers, and slow-speed boosters.

In 1922, Lima built an experimental super Mikado for the New York Central based on the same basic design as the railroad's earlier Mikado

locomotives. This locomotive, Class H-10 number 8000, was a resounding success. It was significantly more efficient than comparable New York Central Mikados but not dramatically heavier or larger. An Alco-built New York Central Class H-7e Mikado, constructed in 1920, weighed 330,600 pounds, whereas Lima's demonstrator weighed only 334,000 pounds while producing nearly 4,500 pounds more tractive effort than the older engine and delivering an additional 11,000 pounds with the booster at slow speeds. (A booster is a small, two-cylinder steam engine that drives an axle on the trailing truck or tender. It was used at slow speeds when the locomotive had ample steam to provide additional tractive effort and cut out when the locomotive reached about 10 miles per hour.) The H-10's performance resulted in greater fuel efficiency and more horsepower. The New York Central was very pleased with the new and improved Mikado and ordered approximately 200 similar locomotives: 75 built by Lima and the remainder by New York Central's regular locomotive supplier, Alco. Woodard and his team did not rest with simply an improved Mikado; they continued to refine and improve upon their steam locomotive design.

THE BERKSHIRE IS BORN

In 1924, Lima introduced a landmark locomotive design that changed the way the industry looked at motive power and ultimately rendered previous designs obsolete. The incremental improvements in steam locomotive technology since the turn of the century had gradually improved locomotive power output, and Lima designed its new locomotive around the principal changes in the technology based on its experience with the H-10 class Mikado. Where the other builders were toying with gimmicks to achieve greater power output, such as Alco's three-cylinder cranked axle designs, Lima went back to basics. It enlarged the firebox.

In the summer of 1991, 4449 heads eastward up the Sacramento River Canyon toward Dunsmuir, California. Southern Pacific 4449 was one of 18 class GS-4 Northerns built by Lima for the railroad in 1941. Southern Pacific's classification system used a simple logic for its abbreviations: the initials "GS" stood for "General Service" or "Golden State."

The distinctive streamlined styling of Southern Pacific's fast passenger locomotives is unlikely to be mistaken for anything else. SP 4449 races through Hooker Creek toward Redding, California, against the glow of the setting sun.

Milwaukee Road hired well-known industrial designer Otto Kuhler to style its streamlined Hiawatha trains. Its 4-4-2 Atlantics and 4-6-4 Baltics (Milwaukee Road did not always use the term "Hudson" for its 4-6-4s) are its best known streamlined steamers, but the railroad also streamlined some its older 4-6-2 Pacific types, such as this one seen at Sioux City, Iowa. *Leon Onofri collection, courtesy Robert W. Jones*

Union Pacific Northern 844 and Challenger 3985 work westbound through Sand Pass, Nevada, on April 25, 1991. Union Pacific purchased 10 4-8-4s from Alco in 1944, No. 834 to 844. They were among the finest 4-8-4s ever built and could easily attain 100 miles per hour on level track.

Since the very beginning, two of the main limiting factors in locomotive design had been the inability of existing railroad infrastructure to handle substantially greater weight and the amount of coal a fireman could shovel. By the 1920s, many railroads had improved their plant to permit significantly larger axle loadings than possible at the turn of the century, while the application of practical automatic stokers had allowed the development of dramatically larger fireboxes. Woodard recognized that greater output could be achieved by increasing the boiler capacity by introducing a larger firebox and boiler. A larger boiler could generate greater steaming capacity and allow for sustained high horsepower at speed. This was the sort of power the railroads needed to haul fast freight, and this is where many earlier designs had failed. Insufficient boiler capacity limited early designs, which would tend to run out of steam at high speeds.

To significantly increase the firebox size, Lima introduced the two-axle outside-bearing trailing truck to carry the additional weight. Thus its new experimental, eight-coupled locomotive was the first 2-8-4 type.

Lima's experimental 2-8-4 locomotive featured an exceptionally large firebox grate (100 square feet), 63-inch drivers, 28x30-inch cylinders, working steam pressure of 240 psi, and a weight of 389,000 pounds. Like its predecessor New York Central Mikado No. 8000, the Lima 2-8-4 was not vastly larger than earlier locomotives. Yet, no other nonarticulated engine could

come close to its output or efficiency. It was an extraordinary machine capable of delivering 69,400 pounds of tractive effort and 82,600 pounds maximum tractive effort with its slow speed booster. The aim of the 2-8-4 was to improve upon the 2-8-2 Mikado type by achieving greater fuel efficiency and to provide greater power when operating at speed. In *The Steam Locomotive in America*, Alfred Bruce states that locomotive output is a function of the amount of energy consumed and the efficiency with which it is applied to the rail. With its 2-8-4, Lima made a marked improvement in both areas and outperformed its super Mikado of a few years earlier. The enlarged firebox grate allowed the 2-8-4 to burn fuel more completely and apply the energy to the rail more efficiently than any other two-cylinder steam locomotive.

From the outset Lima was very pleased with its 2-8-4 demonstrator and designated it class "A-1" as symbol of its great potential. In March of 1925 it sent the engine to a known proving ground for testing—New York

Union Pacific 844 has the rare distinction of never having been retired. For many years it carried the No. 8444 to avoid conflicting with a Union Pacific Electro-Motive GP30 No. 844, but when the diesel was retired, the steam locomotive got its old number back. On August 24, 1996, Union Pacific 844 rolls east through Logan, Iowa, on the old Chicago & North Western main line.

Central's rugged Boston & Albany line—where generations of earlier locomotives had been tested. B&A's long westbound 1.67 percent ruling grade and tortuous profile through the Berkshire Hills of western Massachusetts had a reputation as one of the most formidable stretches of main line in the Northeast. Other grades might be steeper, but the B&A was good test, and it was the most substantial hill on the "Water Level" New York Central.

In the early 1940s, Pocahontas coal carrier Norfolk & Western needed a new type of locomotive to handle its growing passenger consists. Where most railroads would have worked with one of the established builders—Alco, Baldwin, or Lima—to come up with a suitable locomotive, or may have strayed away from steam to the halls of Electro-Motive's La Grange plant, N&W turned to its own mechanical engineers in Roanoke, Virginia, for a design. Norfolk & Western had not purchased a new steam locomotive from the commercial builders since 1927, preferring its own designs, and certainly was not, at that time, going to buy diesels!

Roanoke Shops came up with one of the finest 4-8-4s to ever roll the rails: the streamlined N&W Class J, which featured 27x32-inch cylinders, 70-inch drivers, a 107.7 square foot firebox grate, operated at 275 psi boiler pressure, weighed 494,000 pounds, and delivered 73,300 pounds tractive effort. The N&W built the first five Js in 1941 and 1942, and they were very modern machines with cast steel frames and roller bearings on all reciprocating parts. They also used lightweight rods made of alloy steel and had precision counterbalanced driving wheels

T wo Norfolk & Western Js pause between assignments at Shafer's Crossing near Roanoke, Virginia, on July 31, 1958. These handsome locomotives were used on Norfolk & Western's crack passenger trains: the *Powhatan Arrow* and the *Pocahontas. Richard Jay Solomon*

to minimize reciprocating forces. N&W also felt capable of handling the streamlining themselves, so while most railroads had their styling provided by well-known industrial designers, the J was designed by a little-known employee of the N&W passenger car department, Frank C. Noel. He did well, and the J is considered by many to be one of the most attractive streamlined steam locomotives.

The second order of six Js were built in 1943 and not streamlined because of war-time restrictions on the construction of passenger locomotives; they were listed as freight power. They also lacked the roller-bearing rods.

After the war was over they made a second pass through the shop and were upgraded to match the earlier engines, complete with streamlined shrouds.

By 1950, a number of railroads were claiming complete dieselization, and the Electro-Motive E7 was the standard passenger locomotive. N&W bucked the industry trend and built three more Js. These were the last new steam passenger locomotives built in the United States.

The J class performance was excellent. The Js allowed the railroad to eliminate double-heading on heavy passenger trains, and they were regularly assigned to the most prestigious varnish: Powhatan Arrow, Pocahontas, and the Pelican. Despite the unusually small driving wheels—the J's 70-inch drivers were among the smallest ever applied to a passenger 4-8-4—the engines regularly operated at speeds up to 90 miles per hour and could attain 100 miles per hour in short bursts. In a test, on the Pennsy's Fort Wayne Division, a J handled a 15-car, 1,025-ton passenger train at 110 miles per hour! The Pennsy's Duplex department ought to have been taking notes.

One J, No. 611, escaped scrapping and was preserved. In 1982, it was restored to service and operated in Norfolk Southern's historic steam fleet (NS is the successor corporation to N&W, following a merger with the Southern Railway). For more than a decade it was paraded around the system, hauling passenger excursions and delighting onlookers. However in 1994, a change in Norfolk Southern corporate philosophy resulted in 611's second retirement and today it is just a static display, albeit a very handsome one, at the Virginia Museum of Transportation in Roanoke. It is one of only a handful of preserved streamlined steam locomotives.

After a month of break-in runs, Lima and New York Central staged a well-publicized test of the new locomotive. Two eastbound freights left New York Central's Selkirk Yard 48 minutes apart. The first freight, weighing 1,691 tons, was led by one of the Central's latest heavy Mikados, a Class H-10 built by Lima's competitor, Alco. The second freight led by the Lima demonstrator was significantly heavier, weighing 2,296 tons. There were no unscheduled delays to either train, and Lima's 2-8-4 outpulled and outran the Mikado. Train dispatchers had to switch the 2-8-4 on to an adjacent main-line track, which allowed it to pass the Mikado without either train

having to stop. The 2-8-4 arrived at Pittsfield, some 50 miles from Selkirk, ten minutes ahead of the Mikado—a truly spectacular performance! The New York Central was very impressed and ultimately ordered 55 2-8-4s for the Boston & Albany from Lima. The B&A's 2-10-2s, and Mallets that had enjoyed a brief tenure as the railroad's mountain freight haulers were quickly bumped from B&A through freights in favor of Lima's 2-8-4. This new wheel arrangement was designated the Berkshire type in honor of the railroad on which it was proven, and for 20 years the Lima "Berks" ruled the B&A grades hauling tonnage to and from New England over the grades for

Canadian National was one of the earliest operators of the 4-8-4, taking delivery of its first of the type only a few months after Northern Pacific. CN eventually owned the largest roster of Northerns. Like many railroads that operated 4-8-4s, CN had its own name for the type, and for a time called them Confederations rather than Northerns. *Richard Jay Solomon*

Canadian National's U.S. subsidiary Grand Trunk Western operated a fleet of streamlined 4-8-4s, using them to haul passenger trains between Toronto and Chicago. One of the Trunk's odd looking streamliners is seen at South Bend, Indiana, on November 11, 1950. *Gordon Lloyds, Fred Matthews collection*

Reading class T-1 4-8-4 2100 rolls along a river in eastern Pennsylvania amidst peak fall foliage. In the mid-1940s, the Reading Company built 4-8-4s at its shop in Reading, Pennsylvania using parts from older 2-8-0 Consolidation types and 2-10-2 Santa Fe types. *Richard Jay Solomon*

which they were named. After its successful run on the B&A, the Berkshire prototype went on a nationwide demonstration tour. But, when it was done touring it did not join its sisters in rural western Massachusetts; instead it was purchased by a flatland railroad, Illinois Central.

Lima coined the term Superpower to describe its new locomotive design, and the Boston & Albany Berkshire was just the beginning. The Berkshire type sparked a revolution in the industry and was one of the most popular late-era designs. More than 750 Berkshires were built between 1925 and 1949, and as it turned out Berkshire types were the last new steam locomotive produced by both Lima and Alco.

VAN SWERINGENS AND THE BERKSHIRES

In 1916 two brothers, Oris P. and Mantis J. Van Sweringen, began to assemble a railroad empire, and by 1930 they controlled a number of railroads including the Nickel Plate, Chesapeake & Ohio, Pere Marquette, Erie, Missouri Pacific, and Texas Pacific. The Van Sweringen roads were particularly fond of the Lima's Superpower and especially the Berkshire type. There is no mystery behind this affinity: Lima's plant was located adjacent to the Nickel Plate's main line at Lima, Ohio. John J. Bernet, one of the railroad's top operating officials, embraced Lima's designs. He hopped from property to property looking for ways to improve efficiency and increase profits. An advisory mechanical committee was created and placed in charge of designing and allocating locomotives to the various Van Sweringen properties, and large quantities of Lima's Superpower were part of his magic formula.

Even after the threat of an antitrust action helped break up the Van Sweringen empire, the individual railroads continued to order Lima's steam locomotives. This ended with Nickel Plate Berkshire 779, the very last new steam locomotive built by Lima. Nickel Plate remained loyal to steam longer than most and had ordered 10 new Berkshires to supplement its fleet in 1948, just as many railroads were ordering whole fleets of shiny new diesel-electrics. The Nickel Plate was also one of the last railroads to operate steam in fast freight service. In the mid-1950s it was using its Lima Berks to race freight from Buffalo to Chicago, often outpacing its chief competitor (and one-time owner), New York Central, on its adjacent main lines. (In many places the Nickel Plate and New York Central lines are separated only by a row of telegraph poles.) Repeated again and again was the incongruous scene of a single, high-drivered Nickel Plate Berk with a fast freight in tow—including newly instituted trailer-on-flatcar "piggy back" cars—racing past a long, ponderous New York Central drag freight hauled by a quartet of Electro-Motive streamlined diesels.

THE BERKSHIRE INSPIRES MORE DEVELOPMENT

One of the principal ingredients of the Berkshire's success was its two-axle trailing truck, and this new development had the same effect on locomotive design that the single-axle trailing truck had 30 years earlier. A number of new wheel arrangements were introduced in short order. Soon most new locomotives were equipped with two-axle trailing trucks, and older designs, such as the popular 2-8-2 Mikado, were phased out. The race for greater power was renewed, and for the moment Lima had the edge.

The New York Central adopted the 4-8-4 very late in the steam era. The type had been in service on the Northern Pacific for more than 15 years before the Central considered using it in regular service (in the early 1930s, NYC experimented with an Alco 4-8-4 three-cylinder, high-pressure compound but chose not to adopt the wheel arrangement at that time). While other lines had been using 4-8-4s in passenger service, New York Central had perfected the 4-6-4 Hudson. (As noted in the main text, it also built a fleet of very capable 4-8-2s, which it referred to as Mohawks rather than Mountains.) When the Central finally decided to use the 4-8-4, it was a direct affront to Electro-Motive, which had been promoting its passenger diesels for nearly a decade.

Although Central's Hudsons and Mohawks had performed adequately hauling prewar traffic levels, the surge of World War II movements forced the railroad to develop a more powerful locomotive. New York Central decided to refine and perfect the 4-8-4, while at the time its arch competitor, the Pennsylvania, pursued its Duplex dream. Central built one of the finest 4-8-4s, whereas the Pennsy produced essentially a curious flop. By combining the best attributes of NYC's successful Hudsons and Mohawks, Alco built for the Central a fleet of 26 superbly performing, powerful 4-8-4s called Niagaras rather than Northerns.

New York Central continued to purchase new steam locomotives after World War II, but not for long. The 4-8-4 Niagara— New York Central did not use the term "Northern"—was one of the finest locomotives the railroad ever operated. On October 11, 1952, Niagara 6018 with the *South Shore Express* in tow, races west at Athol Springs, west of Buffalo, New York. *George C. Corey*

The first Niagara was delivered at the end of World War II in 1945. It featured 75-inch drivers, 25x32-inch cylinders, a 100.1 square foot firebox grate, and weighed 471,000 pounds. Its boiler operated at 275 psi, delivering 62,500 pounds tractive effort, and was advertised as delivering 6,000 drawbar horsepower at speed. Subsequent Niagaras were delivered with slightly larger—79-inch—drivers.

They were the epitome of modern locomotive design: their boilers were made from nickel steel, their drive rods were made of lightweight alloy steel, and aluminum was used on less strategic components to reduce weight. Like other modern high-speed steam locomotives, their drivers were precisely counterbalanced to minimize damage from reciprocating forces.

The Niagaras were capable of hauling a 1,000-ton passenger train at 80 miles per hour on level track. Like the Hudson, the Niagara set new standards for availability and utilization, equal to that of Electro-Motive's latest passenger diesels, the post-war E7s. The Niagaras averaged 862 miles per day and more than 26,000 miles per month.

While the Niagaras outperformed the diesels in some respects, the cost of operating the steam locomotives was noticeably higher. To maintain their exceptional availability, the Niagaras required considerably more attention than the E7s. So, despite their stellar performance as steam locomotives, they were quickly displaced from premier assignments and had very short careers.

William Woodard and his team at Lima did not waste any time jumping from the Berkshire to the next new type. By the end of 1925, before the first Boston & Albany Berkshires had reached their home turf, Lima delivered 10 2-10-4s to the Texas & Pacific. These locomotives, appropriately called Texas types, were essentially built to similar dimensions as the Berkshire prototype but with an extra set of drivers and slightly larger boiler and cylinders (29x32 inches as opposed to 28x30 inches on the 2-8-4). As with Lima's other modern super achievers, the T&P Texas type featured a trailing truck booster.

In 1929, the Van Sweringen–controlled Chesapeake & Ohio, then under the direction of Bernet, tested an Erie Berkshire with very favorable results. Based on its experience with the high-drivered 2-8-4, C&O ordered 40 impressively proportioned 2-10-4s from Lima. They featured 29x34-inch cylinders, 69-inch drivers, and a tremendous 122 square foot firebox grate, and they delivered a whopping 108,625 pounds of tractive effort with booster. At the time, they were the largest nondivided drive locomotives in North America. The C&O found that the superpowered Texas types with booster could produce an equivalent amount of tractive effort as its simple articulated 2-8-8-2 Chesapeakes, (known as "Simple Simons" to railroaders), but they used less fuel. As a result, C&O's new T-1 class 2-10-4s quickly displaced the articulateds in heavy coal drag service between the Kentucky coal fields and Toledo, Ohio, much in the same fashion that the Chesapeakes had displaced Mallet compounds only six years before. The C&O's appetite for power was insatiable, and before the end of the steam era, the superpowered Texas types would give way to an even more powerful Lima locomotive: the 2-6-6-6 Allegheny—close to the ultimate in reciprocating steam locomotive development. The C&O T-1 was later duplicated by the Pennsylvania, which classed it J1.

Southern Pacific 4-6-2 Pacific class P-8 No. 2472 leads GS-4 No. 4449 westbound along San Pablo Bay at Pinole, California. Baldwin built the Pacific in 1921, and Lima built the Northern 20 years later. Like many Southern Pacific steam locomotives, both are oil-burners.

Milwaukee Road 4-8-4 No. 261 poses as a Delaware, Lackawanna & Western "Pocono"— that railroad's name for its 4-8-4s— as it rolls through Waukesha, Wisconsin, on a crisp, clear October 10, 1994. The 261 was dressed up as a Lackawanna locomotive for the filming of a Steamtown movie. Steamtown, located in Scranton, Pennsylvania, operates on former Lackawanna trackage.

NORTHERNS AND HUDSONS

Lima's Superpower concept was quickly embraced by the railroad industry, and within two years of the Berkshire and Texas types came two more new super locomotive types: the 4-8-4 Northern and the 4-6-4 Hudson. While the Berkshire and Texas types were intended for freight service, the Hudson and Northern were intended for passenger work. The Northern was the logical expansion of the 4-8-2 Mountain, and this wheel arrangement was developed virtually simultaneously and independently by Alco, Baldwin, and Canadian National. The Hudson type was an expansion of the Pacific type simultaneously developed by Milwaukee Road and New York Central.

NORTHERNS

Northern Pacific needed a better locomotive to haul its popular passenger trains, including its flagship, the *North Coast Limited*. It looked to Alco to

Milwaukee Road No. 261 is a war baby. Restrictions during World War II put a cap on new designs, so Milwaukee Road's last 10 Northerns, delivered in 1944 to help ease the wartime traffic crunch, combined designs from Delaware & Hudson, Rock Island, and Union Pacific. Today, Milwaukee Road 261 is one of several operating Northern-type steam locomotives. It rolls time table directions west along the Mississippi River at Savanna, Illinois on June 24, 1996.

construct a super Mountain type that would meet several special requirements, including the ability to burn low-quality Rosebud coal and make especially long runs. Alco's solution was the first 4-8-4. The two-axle radial-bearing trailing truck enabled Alco to build a larger firebox, which had sufficient grate area to allow even burning of the low grade fuel. The 4-8-4's development was virtually simultaneous with that of the Northern Pacific Yellowstone 2-8-8-4 type, and the two locomotives embraced many of the same concepts.

In early 1927, Alco delivered the first 4-8-4 types to NP. These locomotives had 28x30-inch cylinders, 73-inch drivers, weighed 426,000 pounds, worked at 210 pounds boiler pressure, and featured unusually large fireboxes, with 115-inch grates. They were powerful machines and delivered 61,500 pounds tractive effort. Northern Pacific was pleased with the 4-8-4's performance and regularly assigned them to its heaviest passenger trains between St. Paul, Minnesota, and Livingston, Montana, a distance of nearly 1,000 miles—at the time the longest uninterrupted coal-burning locomotive run in

the world. Northern Pacific had found what it desired in a passenger locomotive and never ordered any other type of steam passenger power.

The 4-8-4 quickly became the most popular "superpower" type, and the most widely built late-era American locomotive. It was regularly operated everywhere in North America except in New England. The new wheel arrangement was christened the Northern Pacific type, a moniker quickly shortened to Northern type. No other locomotive type had a name more likely to incite controversy than the "Northern." The 4-8-4 was known by many other titles as railroads were disinclined to adopt the Northern name. In Canada, 4-8-4s were "Confederations." In the American South, where Northern had Yankee connotations, the locomotives were known as "Dixies." The Delaware, Lackawanna & Western designated their 4-8-4s "Poconos," after the eastern Pennsylvania mountains the locomotives were intended to surmount. Similarly on the Lehigh Valley, 4-8-4s were known as "Wyomings." The

Norfolk & Western continued building steam locomotives into the 1950s and one of its most famous engines, J-Class 4-8-4 611, was completed at Roanoke shops in 1950. Although the streamlined Northern was retired from regular service in 1959, it was preserved and later restored to excursion service in 1982. Here it is seen in October 1994, shortly before its second retirement, ascending Norfolk Southern's Saluda Hill. At 4.7 percent it is the steepest main-line grade in North America. *Brian Jennison*

The New York, Chicago & St. Louis, better known as the Nickel Plate Road, was one of several railroads controlled by the Van Sweringen brothers. The Van Sweringens were partial to Lima's Superpower concept and bought lots of Lima locomotives for their lines. The individual railroads continued with Lima even after the Van Sweringen empire was broken up in the 1930s. Nickel Plate No. 765, a Lima Berkshire built in 1944, rolls toward Buffalo in 1989.

Chesapeake & Ohio called their 4-8-4s "Greenbriars." On the New York Central, one of the last railroads to adopt the type, the 4-8-4 was none other than a "Niagara."

Few types have gained popularity as quickly as the Northern. By the end of 1927, Santa Fe, Lackawanna, and Canadian National had 4-8-4s in service. Where Northern Pacific envisioned the 4-8-4 as a passenger locomotive, Canadian National intended it as a dual-service locomotive. CN's 4-8-4s were relatively light, enabling them to operate on most lines. Ultimately CN and its subsidiaries were the most ardent supporters of the 4-8-4, ordering them until 1940. The CN eventually operated the largest fleet, more than 200 locomotives.

In 1929 the Rock Island ordered 4-8-4s from Alco specifically designed for freight service. These machines were a distinct departure from the passenger locomotives originally ordered by NP. Rock Island's 4-8-4s featured just 69-inch drivers, 26x32-inch cylinders (smaller diameter and longer stroke than NP's), and relatively small fireboxes with just 88.3-inch grates. They were capable of 66,700 pounds tractive effort and featured trailing truck boosters, which provided an additional 13,100 tractive effort for starting heavy trains. Rock Island found the 4-8-4 perfectly suited for its freight operation in the prairies and plains of the Midwest and eventually ordered more than 65 Northern types, giving it the largest roster of the type in the United States.

Alfred Bruce says the Northern type was the ultimate form of eight-coupled locomotive. The type had ample steaming capacity and thus was capable of sustained high horsepower and high-speed operation, making it ideal for both fast passenger service and fast freight service. As a result it was quickly accepted by many lines as a dual service locomotive, assuming the role once held by the 4-4-0. The two-axle lead truck and two-axle trailing truck gave the 4-8-4 superb riding qualities, making it popular with engine crews.

The tremendous power potential of the 4-8-4 encouraged the use of large driving wheels. Where 69-inch drivers were common on Berkshires, and Mountains rarely had drivers larger than 73 inches, 80-inch drivers on Northerns were not uncommon. The Great Northern S-2 class, built by Baldwin, introduced the 80-inch driver 4-8-4 in 1930, and many other roads were quick to follow this pattern.

In 1930, the Timken Company, a manufacturer of roller bearings, saw a great opportunity to increase its sales: railroad rolling stock. There were tens of thousands of railroad locomotives—not to mention freight and passenger cars—all of which ran on traditional friction bearings. Since each locomotive used dozens of bearings, the revenue potential was enormous. All Timken needed to do was convince the railroads that they needed roller bearings. The sticking point was the railroad industry itself, which had a history of staunchly conservative approaches toward new products. Managers were particularly skeptical of "wonder" products that promised to revolutionize the industry, which often proved to be worthless, or worse, detrimental to operation. So, despite Timken's stated advantages of tapered roller bearings, which promised to save the railroads millions of dollars by reducing friction and easing maintenance, the railroads were slow to take advantage of the new product.

Timken wanted to demonstrate the advantages of roller bearings by equipping a locomotive with them, but initial offers to equip existing locomotives were refused. Railroads wanted no part of the test. As a result, Timken decided to order its own new locomotive to demonstrate its bearings. So, it went to Alco and ordered a new 4-8-4—then the state of the art steam locomotive—to its own specifications. Timken's 4-8-4 was a unique machine. Based largely on New York Central locomotive design, it was built to accommodate clearances on virtually all American main lines allowing demonstrations all around the country with few restrictions. Intended for dual service, it featured 27x30-inch cylinders, 73-inch drivers, and an 88 square foot firebox grate. It weighed just 417,500 pounds (less than Northern Pacific's first 4-8-4s of 1927), worked on 250 pounds boiler pressure, and could deliver 63,700 pound tractive effort plus an additional 12,800 pounds with booster. It was a compact but powerful Northern.

In 1930, new locomotives were relatively expensive, so it was highly unusual for a nonrailroad to purchase one, particularly a specially designed engine such as the 4-8-4 Timken ordered. To help defray the costs, Timken arranged with 52 individual parts suppliers to contribute to the engine without billing until after the locomotive had completed its tests and could be sold.

As demonstrator for Timken's product it had a clever name: the Four Aces. It was numbered 1111 and displayed playing card symbols—heart, spade, diamond, and club—on its sand box number boards. It was painted dark green with gold stripes, and its owner's name was printed in bold serif letters on the tender. There was no mistaking this engine for any other!

The Four Aces was delivered in April 1930 and spent 21 months touring the United States, running on 13 different railroads. In that time it accumulated more than 100,000 miles and worked in all kinds of service. It hauled both fast passenger and heavy freight trains alike, achieved a top speed of 88 miles per hour, and hauled a 132-car coal train up a 2 percent grade.

To demonstrate the virtue of its bearings, Timken arranged to have a team of three young women pull the engine with a rope, in front of eager reporters. The stunt was effective and drove home the point: a locomotive on roller bearings was easier to move than one with conventional friction bearings. Reduced friction meant the locomotive would have greater starting power and would require less lubrication and less maintenance. It was also far less likely to suffer the dreaded "hot box"—a costly and sometimes disastrous flaw caused by an overheated journal bearing. Roller bearings were no gimmick and not just a cheap trick either: they really worked. After its first 100,000 miles, Four Aces' bearings showed no appreciable signs of wear.

The locomotive investment paid off: soon roller bearings were a standard item on most new locomotives. Some were later equipped with roller bearings on the side and main rods and the valve gear in addition to the axles. Timken went on to sell roller bearings for all railroad rolling stock, and today roller bearings are standard equipment on the axles of all railroad equipment.

The Four Aces had a long productive career after its brief stint as a Timken advertising model. Its firebox was damaged while running on the Northern Pacific, so the railroad bought the locomotive and it joined NP's pioneering roster of 4-8-4s. It was renumbered 2626 and served the NP for nearly 25 years before being retired in 1958.

To demonstrate the advantages of its roller bearings, Timken had Alco build it a Northern type that could operate on most North American main lines. The locomotive was No. 1111, nicknamed the Four Aces. Stylized versions of the four playing card symbols— spade, heart, diamond, and club— were painted on the locomotive's sand box and displayed in the number boards. *Builder photo, author collectio*

Under the direction of George H. Emerson, Baltimore & Ohio's Mt. Clare shops built several experimental locomotives with water-tube fireboxes, including this semi-streamlined Hudson type named *Lord Baltimore*. The B&O took many of its styling cues from British locomotive practice, including the skirting outside the drivers and door fasteners on the front of the smokebox. *John P. Hankey collection*

By the early 1940s the 4-8-4 had been developed into the ultimate conventional reciprocating steam locomotive. The refinement of the locomotive's proportions and the introduction of technological innovations allowed designers to produce truly awesome steam locomotives. Among the finest 4-8-4s were those built for Southern Pacific, Santa Fe, Union Pacific, Norfolk & Western, and New York Central.

HUDSONS

The 4-6-4 emerged simultaneously with the 4-8-4 in 1927. While the 4-8-4 was the optimum application of the four-coupled steam locomotive, the 4-6-4 represented the ultimate development of the three-coupled locomotive. Both new locomotive designs were originally intended for passenger applications, but the 4-8-4 became a dual-service steam locomotive, while the 4-6-4 was refined for a single, highly specific application. Milwaukee Road and New York Central worked on the 4-6-4 independently but at roughly the same time. The Milwaukee Road drew up plans for a 4-6-4 first, but could not afford to build one until 1929, while New York Central went ahead and completed its machine.

NEW YORK CENTRAL HUDSON

During the mid-1920s New York Central was hauling a growing volume of passenger traffic, and it was second only to the Pennsylvania Railroad in passengers carried.

Its famous "Water Level Route" connecting New York City and Chicago by way of Albany, Utica, Syracuse, Rochester, Buffalo, Erie, Cleveland, and Toledo, was one of the busiest passenger routes in the United States. Its track structure was immaculate, and its level profile encouraged fast running.

New York Central competed with the Pennsylvania in the New York City to Chicago corridor. Running time was key to the Central's market share and it perfected the heavy Pacific type, regularly hauling 9-car trains

at 80 miles per hour with them. But the Central needed to haul longer trains at speed and wanted to avoid double heading, an expensive and poor use of resources. Complicating the Central's situation were abnormally restrictive clearances—it could not pass anything much higher than 15 feet on the water level route, making a larger Pacific type prohibitive.

New York Central's experience with subsidiary Boston & Albany's 2-8-4 Berkshires revealed the strategic power potential available by using a two-axle trailing truck. As with the expansion of the Mikado into the Berkshire, the two-axle trailing truck would allow a 4-6-4 type to carry a larger firebox than a 4-6-2 and therefore have more steaming ability. New York Central's chief engineer, Paul W. Kiefer saw the 4-6-4 type as the solution for New York Central's heavy passenger trains and was largely responsible for the design of the engine. He worked with Alco to build a powerful engine that could accommodate New York Central's clearances and outperform the railroad's already excellent Pacifics.

The prototype 4-6-4, class J-1, was delivered to the New York Central on Valentine's Day, 1927. Like the first Berkshire, this locomotive was clearly a landmark machine. It featured 25x28-inch cylinders, 79-inch drivers, and weighed 565,200 pounds. Its boiler worked at 225 psi. It could deliver 42,300 pounds tractive effort and an additional 10,900 pounds with trailing truck booster. More significantly, the two-axle radial-bearing trailing truck allowed for a firebox that was 28 percent larger than that on a comparable New York Central 4-6-2 Pacific. The firebox grate was 20 percent larger and provided 13 percent more heating surface.

The locomotive's performance was outstanding; it could go 26 percent faster and produce nearly 25 percent more power than the Pacific. This was exactly the machine New York Central sought. It was designated the Hudson type after the famous river that New York Central closely followed between New York City and Albany. Powerful, fast, and fuel efficient, these machines could haul the Central's long fast passenger trains along the Water Level Route without the need for double heading.

During the next decade, the Central continued to perfect the Hudson, ultimately ordering 275, more than half of all American-owned Hudsons. The zenith of the design, New York Central class J-3a, exhibited markedly better performance than the prototype. This locomotive featured 22.5x29-inch cylinders, 79-inch drivers, and a firebox 60 percent larger than the Pacific. It was the best that New York Central could expect from a six-coupled locomotive.

New York Central's Hudsons were noted for their exemplary availability and miles operated between major overhauls, setting new standards for the industry. The J-3a's averaged 232,768 miles between major overhauls.

MILWAUKEE'S "BALTICS"

Although Milwaukee missed its opportunity to build the first 4-6-4, it eventually took delivery of the type in 1929, which it referred to as "Baltics," rather than New York Central's lexicon. Milwaukee's most famous 4-6-4s were six streamliners built by Alco in 1937-38 with 84-inch

On April 13, 1947, Boston & Albany No. 1409, an A-1a Berkshire built by Lima in 1926, leads 47 cars of freight westbound through Middlefield, Massachusetts. The ruling grade westbound to Washington Summit is 1.67 percent. To assist the train over the grade, a Mikado type was cut in on the rear in Chester as a helper. The Boston & Albany main line through the Berkshires was the proving ground for Lima's 2-8-4 type. *Robert A. Buck*

drivers. These locomotives were true speed demons and regularly hauled the fastest steam trains in the world between Chicago and Minneapolis. They averaged 81 miles per hour between terminals and could operate at sustained speeds in excess of 100 miles per hour!

RELATIVELY FEW HUDSONS BUILT

A number of railroads owned small fleets of Hudsons to haul their premier passenger trains including Burlington, Chesapeake & Ohio, New Haven, and Santa Fe. The Baltimore & Ohio even built an experimental Hudson with a watertube boiler.

While the Hudson was an excellent performing machine, it never enjoyed the widespread popularity of other types; only a total of 487 Hudsons were built for service in North America, less than half of the Northerns, and less than one-tenth of the Pacifics. The Hudson was a locomotive designed for a specific application—to haul fast heavy passenger trains—and was not well suited to other tasks. Northerns were more easily adapted to freight service, and Pacifics could find work on local passenger runs, but Hudsons were really only good for speed (although some did find freight work toward the end of their careers). Also the passenger road diesel became available in the late 1930s and cut into new locomotive orders that may have been Hudson types from that time on. The result was that Hudsons were not ordered in large numbers, and were often the first steam locomotives retired when the new passenger diesels arrived on the property.

STREAMLINERS

Some of the best known steam locomotives are the flashy streamliners of the 1930s and 1940s. These exotic looking engines, while relatively few in number compared to the vast hordes of utilitarian workhorses, were at the forefront of public attention. They were used to haul the most deluxe, premiere passenger trains: New York Central's *Twentieth Century Limited*, Milwaukee Road's *Hiawatha*, Pennsylvania's *Broadway Limited*, and Southern Pacific's *Daylight*. They were featured prominently in advertising and were popular with model makers and authors of children's books. (In some cases the authors and artists were the same people who designed the actual streamlining. Noted designers Raymond Loewy and Otto Kuhler both produced books on railroad

Water tanks were standard fixtures along the railroad in the days of steam. They were spotted at strategic locations along the right of way, to allow locomotives to refill their tenders. Boston & Albany No 1400, the first production Berkshire type, pauses at the tanks in West Brookfield, Massachusetts. *Robert A. Buck*

The New Haven bought 10 streamlined 4-6-4s, class I5, from Baldwin in 1937. Known as Shoreliners, they were painted black and silver, and they hauled New Haven's fast passenger trains between Boston and New Haven, Connecticut. The New Haven's main lines between its namesake and New York City were electrified, so passenger trains would change from to steam to electric power at New Haven. *George C. Corey*

Two Baltimore & Ohio class P-7 Pacifics seen in Philadelphia on November 29 graphically illustrate the styling difference between streamlined and non-streamlined steam locomotives. With the exception of the shrouds, both locomotives are nearly identical mechanically. *Charles A. Brown photo, collection of Robert A. Buck.*

Streamlined J-3a No. 5454 leads New York Central's *Twentieth Century Limited* toward Chicago along the Hudson River at the Bear Mountain Bridge in the summer of 1939. Henry Dreyfus provided the styling for 10 New York Central J-3a Hudsons, Nos. 5445 to 5454, which Alco built in 1937 and 1938. These locomotives featured disc drivers rather than conventional spoked drivers. *Frank Quin, Jay Williams collection*

locomotives.) Streamlined styles were varied, distinctive, and colorful. The streamliner represented renewed hope for the railroads during otherwise desperate times. They conveyed speed, comfort, and style. Most of all they indicated the railroads were a modern and efficient means of transport.

The streamlined concept dates back to at least 1865, when Massachusetts inventor Reverend Samuel R. Calthrop patented an air resistant train. There is no evidence of any attempt to build Calthrop's train, and the idea lay dormant until the turn of the century when the Baltimore & Ohio built an ill-fated experimental streamlined trainset called the *Windsplitter* (but featured a locomotive of conventional design).

The first truly streamlined steam locomotive may have been a Henschel 4-4-4 three-cylinder compound built in 1904 for the Prussian State Railways. In 1905, the McKeen Motor Car Company began building internal combustion engine powered streamlined rail cars. The company's founder,

William McKeen, was inspired by Naval torpedo boat designs he saw at the 1904 St. Louis World's Fair, and was encouraged by Union Pacific President Edward Harriman to apply the concept to a rail car. These cars enjoyed a limited popularity on the Union Pacific, McKeen's employer, and on affiliated railroads. The McKeen cars did not have a significant impact on the industry, but they seem to have had some effect on future streamlining.

In 1927, industrial designer Otto Kuhler drew up plans for a streamlined New York Central Hudson, but the concept did not interest the railroad at that time. In 1934 there was a sudden, renewed interest in streamlined trains. Two internal combustion-powered lightweight articulated trains, Burlington's *Zephyr* and Union Pacific's M-10000 (later the *City of Salina*), toured the nation creating interest in high-speed rail travel (see Diesel Debut, chapter 7). These trains were aerodynamically designed to reduce air drag at high speeds. The interest in streamlining caught on very quickly. That same year the

Boston & Albany Hudson No. 614 charges along with a heavy consist. The Hudson type was designed as a fast passenger locomotive. When diesels replaced the Hudsons on crack passenger trains, some assumed freight duties for a short time, but most were scrapped. *Ken Brennan, author's collection*

During the 1920s, builders were searching for ways to get greater power and efficiency from the reciprocating steam locomotive. One of Alco's solutions was the three-cylinder simple engine. The center cylinder powered a cranked axle. Union Pacific bought 88 enormous three-cylinder locomotives in a unique 4-12-2 wheel arrangement. The first 4-12-2, No. 9000, is seen during set-up activities at Omaha, Nebraska, in 1926. *Author collection*

Milwaukee Road was the first to order new streamlined steam locomotives. Its four 4-4-2 Atlantics, built by Alco between 1935 and 1937, were used in high-speed passenger service on its Chicago to Twin Cities main line. They regularly operated at speeds well in excess of 100 miles per hour and were among the fastest steam locomotives ever built. Milwaukee Road 4-4-2 No. 3 leads train No. 100, the *Afternoon Hiawatha*, on October 10, 1938. *Graham, Jay Williams Collection*

Pennsylvania Railroad streamlined its prototype GG1 electric (a design later refined by famed industrial design Raymond Loewy).

Later in 1934, Norman F. Zapf designed aerodynamic shrouds that were applied to a three-year-old New York Central Hudson, No. 5344, and this locomotive, named the *Commodore Vanderbilt* after the railroad's founder, is generally considered the first American streamlined steam locomotive. Zapf intended the shrouds to improve the locomotive's performance; aesthetics were a secondary concern. The shrouds disguised the locomotive's mechanical parts (which made maintenance difficult). But tests indicated a slight improvement in the engine's performance at speed. The *Commodore Vanderbilt* was assigned to the famous *Twentieth Century Limited* and operated between Croton-Harmon, New York, and Chicago (nonstreamlined electrics hauled New York Central trains between Grand Central Terminal and Harmon in order to comply with New York City's ban on steam locomotives).

In 1935, the Milwaukee Road took delivery of three 4-4-2 Atlantics that featured 84-inch drivers and aerodynamic shrouds designed by Otto Kuhler (a fourth locomotive was delivered in 1936). These were the first American steam locomotives built new as streamliners. They were placed in high-speed passenger service between Chicago and Milwaukee where they regularly maintained speeds well in excess of 100 miles per hour. Some authorities state that these Atlantics were probably the fastest steam locomotives ever to operate in North America.

By the late 1930s a number of railroads were operating streamlined steam locomotives. Many of these later designs were more aesthetically pleasing, tended to accentuate a locomotive's form rather than cover it up, and allowed better access for ease of maintenance. In most cases, however, this later streamlining only promoted the illusion of speed; it did not significantly reduce wind resistance and did little to improve the locomotive's performance. The Hudsons and Northerns were the most common types to receive streamlining, although a number of railroads dressed up older Pacifics and Mountains with streamlined shrouds. The most visually striking streamliners included New York Central's 10 J-3a Hudsons with shrouds designed by Henry Dreyfuss; New Haven's 10 I-5 "Shoreliners" (4-6-4s); a Pennsylvania Railroad K4s Pacific and the S1 and T1 Duplexes shrouded by Raymond Loewy; Southern Pacific's *Daylights*, epitomized by the classy, World War II era class GS4 Northerns; and Norfolk & Western's passenger locomotives typified by its outstanding J-class Northerns.

Few steam locomotives received the streamlined treatment after World War II, and many streamlined locomotives lost their shrouds when railroads found the shrouds interfering with maintenance. Furthermore, as diesels began to claim the choice passenger assignments, streamlined steamers often ended up on less-prestigious runs, and some were even bumped into freight service. Although the tenure of streamlined steam locomotive was relatively short-lived, its image is one of the most enduring legacies of the steam era.

6

SPECIAL SERVICE ENGINES

The conventional steam locomotive designed for main-line and branch-line freight and passenger service was not always best suited for more specialized applications, so a number of designs were developed for specific situations. These included engines designed to accommodate unusual working conditions found on industrial lines, construction tracks, logging railways, street and elevated railways, inclined rack railroads, narrow gauge lines, and even the larger railroads' special needs such as commuter service and inspection trains. While special service steam engines were sometimes built by the large locomotive builders, several smaller locomotive manufacturers focused specifically on their construction.

URBAN TRANSIT—DUMMY CARS

"THESE MACHINES [DUMMY CARS] ARE NEARLY NOISELESS IN OPERATION: SHOW NO SMOKE WITH THE USE OF ANTHRACITE COAL OR COKE, AND SHOW LITTLE OR NO STEAM UNDER ORDINARY CONDITIONS OF SERVICE. THEY CAN BE RUN AT TWO OR THREE TIMES THE SPEED OF HORSE CARS AND DRAW ADDITIONAL CARS." —FROM A BALDWIN LOCOMOTIVE WORKS ADVERTISEMENT IN 1890.

Beginning in the 1860s, street railways were searching for a better way to move their passengers through the nation's ever more crowded city streets. In many cities, lines sprung up that used horses to haul small lightweight coaches on tracks in the street. These "one horsepower prime movers" had limited pulling capacity, and alternatives were sought. One concept was to use small steam locomotives instead of animal power to haul the coaches. Due to fears of locomotives startling horses in

Like most builders, the Heisler Locomotive Works attached its name to the locomotives it built. This engine was Louise Lumber Company No. 2, which now serves the Silver Creek & Stephenson Railroad at Freeport, Illinois.

Many steam locomotives were designed for specialized services. The Denver & Rio Grande Western operated a fleet of outside frame three-foot gauge Mikados on its lines in Colorado and New Mexico. These were among the largest narrow gauge engines in America. During a late-summer thunder shower, former Rio Grande No. 484, built by Baldwin in 1925, hauls a Cumbres & Toltec passenger train around Tanglefoot Curve near the summit of Cumbres Pass in southern Colorado.

Tenderless tank switchers were well suited to operate in the narrow confines of factories and small yards found along the waterfront. Brooklyn Eastern District Terminal operated a fleet of tank engines built by the H.K Porter Company. On January 22, 1959, BEDT No. 13 works the car ferry at the railroad's main yard in Brooklyn, New York, against a backdrop of the East River and the Manhattan skyline. *Richard Jay Solomon*

Cass Scenic Shay No. 5 at Cass, West Virginia, on July 14, 1981. Shays were built in both two-cylinder, two-truck, and three-cylinder, two-, three-, and four-truck varieties. No. 5 is an example of the three-truck Shay. Cylinders were located on the engineer's side of the locomotive, which gave the engines a lopsided appearance. *William R. Mischler, collection of Brian Jennison*

the street and offending Victorian-era aesthetic sensibilities, designers created a shroud that resembled a horse car. These vehicles, known as steam "dummies" concealed a small locomotive. The engine's firebox, boiler, smoke stack, cylinders, and running gear were all hidden from sight, and the small engine could tow a coach through the city streets on rails without upsetting animals or people. Some larger dummy cars had space for passengers as well. While dummies achieved a limited popularity in some American cities, they were rendered obsolete with the development of the electric streetcar in the late 1880s, and by the turn of the century most had been retired.

FORNEYS

Tenderless locomotives called tank engines had been built since the very beginning of steam locomotive design. However, they had not been widely adopted for several reasons: they could carry only a limited amount of fuel, which greatly restricted the distance they could travel; and, the entire weight of the engine and tender rested on the driving wheels, which resulted in a loss of tractive effort as the locomotive consumed fuel and therefore got lighter.

In 1866, Matthias Forney patented a type of tank engine that partly overcame these flaws. He extended the frame of the locomotive to include a small tender, thus giving the locomotive added fuel and water capacity while taking the weight of the fuel off the drivers. The engine had a relatively short wheelbase, making it ideal for urban applications where sharp curves were prevalent. The Forney locomotive used an unorthodox 0-4-4T wheel arrangement.

Forney was not a novice locomotive builder; he had learned about steam locomotive construction from Ross Winans and later worked for the Baltimore & Ohio. (He later became editor of the *Railway Gazette*.) He was a staunch proponent of the tank engine concept but did not find a receptive market among the railroads. A few lines bought his engines for suburban commuter services, but they were unwilling to embrace his concepts fully. Large railroads were not the only users of steam locomotives, and Forney found another market for his product: urban elevated railways, which were just being developed in the 1870s.

Between 1868 and the turn of the century, New York City, Brooklyn (then an independent city), and Chicago began building elevated railways to relieve congestion in the city streets. These lines rode primarily on iron and steel structures above street level and featured many short grades and tight curves. The Forney type was perfectly suited for these elevated railways. It was relatively lightweight and adept at negotiating tortuous, steep track. Hundreds of Forneys were built for urban rapid transit service. Typically a Manhattan Elevated Railway Forney type weighed about 30,000 pounds, considerably lighter than a typical 4-4-0 of the period, which weighed about 64,000 pounds. The Forney had tiny (10x14-inch) cylinders, proportionally small (38-inch) driving wheels, and a firebox intended to burn anthracite coal to minimize pollution. Baldwin built Forney types in a Vauclain compound arrangement for use in Chicago.

Central Railroad of New Jersey used double-ended tank locomotives on its suburban commuter passenger runs. Double-ended locomotives saved the railroad money because it did not need to turn the engine at the end of each run—particularly advantageous when serving large stub-end passenger terminals such as Jersey Central's Jersey City facility. This photo is from a builder's card and the engine's vital statistics are on the back. *Author collection*

The Forney's tenure above the streets of New York, Brooklyn, and Chicago was very short. The elevated lines found electric power more suited to their operations, and by 1900 nearly all the lines were electrified, sending the unneeded steam engines to scrap. Some Forneys were also built for industrial and logging lines, and these survived longer. While his locomotive design achieved only limited popularity, Forney's reputation in the industry is probably best known for his book *Catechism of the Locomotive*, published in 1873—the most thorough treatise on American steam locomotives of the day.

Suburban Tank Engines

The tank engine concept was ideally suited for service on relatively short suburban commuter runs, and a number of eastern carriers used bidirectional tank engines on their short passenger runs. Because the engine and tender were combined on the same frame, high-speed reverse moves could be made without risk of derailment, with leading and trailing trucks giving the locomotives added stability. Their use was restricted to very short runs because of the small tenders, which limited the distance the locomotives could travel between refueling stops. The tank engines could run in both directions, which made it unnecessary to turn the engine when it reached the end of its run. This reduced operating costs, as few turntables and terminal facilities were needed. The Central Railroad of New Jersey and Boston & Albany were both strong proponents of this design in the twentieth century and owned sizable fleets to power commuter operations. The B&A's five 4-6-6Ts, Class D-1a, were the largest and last of the commuter tank engines built for operation in the United States. These stocky looking beasts were built by Alco's

Schenectady Works in 1928, with 23.5x25-inch cylinders and 63-inch drivers, and producing 41,600 pounds tractive effort. As with many suburban locomotives, these were designed to rapidly accelerate relatively heavy passenger trains with frequent station stops—typical commuter train operation. They normally ran to Riverside over both the winding Highland Branch and the Boston & Albany main line.

Tank Switchers

The 0-4-0T and 0-6-0T with a saddle water tank were both popular switcher types for industrial service (switchers are used for very short runs or to move cars around the yard). The 0-4-0T and 0-6-0T featured a very short wheelbase to negotiate sharp curves. The entire weight of the locomotive was on the drivers to obtain maximum tractive effort. These locomotives were popular with construction contractors and other firms that needed small, high tractive effort locomotives. Many railroads owned small tank engines for switching small yards, industrial parks, and harborside waterfront trackage. Switchers of this sort might also be found at passenger terminals and coach yards where the length of the locomotive was a consideration.

A variation of the tank locomotive was the fireless-pressurized engine. Instead of a traditional firebox and boiler, this locomotive had a large insulated tank that was charged with high-pressure, superheated water from a stationary boiler. This engine could operate for a limited time by releasing steam from the tank into its cylinders, which generally operated at low pressure—just 40 to 50 psi. Since the boiling point of water is raised with an increase in pressure, as the pressure in the tank decreased the water continued to boil, giving the locomotive workable steam for several hours.

The geared Shay was commonly found working on remote lumber hauling lines. It was the most popular of the three most common types of geared locomotives. Ely Thomas Lumber Company Shay No. 2, at Fenwick, West Virginia, on June 1, 1958, was built for the Enterprise Lumber Company in Simms, Louisiana. It is now displayed at the Railroad Museum of Pennsylvania in Strasburg along with examples of Climax and Heisler geared locomotives. *Richard Jay Solomon*

The flexibility and adhesion offered by a geared locomotive were well suited to lumber-hauling railroads, which often had very rickety track structure. Tracks were built to haul forest products out of the woods, and as the timber was harvested the tracks were moved or abandoned. On May 31, 1958, Elk River Railroad Shay No. 19 rolls through a creek bed in West Virginia, typifying the temporary nature of the lumber hauling railroad. *Richard Jay Solomon*

Obviously, this type of locomotive was only suited for short runs, but it was preferred for service in factories and other situations where a live locomotive spewing smoke and fumes was undesirable.

Switchers of all kinds were generally eclipsed by their much larger, flashier brethren in heavy freight service or fast passenger service on the main line. The lowly yard goat was rarely noticed, except for the unsightly smoke it caused. When the diesels came, the switchers were often the first steam engines to go.

RACK RAILWAY ENGINES

Adhesion grades steeper than 5 percent (a gain of 5 vertical feet for every 100 traveled horizontally) are not practical for conventional, rod-driven steam locomotives. So, to build a steeper railway line, a center cogged rail or rack is used to achieve traction. The rack is engaged by a geared drive wheel on the locomotive. To accommodate the steep grade and rack, specialized steam locomotives were developed.

The Manitou & Pike's Peak Railway in Colorado was one of several steam-operated rack railways in the United States. It used specially designed Vauclain Compound steam locomotives. The high-pressure cylinders on the bottom exhausted steam directly into the larger low-pressure cylinders above to improve the efficiency of the locomotives. Manitou & Pike's Peak No.1 is displayed at the Colorado Railroad Museum in Golden.

The Mount Washington Cog Railway is an all steam-powered rack railway that climbs to the top of its namesake mountain, an elevation of 6,288 feet above sea level. Its grade averages an astounding 25 percent; 5 percent would stall almost any train on an adhesion grade. To compensate for the steep grade, the railway's locomotives have their boilers at an angle to the frames, which helps keep a safe level of water over the crown sheet. Also, the locomotives always face uphill. *Richard Jay Solomon*

Wiscasset, Waterville & Farmington No. 2 seen at Wiscasset, Maine, is an excellent example of an 0-4-4T Forney type. The WW&F was a two-foot gauge line that connected with the Maine Central at Wiscasset. Matthias Forney advocated putting the entire weight of the locomotive on the drive wheels, while putting the weight of the fuel and water on the trailing truck. *Stanwood K. Bolton collection, courtesy of George C. Corey*

The largest Shay ever built was also the last. Western Maryland No. 6 was constructed by Lima in 1945 and ran for only a few years before being retired. Today the big three-truck Shay operates on the Cass Scenic Railroad. *John P. Hankey collection*

Rio Grande Mikado No. 463, one of the diminutive K27s , a type of locomotive known affectionately as a "Mudhen," hauls a Cumbres & Toltec freight train for photographers at Broad Spur on June 24, 1995. The K27s were one of several classes of Rio Grande narrow gauge Mikados that feature outside frames and counterweights. *Brian Jennison*

Although rack railways attained some popularity overseas, they were not widespread in the United States. A few American rack railways were built and required very specialized steam locomotives. The Mount Washington Cog Railway in New Hampshire and the Manitou and Pike's Peak Railway in Colorado are the most famous American rack lines, and their sole purpose has been to haul sightseers up the mountains.

The Mount Washington line still uses steam power, diminutive 0-2-2-0s, weighing only 26,000 pounds. They use two pairs of cylinders set back-to-back between the driving wheels, with each pair powering one set of wheels. The gear that engages the rack is set between the driving wheels and driven by a jack shaft. The boiler is set at a sharp angle to the frame of the locomotive to keep the water level over the firebox crown sheet level when on the grade—on Mount

Washington the grade averages an astounding 25 percent! The locomotives always face upgrade, and they back down when descending the mountain. When descending, train speed is held in check by maintaining back pressure in the locomotive cylinders. Today the Mount Washington line is still 100 percent steam powered and has continued to build new steam locomotives into modern times.

The Pike's Peak line employed a specially designed variation of Baldwin's four-cylinder Vauclain compound. The cylinders powered a jack shaft connection that indirectly connected to the driving wheels and cog drive. The locomotive used an outside frame, with siderods that drove crankpins and counterweights beyond the frame. Like the Mount Washington engines, the boiler was placed at an angle to the frame. While diesels haul most trains today, one steamer is occasionally used.

Denver & Rio Grande Western class K27 463 leads a "photo freight" westbound on the Cumbres & Toltec in the Toltec Gorge. The train is exiting the rock tunnel on June 24, 1995. *Brian Jennison*

The Heisler Locomotive Works built geared locomotives in Erie, Pennsylvania. Heislers use two cylinders arranged cross-wise below the boiler at a 90-degree angle to each other that power a crankshaft that powers the drive wheels through gearing on each axle. Louise Lumber Co. No. 2, a 36-ton two-truck Heisler, is now used in excursion service by the Silver Creek & Stephenson Railroad at Freeport, Illinois.

NARROW GAUGE LOCOMOTIVES

Narrow gauge lines enjoyed considerable popularity in the United States before the turn of the century. The lightweight nature and small proportions of narrow gauge lines and their ability to negotiate sharper curves and steeper grades than standard gauge lines made them more cost efficient to build. They were often chosen to serve remote regions where standard gauge lines would have been prohibitively expensive to construct. The "standard" American narrow gauge was three feet, although a number of other gauges were also used.

Prior to the turn of the century, most American narrow gauge railroads used proportionally small versions of 4-4-0s, 2-6-0s, and 2-8-0s, most of which did not employ designs that were notably different from their larger cousins. These machines' narrow inside frames severely restricted firebox size, so the firebox grate needed to be enlarged to increase the engine's power. Later narrow gauge locomotives, notably those built for the Denver & Rio Grande Western, solved this problem with several important designs. Beginning in 1903, Rio Grande took delivery of Mikado types that used outside frames and outside crankpins and counterweights operated by main and side rods (similar to those described on the Manitou & Pike's Peak engine) instead of the con-

ventional arrangement used on standard gauge locomotives. The firebox was supported by the rear trailing truck, which allowed for a larger grate and greater combustion area and made it a substantially more powerful locomotive.

Rio Grande had the most extensive and longest lived common carrier narrow gauge system (as opposed to an industrial railroad), and its three-foot gauge engines were among the largest nonarticulated narrow gauge locomotives in North America. Most were built by Baldwin, although some were Alco products and a few, the monstrous K37s, were rebuilt by Rio Grande from standard gauge Baldwin 2-8-0s.

GEARED LOCOMOTIVES

The conventional reciprocating rod-driven steam locomotive proved less than ideal when operating in lumber service and other specialized industrial applications where poor track, steep grades, and slow speeds were the norm. So several types of geared locomotives were developed specifically to provide high tractive effort and high adhesion when operating at slow speeds on poor track. These locomotives were driven by a crankshaft that powered the trucks by a network of gears and differed primarily in the arrangement of the pistons to the shaft. Geared locomotives could easily negotiate grades of up to 10 percent and would hold the rail on track that would have derailed any conventional locomotive.

The first and most popular geared locomotive was designed by lumberman Ephraim Shay in 1878. Early Shays, built by the Lima Machine Works of Lima, Ohio, used two vertical cylinders on the engineer's side to turn a horizontal crankshaft that powered two pivoting two-axle trucks at each end of the locomotive. The shaft turned the wheels by way of a

A close-up view of a Rio Grande K36 Mikado displays its distinctive running gear. Rio Grande's narrow gauge Mikado types used outside frames and outside crankpins and counterweights instead of the conventional arrangement found on standard gauge locomotives. This arrangement allowed for a larger, more powerful narrow gauge locomotive.

network of gears. In 1885, Lima expanded this arrangement by using a three-cylinder engine to drive three two-axle trucks. More than 30 years after Lima entered the locomotive business by building Shays, it reorganized into the Lima Locomotive Works and became one of the leading manufacturers of main-line steam locomotives. Lima continued building Shays until 1945, when it delivered Western Maryland No. 6, the largest of the type ever built.

The other two popular types of geared locomotives were built by the Climax Manufacturing Company of Corry, Pennsylvania, and the Heisler Locomotive Works of Erie, Pennsylvania. Climax began building locomotives in 1884. They used a pair of steeply angled cylinders situated beside the boiler to drive the crankshaft. Heisler used two cylinders arranged crosswise below the boiler at a 90-degree angle. Heislers were built in both two-truck and three-truck varieties.

Geared locomotives were popular with lumber companies and could be found everywhere that timber was harvested, particularly in northern New England; the Appalachian regions of Virginia, West Virginia, and Kentucky; the upper Midwest; and northern California and the Pacific Northwest. Because of their unique hauling abilities, gear locomotives working on forested logging spurs often outlasted their conventional cousins working out on the main lines. A number of geared engines continued to perform well into the 1960s.

The 0-4-0T was a popular switcher type. The full weight of the engine was on the drivers, and its short wheelbase was advantageous in tight curves. New York & New England No. 72 was built by the Taunton Locomotive Works in 1873 for the Hartford, Providence & Fishkill. In the 1870s, even the most utilitarian equipment was made to look attractive. Note the decorative trim on the smoke stack, headlights, and sand and steam domes. *Author collection*

Steam dummies were used on street railways to disguise the locomotive in an effort to avoid frightening horses and offending sensitive Victorian aesthetic sensibilities. The advent of the electric streetcar eliminated the need for steam dummies, and most were gone by the turn of the century. Brooklyn City Railroad No. 15 New Utrecht poses with its crew. Imagine riding through the streets of Brooklyn in a small coach hauled by this diminutive engine. *Author collection*

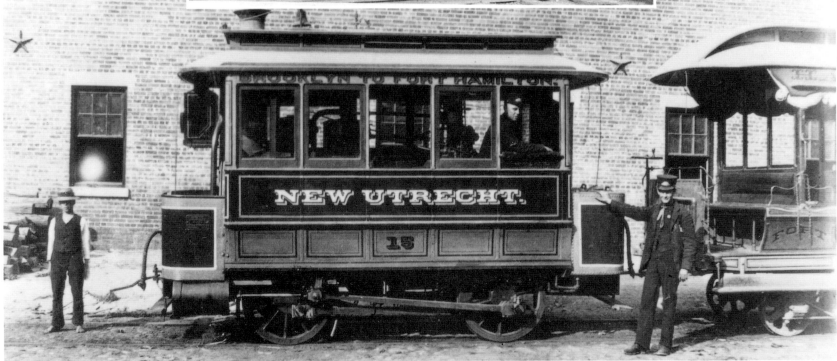

The Cass Scenic Railroad in West Virginia operates a fleet of Shay-type geared locomotives. The Shay type, built by Lima, was the first successful geared logging locomotive and the dominant type. *Richard Gruber*

7

DIESEL DEBUT

In the summer of 1935, out on the open prairie of eastern Colorado, the engineer of an eastbound Chicago, Burlington & Quincy freight takes the siding as per his orders. He must wait here for a westbound passenger train. Leading the freight is a big 2-10-2 Santa Fe type built by Alco's Brooks Works to United States Railroad Administration guidelines. It's a big locomotive designed for moving freight at moderate speeds.

Protecting the east end of the siding are a pair of lower quadrant semaphores, automatic block signals that show clear when the blade is lowered at a 45 degree angle and stop when the blade rises to a level position. A breeze blows lightly across the prairie and some curious crows circle. Several minutes after the train has completely entered the siding, clearing the main line, the signal arms at the east end rise from "clear" to "stop" with an audible clunk.

Train orders, issued from the dispatcher and delivered by an agent, authorize train movements, not these signals. The signals are merely added protection to prevent collisions.

In a few more minutes a headlight appears on the horizon. It's the Denver-bound *Zephyr*, and it's moving *fast*. In a flash of glinting stainless steel, the *Zephyr* races past the long freight. This shiny passenger train is a revolution on wheels. There is no tell-tail wisp of steam following this train. A harbinger of things to come, it is the first diesel–electrically powered passenger streamliner. The semaphore clears, and the freight, manually lined out of the siding, continues east. It's just another day on the Burlington, but in a few short years big steamers like this old Santa Fe type will have been entirely supplanted by diesel-electric descendants of that shiny streamlined *Zephyr*.

DAWN OF THE DIESEL

In 1925, just as Lima introduced its Superpower, the latest and greatest in reciprocating steam power, another type of motive power entered the railroad scene. The Central Railroad of New Jersey purchased what is considered the first commercially produced diesel-electric loco-

---

Most late era steam locomotives were equipped with Timken roller bearings on their axles, which improved the efficiency and dependability of a locomotive by reducing friction. They also greatly reduced the chance of a "hotbox," which could result in a catastrophic bearing failure that could cause a derailment.

The railroads had been searching for a practical alternative to steam locomotives for decades before the introduction of the diesel-electric. Early in the twentieth century the New York, New Haven & Hartford pioneered practical high-voltage overhead electrification using 11,000 volts alternating current. At Stamford, Connecticut, on August 9, 1958, an EP-4 electric leads a fast passenger train between New Haven and New York City. *Richard Jay Solomon*

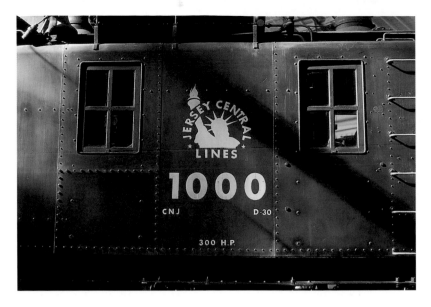

Central Railroad of New Jersey No. 1000 is considered the first successful commercial diesel-electric locomotive. Built by a consortium of Alco, General Electric, and Ingersoll-Rand, the little 300 horsepower boxcab went to work in the Bronx in 1925. It was a harbinger of things to come: by 1960 diesels had supplanted steam. Today CNJ 1000 is proudly displayed at the B&O Railroad Museum in Baltimore.

A number of railroads experimented with electrification, including the Virginian, which had been seeking ways to move greater tonnage with a single crew. It experimented with some of the largest steam locomotives ever built: 2-10-10-2 Mallets and a Triplex. Two streamlined General Electric EL-2Bs lead Virginian tonnage through Roanoke on July 30, 1958. The economy of the diesel-electric (in effect, electrification without expensive catenary and power plants) put an end to many electric operations, including Virginian's. *Richard Jay Solomon*

Contrast in technological development: a brand-new SD70MAC diesel-electric—the latest in diesel-electric technology—meets Milwaukee Road 4-8-4 No. 261 at Galesburg, Illinois, on June 23, 1996. Diesel technology has come a long way since 1925. Today's modern diesels use alternating current traction motors and can produce up to 6,000 horsepower. This SD70MAC and No. 261 can both produce roughly 4,000 horsepower. The shopmen at Galesburg were impressed with the 1944-built steamer!

motive, a 300 horsepower switcher built by a consortium of Alco, General Electric, and Ingersoll-Rand. A diesel engine generated current, which was used to power electric traction motors. The locomotive was not much to look at—just a box with wheels—but it was the harbinger of the future.

While the Lima Berkshire A-1 was a spectacle and was paraded around the country, CNJ No. 1000 was quietly put to work on the waterfront yards in the Bronx. It performed well, and by the late 1920s the diesel electric had established a reputation as a viable switching locomotive. Co-builder Alco may have recognized the potential of the diesel at the time of CNJ 1000's construction, but felt the real locomotive business was still in steam, and that this boxcab diesel was a mere sideshow. Alco and GE were partners in

the construction of straight electric locomotives, where Alco provided the frame and running gear and GE provided the electrical components. So this odd little switcher was not unlike other cooperative ventures. The diesel had a long way to go before becoming a practical alternative to steam as a road locomotive. In the late 1920s the Canadian National tested a diesel-electric designed for road service, but it was deemed a failure.

Since before the turn of the century, railroads had been searching for a suitable alternative to the steam locomotive, one that would provide a more powerful, efficient way of running trains. Electricity was considered a prime possibility as replacement power, but it was assumed that the power plants would be located off-line, not on the trains themselves.

A variety of electrification schemes had been tried in heavy railroad applications. The Baltimore & Ohio is credited with the first steam railroad electrification: a short overhead system installed in the new tunnel under Baltimore in 1895. Electrification had its merits, and by the 1920s several eastern railroads had electrified heavy suburban commuter lines with considerable success. Some lines went further: for example, the New Haven electrified its busy four-track main line from New York City to its namesake city with superb results. It handled both freight and passenger trains with electric locomotives. In the West, the Milwaukee Road electrified two long segments of its mountainous Pacific Extension, totaling 656 route miles. This system's promoters hoped this would be the prototype for main-line electrification around the nation. Another popular electrification application was in long tunnels, where there were problems from noxious fumes. In New York City, electrification was mandated following a disastrous collision in 1902 caused by a smoke-filled tunnel on the Grand Central approach.

The most ambitious electrification plan was launched by the Pennsylvania Railroad, which in the late 1920s began electrifying its busy multiple-track main line from New York to Washington, with the beginnings of a potential electrification between Philadelphia and Pittsburgh. Electrification was not new to the PRR. It was among the pioneer promoters of electrification as a motive power solution, and over the previous 25 years had electrified several of its heavily traveled lines. Nonetheless, the electrification of its New York-Washington corridor was an enormous undertaking. It was *the* busiest passenger route in North America and an extremely heavy freight route too. The expenditure needed to electrify the corridor was tremendous, but the potential savings justified the cost in the eyes of railroad management.

Large-scale electrification had many benefits. Electric locomotives (often called motors, because they only transmitted—rather than generated—power) could provide greater tractive effort, particularly when starting a train. They could accelerate faster than steam locomotives and maintain high speeds more efficiently. In areas of high traffic density there was a clear fuel savings. Electric motors were less costly to operate, they required far less maintenance, and they could run as multiple units, which allowed a single crew to haul more tonnage. They were also cleaner than steam locomotives, which made them popular with the riding public.

The capital investment needed for electrification made wide-scale application prohibitively expensive. While the long-term investment of electrification might pay off in greater efficiency, installation costs discouraged most lines from employing it. It is doubtful that electrification alone would ever have made the steam locomotive fully obsolete in the United States. Many long and lightly traveled branch lines would no doubt have remained steam-powered had other technology not come along.

GASOLINE-ELECTRICS

The self-propelled gasoline-electric motor car was developed prior to World War I. By the 1920s several manufacturers were producing these cars, commonly known as "doodlebugs." Railroads employed the inexpensive

Steam had a great reprieve during World War II. The railroads were saturated with traffic and in desperate need of motive power. The War Production Board restricted diesel-electric production and a number of lines bought new steam locomotives when they might have purchased diesels. Milwaukee Road purchased ten 4-8-4s from Alco in 1944 including No. 261.

Steam locomotives require intensive maintenance and servicing and several hours of preparation for service. Dieselization enabled railroads to greatly reduce their labor force because the diesel-electrics required far less maintenance and each diesel unit usually replaced more than one steam locomotive. An engineman oils the crossheads and valve gear on Northern Pacific Ten Wheeler 328, as the boiler pressure slowly rises.

cars in light branch-line passenger service to reduce costs. While these light-weight cars were not viewed as a significant development for main-line rail-roading, they were an important part of a technological convergence that made the development of the road diesel-electric possible in the 1930s.

ELECTRO-MOTIVE AND GENERAL MOTORS

One of the leading producers of doodlebugs was the Electro-Motive Corporation, which used gasoline engines built by the Winton Engine Company. In 1930, automobile manufacturer General Motors purchased both EMC and Winton, which also built diesel engines.

In 1934, EMC provided the power plant for the latest fad in passenger service: the lightweight streamlined articulated train. Two diesel train-sets debuted that year, both on western lines. These were Union Pacific's M-10000 (later the *City of Salina*) powered by a Winton distillate engine (one that used spark plugs for ignition) and Burlington's Budd-built, stain-less steel *Zephyr*, powered by a Winton diesel engine (making it *the* first diesel-electric passenger train). Both trains toured the country before entering regular revenue service.

Many railroaders may have dismissed the *Zephyr* and *City of Salina* as gimmicks. *These lightweight trains are little more than overgrown motor-cars, right? Real work requires real power, and that, as everyone knows, is provided by steam locomotives.* But railroad managers took them a lot more seriously. These "gimmicks" might just save the industry. The *Zephyr* and *City of Salina* were intended to attract passengers back to the rails. First electric interurbans, then automobiles, and then airplanes had distracted the traveling public. Furthermore, the Great Depression seriously affect-ed ridership, and the railroads felt they needed a radical solution to get attention. It was an age of wild stunts, so why shouldn't railroads try some-thing new? The response to the new sleek streamliners was enormous. The trains were so popular that neither Burlington nor Union Pacific had anticipated the crowds. There were not enough seats on the short stream-lined trains to carry the potential ridership. They needed bigger trains, and bigger trains meant more powerful engines.

Electro-Motive had faith in a great need for internal combustion power and met the challenge. Also, while the first streamliners were semi-permanently coupled articulated sets, later "power cars" were separate locomotives. Electro-Motive abandoned the distillate engine as a railroad power plant and instead refined and applied Winton's two-stroke diesel engine. By the late 1930s, EMC was building diesel-electric passenger locomotives that were matching and exceeding the hauling capabilities of the latest steam locomotives—Northerns and Hudsons—and often were outrunning the steamers with heavy consists. The railroads were not uni-versally impressed and some lines remained loyal to steam power despite the performance of the diesels. Traditionally the railroad industry had been slow to accept or adopt change and many radical motive power concepts had come and gone, but most railroads were quick to realize that diesel was more than just a passing fad. It was the future of American motive power.

An important evolutionary development came in 1939: Electro-Motive introduced its FT freight locomotive—a 5,400-horsepower, four-

While the cost of diesel-electric operation may be more practical from a business perspective, steam is king (aesthetically anyhow) in the eyes of many railroad observers. Several railroads and organizations recognized this and restored locomotives to excursion service after they had been retired from their regular duties. Southern Railway Mikado No. 4501 was returned to service in the 1960s. It catches the glint of the sun on June 9, 1974, while running between Danville, Virginia, and Louisville, Kentucky. *John Gruber*

As railroads retired their last steam locomotives, they often ran farewell excursions for the legions of loyal steam fans. It was the end of an era, and many wished to see steam at full throttle one more time. Southern Pacific GS-6 No. 4460 makes lots of smoke and noise for a photo lineup east of Truckee, California, on October 19, 1958. Today this locomotive is preserved at the Museum of Transportation in St. Louis. *Fred Matthews*

In the 1960s, the Reading Company ran many steam trips with its fleet of T-1 class 4-8-4s. Known as "Iron Horse Rambles," these popular trips gave those who may have missed steam in regular service the opportunity to see big steam in action out on the main line. Two Reading T-1s lead an October 1963 excursion in eastern Pennsylvania. *Richard Jay Solomon*

unit streamlined diesel-electric. The FT was no gimmick, it was not a fad, it was a *real* locomotive. Before EMC demonstrated the FT to the railroads it worked out its most serious bugs, so the FT pleased its promoters and demonstrated its superior qualities as a locomotive. It matched or outperformed steam in virtually every situation in which it was tried.

Again the response was not universal—some lines didn't run the FT—but many railroads did and were soon convinced. The FT was just the locomotive they had been waiting for. It was efficient, powerful, and clean. Electro-Motive soon had dozens of orders for its new product. By 1940, the diesel-electric had demonstrated its superiority over conventional steam. It offered many of the advantages of electrification at a much better price and without the up-front costs of overhead wire and electric power plants. The steam locomotive was doomed.

STEAM REPRIEVE

Just as it appeared that railroads were going to march ahead into the bright new world of diesel traction along came one last chance for steam to show its might: the Japanese bombed Pearl Harbor and the United States entered World War II. During the war, materials and factory output were strictly controlled by the government under the War Production Board. One of the crucial components required in manufacturing diesel-

electrics was copper, a metal of great strategic importance, and diesel engines that might have been used in locomotives were used in ships and submarines instead.

While Electro-Motive was allowed to build a few diesels, much of its production capacity was turned toward the war effort. Railroads that ordered new diesels would just have to wait until the war was over.

The war created an enormous surge in railroad traffic, and the need for new motive power had never been greater. Traffic levels rose to unprecedented heights. Ten years of deferred maintenance and few new locomotive deliveries during the 1930s Depression complicated the motive power shortage during the war. A total of *six* new locomotives had been built in 1932 and only *one* in 1933. This was the low point, and locomotive orders picked up a bit towards the end of the 1930s, but railroads were hesitant to place large orders for new locomotives while traffic levels were still thin, and the yards were filled with aging but serviceable clunkers. So, when war traffic hit, many locomotives were more than twenty years old and some were more than forty years old. The railroads were not prepared for the traffic, and they scrambled for power. Just about any old teakettle that could run was rebuilt and fired up. Locomotives that had been written off as scrap were reinstated to service. The War Production Board was more generous with its allocation of new steam locomotives than it was for new

During the late 1950s it was not uncommon to find cold steam locomotives stored on sidings. Often the diesel-electrics had assumed the duties of the old steam engines, but the price of scrap metal did not warrant immediate scrapping. In November 1956, two Southern Pacific 2-8-0 Consolidations sit lifeless along the Carquinez Straits at Port Costa, California. *Fred Matthews*

diesels. Where the railroads wanted new Electro-Motive diesels, they instead received new 4-8-4s, 2-10-4s, and other superpower to carry them through the war. The War Production Board also frowned on the development of new locomotive designs. So builders often pulled out old blueprints instead of designing new locomotives. This applied to diesel design too: the steam builders, Alco, Baldwin, and Lima, were discouraged from developing their own road diesels to compete with Electro-Motive's FT.

After the war, when restrictions were lifted, American railroads were faced with a largely worn out fleet of locomotives of somewhat obsolete designs. While a few lines such as the Chesapeake & Ohio, New York Central, Nickel Plate Road, and Norfolk & Western ordered new steam, most lines opted for diesels. The diesel-electric's advantages were undeniable, and despite the efforts to save the external-combustion engine, the age of steam in the United States was over. The traditional builders of steam locomotives, Alco, Baldwin, and Lima, continued to build steam for a few years, but they all introduced diesels in their catalogs with limited

Many steam locomotives were not scrapped following their final runs. Southern Pacific GS-4 4449 was one of many SP locomotives preserved; for many years it sat in a park in Portland, Oregon. In the 1970s it was pulled from its static perch and restored to service as one of the American Freedom Train locomotives. In April 1977, No. 4449, wearing patriotic colors, rolls through familiar territory as it passes Mission Tower in Los Angeles. *Fred Matthews*

degrees of success. Ultimately they all went out of business. Lima and Baldwin merged and then exited the new locomotive business in 1956, while Alco struggled on into the late 1960s. Alco's Canadian subsidiary Montreal Locomotive Works lasted into the 1970s.

EFFICIENCY, VERSATILITY, STANDARDIZATION

The superior efficiency and performance of diesel-electrics versus steam was one of the diesel's initial selling points. The diesel engine is a significantly more efficient heat engine than the reciprocating steam engine. At optimum performance, the modern steam locomotive can theoretically produce a maximum of 12 percent thermal efficiency, but 6 to 8 percent is the maximum achievable in actual operation. Thermal or heat efficiency is a measure of how well an engine converts its fuel to the work required. The

ting personnel costs. Railroads were also able to eliminate many short helper grades, resulting in additional savings. (Until the development of safe remote radio-controlled operation, however, manned diesel helpers were still common practice on steep mountain grades, and even with the advent of safe radio control, some railroads still preferred to operate manned helpers.)

Diesels gave the railroads great flexibility in operation and provided significant simplification in motive power application. The individual diesel-electric was very versatile. For years railroads had maintained a different type of locomotive for every application. Most railroads had a least a dozen different types on the roster. For example, on the eve of dieselization, Southern Pacific was operating 17 different types of steam power with numerous subclasses. The diesel's ability to generate maximum power from the start eliminated the need to match locomotive to application, and specialized designs for individual railroads were unnecessary. In the early 1940s, Electro-Motive established just three basic types of diesel-electrics: switcher, road freight, and road passenger. These types later evolved, and the road switcher was introduced, a locomotive which was suited for a variety of tasks. There were specialty diesel-electrics, but these were very few in number relative to the dominance of standard types.

Because there were fewer, more versatile models, adoption of the diesel imposed a system of standardization that 100 years of steam locomotive design had been unable to achieve. While some railroads, such as the Pennsylvania Railroad, had standard locomotive types and interchangeable parts, many railroads did not. Every railroad's locomotives were somewhat different, and there were often serious design differences from class to class on locomotives of the

In 1936, Baltimore & Ohio bought the first streamlined passenger road diesels that were not semipermanently coupled to a lightweight train set. Electro-Motive Corporation's pioneering model EA was an 1,800 horsepower cab unit that set the pattern for thousands of passenger diesels to follow. Today the hollow shell of the first EA, No. 51, is preserved at the B&O Railroad Museum in Baltimore.

steam engine experiences a tremendous heat loss in its firebox, boiler, and cylinders and is further hampered by incomplete fuel combustion.

A diesel engine's thermal efficiency is roughly four times greater than that of a steam engine. Furthermore, a steam locomotive's optimum power output is produced at higher speed than diesels: steam locomotives with drivers in the 69-inch range produced their maximum horsepower in the mid-40 miles per hour range, while early diesels produced maximum horsepower in the 10-20 miles per hour range. As a result these diesels could start a train easier than a steam locomotive could.

The diesel-electric was more cost effective than steam for several reasons. Multiple-unit operation, which allowed one engineer to control many diesel units, and the diesel-electrics' ability to start a heavy train without assistance allowed the railroads to haul more tonnage with fewer crews, thus cut-

In 1938, Burlington's *Pioneer Zephyr* train set, running as the *Advance Denver Zephyr*, splits a set of lower quadrant semaphores after passing a steam-powered freight on the plains of eastern Colorado. This diesel-electric-powered *Zephyr* represented the future of American railroading. *Otto C. Perry, Denver Public Library Western History Department*

A set of Electro-Motive FT diesel-electrics is surrounded by the steam and smoke of dozens of steam locomotives at Willard, Ohio, on March 19, 1949. The FT was the first practical road diesel designed for freight service. When Electro-Motive introduced it in 1939, it spelled doom for thousands of steam locomotives. The FT is easily identified by its row of four porthole windows on the side of the locomotive. *Bruce Fales, Jay Williams collection*

same type on an individual railroad. Efforts by the USRA during World War I to create standard designs for American railroads were largely disregarded after the war. Electro-Motive diesels on the Northern Pacific, however, used the same parts as those on the Maine Central and the Florida East Coast. For the first time railroads came close to having a standard parts supply for the entire industry. The only problem was a lack of interchangeable parts among diesels of different manufacturers. Railroads that bought diesels from a variety of builders would often find themselves at a disadvantage in the parts department.

Diesels require far less maintenance than steam, which resulted in dramatically lower operating costs. It can routinely take hours to prepare a steam locomotive for its daily run, but a diesel can be made ready in a matter of minutes. Furthermore a diesel does not require the labor-intensive ongoing maintenance that a steam locomotive does. Steam locomotives need to have their various reciprocating parts lubricated every few hundred miles; diesels do not. Finally, steam locomotives require an inordinate amount of heavy maintenance. Boilers must be maintained, flues kept clean, fireboxes patched, and so on. While diesels do require maintenance, they can run far longer between major overhauls. For some railroads the comparison between steam and diesel maintenance was exaggerated because they were using worn out, antique steam locomotives, rather than more modern efficient engines. New York Central's Hudsons may have averaged more than 20,000 miles a month on the road, but most older steamers averaged far less than that and could not come close to the availability offered by diesel-electrics.

Railroads also found that they did not need as many locomotives. Many lines found that each diesel-electric could effectively replace 10 to 12 steam locomotives. This, combined with a reduced need for maintenance, allowed railroads to trim maintenance forces and consolidate shops, which produced additional savings quickly. In the days of steam, railroads maintained major shop facilities relatively close to one another, and it was not unusual to have repair facilities at every major crew change point, which were routinely about 100 miles apart. Another advantage to diesel operation was their ability to run longer between fuel stops. Where steam locomotives required both fuel and water at frequent intervals, diesels did not. The constant need to stop for fuel and water delayed trains. A few lines, such as the Pennsylvania and New York Central, employed track pans to enable their locomotive to scoop water at speed, but this was the exception to conventional practice. Thus diesels sped up running times on both passenger and freight schedules, allowing railroads to improve service.

Diesels were noticeably cleaner than steam engines. This was pleasing to operating crews, who also found the new diesels more comfortable to operate than steam. Since the diesels did not belch towering columns of thick black smoke, they were viewed as a big improvement for passenger trains. Cleaner exhaust emissions had been the initial justification for little CNJ 1000, which worked in New York City where coal smoke was restricted.

Lastly, the diesel brought a new image to the railroads at a time when they were desperately looking to attract public attention. The traditional reciprocating steam locomotive had come to be viewed as inefficient, old fashioned, and obsolete. To compete with automobiles and airplanes, the railroad felt they needed to modernize. Replacing old fleets of inefficient steam locomotives with new, faster, cleaner, more efficient, modern diesels pleased management and stockholders alike.

At Rigby Yard in Portland, Maine, Boston & Maine's Electro-Motive F2, No. 4258, presides over B&M Pacific No. 3713, as the steam engine readies for its final run to Boston on April 26, 1956. While not the last run of Boston & Maine steam, it was a symbolic event that marked the end of steam on the Boston & Maine. Pacific 3713 is scheduled for restoration at Steamtown in Scranton, Pennsylvania, and may run again someday. *George C. Corey*

DIESEL-ELECTRIC SUPPLANTS STRAIGHT ELECTRICS

The diesel allowed the railroads to enjoy many of the benefits of electrification without the enormous expense of overhead-wire electrification. As a result the diesel-electric not only ended steam operations but put a stop to virtually all new main-line electrification in the United States. Furthermore, the costs of diesel operation were so advantageous that many stretches of electrification were phased out.

On November 7, 1954, two Central Vermont 2-8-0s work hard, climbing State Line Hill at Smith's Bridge on Stafford Hollow Road in Monson, Massachusetts. The Central Vermont Railway, a Canadian National subsidiary, was among the last operators of main-line steam in New England. While diesels were used on some runs, steam remained until 1957. *George C. Corey, Robert A. Buck collection*

Some lines were fully dieselized before 1950, while others maintained steam locomotives well into the 1950s. Ultimately all revenue steam succumbed to the diesel-electric. The Central Vermont was among the last steam users in New England, and also the owner of the heaviest steam locomotives in the region—10 Alco-built 2-10-4 Texas types built in 1928. Central Vermont 2-10-4 No. 700 leads freight No. 430 southbound near Claremont Junction, New Hampshire, on November 30, 1952. *George C. Corey*

TAKE IT OR LEAVE IT

Electro-Motive built locomotives as parent General Motors built automobiles, in an assembly-line fashion. So rather than cater to individual railroad whims and produce custom locomotives to fit each line's special needs, Electro-Motive mass-produced diesels in standardized models. The only distinct attributes were superficial external appearance: paint color and placement of exterior trappings such as lights and bells. The FTs that hauled Boston & Maine tonnage along the Deerfield River and through the Hoosac Tunnel were, for all practical purposes, the same as those used by the Western Pacific to haul freight across the Nevada deserts and through the Feather River Canyon. For these same jobs the railroads had distinctly different steam power. The B&M's late steam preference had been Berkshires, while the Western Pacific had preferred 2-8-8-2 simple articulateds.

RAPIDLY CHANGING CHARACTER OF AMERICAN RAILROADS

Several sociocultural factors helped to doom steam quickly. A series of coal strikes following World War II caused coal prices to skyrocket and swayed public sentiment against the coal industry. This aggravated the already significant gap between coal and oil prices, and the discovery of huge Saudi Arabian oil fields in the 1950s kept oil prices very low for another 20 years.

The diesel changed the character of railroading in many ways. Following complete dieselization, steam locomotive shops and roundhouses were phased out, closed, and demolished. Many diesels were designed for bidirectional operation, making the once-common turntable an anachronism. On-line coaling and watering facilities were abandoned and dismantled. To speed fueling on heavily traveled lines, some railroads had operated elaborate mainline fueling facilities, complete with huge coaling towers and water tanks. The diesels passed these by—no need for coal on an Electro-Motive product. In a few cases, the skeletal remnants of these facilities remain today as a reminder of the steam era.

The diesel revolution was relatively swift. By the mid-1950s, diesel-electrics were hauling most American trains. While a few steam holdouts, such as Norfolk & Western, maintained full-scale steam operations into the late 1950s, by 1960 main-line steam in the United States was a thing of the past.

Diesels brought a locomotive standardization that had never existed in the steam era. Where Boston & Maine hauled its tonnage with 2-8-4 Berkshires, Western Pacific used Mallet compound 2-6-6-2s and simple articulated 2-8-8-2s. But both railroads replaced their freight steam with Electro-Motive FT diesels. In 1947, a WP 2-8-8-2 works eastbound with a freight at the Williams Loop, near Spring Garden, California. *Fred Matthews, courtesy of Sundance Publishing*

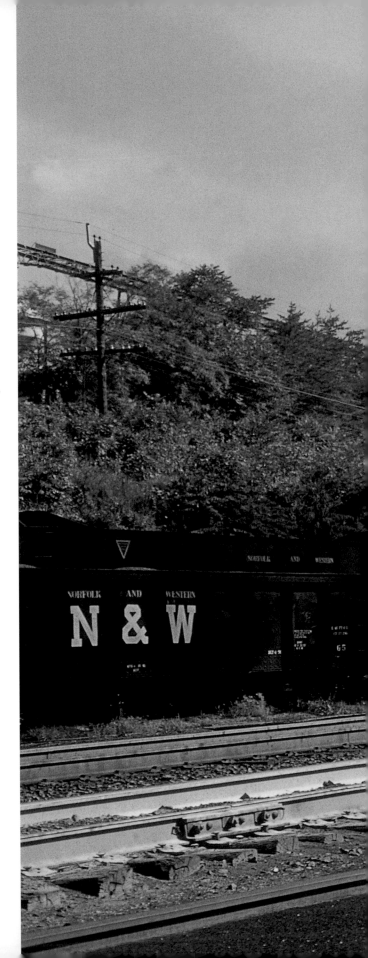

8

STEAM TECHNOLOGY IN THE DIESEL AGE

5741

Shortly after the end of World War II, in the cornfields of eastern Indiana, a brand-new Chevy pulls toward a rural grade crossing with Pennsylvania Railroad's Fort Wayne Division. The last glow of the winter sun is fading, leaving just a trace of orange on the westward horizon amidst a blue-gray sky. In the nearby fields, frost is forming on the dead stalks of corn left over from the autumn harvest. At the crossing, the familiar crossbucks read "Stop, Look & Listen."

The Chevy rolls to a stop, and its driver—always cautious as he approaches this busy main line—looks to the east, and there he notes a distant headlight. There is so much traffic on this line and the track so tangent, it seems as if there is always a headlight in the distance. However, before he eases his new truck across the tracks, he glances to the west, where he sees another train bearing down at him, at great speed. It's the eastbound *Trail Blazer*. Moments later, in a blur of drivers, steam, and smoke, the train hits the crossing at more than 100 miles per hour. The Chevy driver catches a glimpse of the Pennsy's trademark keystone low on the pilot of the new streamlined engine, followed by two sets of 80-inch drivers, and a long passenger train.

For a brief moment he has a vision of the future: that was one of those new streamlined steamers he had been seeing in Pennsy's wartime advertising for the past couple of years. Indeed it is one of the latest, most advanced steam locomotives in the world, a peculiar, unorthodox machine called a Duplex—fast and very powerful. Where most passenger trains need two of the older K4s Pacifics, this train was doing just fine with a single Duplex. Right after the eastbound *Trail Blazer* clears, the westbound train hits the crossing—one of the PRR's lesser limiteds led by a trio of new Electro-Motive E7 diesels. The vision of the Duplex fades as *this* train races westward into the night.

The Pennsylvania Railroad herald was a gold and red keystone. Most of PRR's later steam locomotives displayed this symbol with the engine number on the front of the locomotive.

Norfolk & Western used conventional reciprocating steam in heavy main-line service longer than any other railroad in the United States. While the PRR was experimenting with Duplexes, N&W was refining conventional steam power. It continued to build Mallets into the early 1950s. On August 1, 1958, N&W Class Y6a Mallet No. 2156 leads another Y Class on a heavy westbound freight train at Blue Ridge, Virginia. *Richard J. Solomon*

THE DUPLEX

Beginning in the early 1930s, Baldwin began to promote the Duplex locomotive as its answer to Lima's superpower concept. It proposed a nonarticulated locomotive with two complete sets of running gear designed for high-speed passenger service. The advantage of this design was a lighter piston thrust and lighter main and side rods, which would result in less damaging reciprocating forces, permit smoother riding qualities at higher speeds, and theoretically require less maintenance.

While a novel approach to locomotive design in America, the idea was not original to Baldwin. The French had built some nonarticulated Mallets in 1932. For the most part, the American railroads paid little interest to the concept, as during the 1930s traffic was down and few new locomotives were built. When railroads did get new power, they preferred more conventional designs over radical new concepts.

As it turned out, the first Duplex was not built by Baldwin but by Baltimore & Ohio's innovative Mt. Clare Shops, which had been pondering Baldwin's concept and decided to take its own approach to the idea. The resulting highly unorthodox machine, Class N1, followed in a line of modern progressive experimental locomotives developed by Mt. Clare, under the inspiration and direction of George H. Emerson, that used high-pressure water-tube boilers. Notable were 4-4-4 *Lady Baltimore* and Hudson type *Lord Baltimore*. The B&O Duplex was completed in June 1937 and named *George H. Emerson* after its designer.

It was a rigid frame 4-4-4-4 type, with two pairs of 16x26.5-inch cylinders placed in an unusual arrangement to avoid an exceptionally long wheelbase. While the front set was placed in the normal position, the rear set rode below the firebox and faced backward. Like other B&O experimentals, it used a water-tube boiler; this one operated at 350 psi. It weighed roughly 386,500 pounds, with the tender about 736,500 pounds. Its 76-inch drivers could pro-

duce 65,000 pounds of tractive effort and an estimated 3,900 horsepower. It was a very lightweight engine for its potential power, allowing it to run virtually anywhere on the B&O. The locomotive's main rods weighed only 50 percent of those used by a B&O Mountain type, which produced equivalent tractive effort. And the whole locomotive weighed less than the 4-8-4 Northern types that it was intended to outperform. The first Northern Pacific 4-8-4s of 1927 weighed 426,000 pounds (739,000 pounds with tender), had 73-inch drivers, and produced a tractive effort of 61,500 pounds, slightly less than B&O's Duplex. Santa Fe's Northern types, built in 1938 with 80-inch drivers, produced a slightly higher tractive effort of 66,000 pounds, but weighed significantly more than the Duplex; the engine alone weighed 510,000 pounds, and the tender an additional 451,000 pounds. This was more than B&O's first Mallet types.

In tests, the *George H. Emerson* achieved speeds of 85 miles per hour effortlessly and could operate in excess of 90 miles per hour. Performance was marred, however, by the tendency of its two engines to operate in sync with one another, an undesirable characteristic that produced a harmonic vibration and caused a rough ride. The engine was also prone to slippery operation. Starting up and on curves, one engine would loss traction and slip. Its water-tube firebox also presented more than its share of maintenance difficulties. In addition, crosshead and guide placement on the rear engine caused it to collect much dust and dirt, resulting in excessive wear.

The economy and performance of the diesels put an end to B&O's steam locomotive experiments. In 1943 the *George H. Emerson* was sidelined, having never been duplicated, and in 1950 it was cut up. However this was not the end of the story; the Duplex concept led to one of the strangest and one of the most intriguing developments of the late steam era.

Pennsylvania Railroad No. 6111 was one of the first two T1 Duplexes built by Baldwin in 1942. These rigid-frame high-drivered streamliners were intended as the next generation of high-speed passenger power on the PRR. Fifty T1s were built after World War II, but the locomotives developed serious problems and had very short careers. *California State Railroad Museum collection*

Pennsylvania Railroad Sets Out to Save the Steam Engine

In the late 1930s, the Pennsylvania Railroad, which had not built or ordered any new steam locomotives since the last of its M1 Mountains were delivered in 1930, suddenly took a renewed interest in steam technology and embarked on what may seem an ultimately futile but innovative and bold path in the development of the Duplex. Historian John P. Hankey says, "The Pennsylvania Railroad had the talent, power, and justification to see if steam could compete with the diesel."

Today it might be difficult to appreciate or comprehend the vast scope of the Pennsylvania Railroad during its heyday. It was among one of the most powerful corporations in the world, and for many years it was the single largest passenger carrier—by any mode—in the United States. Statistically speaking, you were more likely to ride a Pennsylvania Railroad train than any other. In addition to its vast passenger operations, the railroad moved a phenomenal volume of freight, the largest portion of which was coal.

The railroad itself was one of the largest consumers of coal in the world as nearly all of its locomotives burned this traditional fuel. The PRR operated the largest fleet of steam locomotives in the United States. At its peak in 1920, this represented 7,667 locomotives; in 1930, some 5,671 engines. In 1920, its total mileage reached 11,107, considerable for the time. The railroad stretched from New York to Washington, from Philadelphia to Chicago, with lines to St. Louis, Buffalo, Cleveland, and Mackinaw City, Michigan, among other places. Probably its most impressive asset was its multiple-track main-line across New Jersey and Pennsylvania, known as the Broad Way (hence, the origin of its flagship train, the *Broadway Limited*).

In addition to its own lines and wholly owned subsidiaries such as the Long Island Rail Road, the PRR maintained a strong financial interest in several other principle eastern carriers, including Norfolk & Western, Wabash, and Lehigh Valley.

It has been said that at the height of the PRR's influence, if one made casual reference to the "President," clarification would have been necessary: the president of the Pennsylvania Railroad or the president of the United States? The PRR was more than just a railroad. It was an empire.

In the early part of the century the mighty PRR, decisive industrial giant and self-proclaimed "Standard Railroad of the World" (a misleading title because PRR's standards were often in direct contradiction to the rest of the industry), had been on the forefront of innovative steam locomotive design. But by the 1930s, while other lines such as its chief competitors New York Central and Baltimore & Ohio had been experimenting with innovative new steam locomotives, the PRR was content to use designs it had refined 20 years earlier.

Pennsy's conservative locomotive policy was predicated on refining existing designs and mass-producing them rather than buying 10 each of every new-fangled contraption that came on the market. While the railroad would investigate promising new types on a limited basis, it was hesitant to invest heavily in unproven radical types. Instead, it looked for ways to improve upon existing designs. This policy dated back to 1867, when

Pennsylvania Railroad J1 No. 6488 rolls northbound across the Baltimore & Ohio at Attica Junction, Ohio, on July 29, 1957. During the Second World War the War Production Board prevented PRR from developing its own locomotives and forced it to build locomotives of a proven design. So the Pennsy adapted the plans for Chesapeake & Ohio's T1 Texas type to its own practices. *George C. Corey*

Two PRR I1s Decapods lead a freight at Snydertown, Pennsylvania, on March 31, 1956. The train is headed for the Lehigh Valley Railroad interchange at Mount Carmel. The I1s Decapod exemplified PRR's practice of locomotive standardization: the railroad owned 598 I1s locomotives all built to the same design. In PRR classification terminology, a small "s" is part of the locomotive designation, indicating the locomotive is superheated. Pennsy ended this practice in the mid-1920s, when universal superheating became the rule; this was just prior to the advent of its M1 4-8-2s. *George C. Corey*

A General Electric press release promoting its new steam-turbine-electric, dated December 19, 1938, read: "Erie, PA.-Shaped like a giant projectile, and concealing 5,000 horsepower beneath its sleek stream-lining this new-type locomotive, carrying its own steam-turbine plant and capable of whisking a transcontinental train of 15 standard Pullman cars from Chicago to the west coast at speeds up to 125 miles an hour. . . ." GE's locomotive was one of several attempts to promote the steam turbine in the United States. *Stephen A. Solombrino collection*

On December 30, 1956, PRR M1b No. 6899 leads an eastbound freight along the Susquehanna Division at Nisbet, Pennsylvania. The PRR was content to build 4-8-2 Mountain types until 1930, while other railroads were buying more advanced designs. Later, when the PRR did try to improve the efficiency of the steam locomotive, it chose to advance the Duplex concept. *George C. Corey*

Alexander Cassatt, then in command of the railroad's motive power, had introduced a system of standard locomotive classes. Originally there were just three standard classes, but by the early 1890s there were more than 20. In 1876, less than 10 years after locomotive standardization began, more than 50 percent of PRR's fleet were of standard types, and by the turn of the century, nearly the entire roster was standardized, save for a handful of locomotives acquired through mergers.

When other lines were experimenting with various compounds, PRR instead refined the 4-4-0 and 4-4-2 designs. When the Mallet compound looked like the solution for hauling heavy freight trains, PRR shied away from it, despite its stiff grades and heavy coal tonnage. PRR owned only a handful of Mallets and retired them early. While the Pennsylvania was one of the first lines to experiment with single expansion "simple" articulateds (it designed an extremely powerful simple articulated in 1919, at the time the most powerful locomotive in the world), it never embraced the type in regular service. Its few experimentals worked off their miles in obscurity as helpers.

When the Mikado came of age as a freight hauler, PRR was slow to adopt it; instead it continued to build the proven Consolidation type. When it finally embraced the Mike, it built them en masse. While other lines owned a dozen different classes of Mikados, PRR had just two, the L1s and L2s. The L1s was PRR's own design and it had 571 nearly identical locomotives. The L2s was a USRA design foisted upon the railroad during the traffic surges of World War I. Pennsylvania owned just a handful.

The 2-10-0 Decapod was not a particularly popular locomotive on most American lines, but Pennsy owned 598 of them—more than all the other Decapods in America by a large margin, and all were Class I1s.

Built in 1954, Norfolk & Western's *Jawn Henry* was the last serious attempt to advance the steam turbine in the United States. The locomotive and tender weighed 1,172,000 pounds and was rated to deliver 175,000 pounds starting tractive effort. In tests, it produced 199,000 pounds at 1 mile per hour. N&W considered buying a fleet of turbines, but found the cost per unit too high when compared to diesel-electrics. *N&W builder card, Ed King collection*

At 12:34 p.m. on November 20, 1947, PRR T1 Duplex No. 5545 leads train No. 95, the *Mail & Express,* past Sugar Run, Pennsylvania, on its climb toward the summit of the Alleghenies at Gallitzin. This Baldwin-built T1 was one of the later production locomotives that featured more subdued styling than earlier models. The long tapered "chiseled" nose and rounded pilot with portholes has given way to a stubbier, more utilitarian appearance. *Bruce Fales, Jay Williams collection*

In the late 1930s the Pennsylvania Railroad set out to develop the next generation of steam locomotive. With the help of the three commercial builders, PRR came up with the 6-4-4-6 Duplex type, Class S1. Although an awesome-looking machine, its usefulness·was hampered by its tremendous size. The PRR S1 leads the *Trail Blazer* on the south side of Chicago. *California State Railroad Museum collection*

Pennsylvania's quest for locomotive standardization had led it to ignore the recent developments of Lima Superpower and other innovations. In the mid-1930s, when the New York Central was breaking new ground with its supermodern J-3 Hudson types, PRR was content to look for ways to improve upon its once state-of-the-art K4s Pacific, by then a 20-year-old design. It modified the K4s Pacific in dozens of ways to improve the design: adding smoke deflectors, trying roller bearings, streamlining some, equipping one with Franklin poppet valves and another with rotary cam poppet valves. The railroad built two K5 Pacifics in 1928 but never duplicated them.

As Superpower was revolutionizing other fleets, PRR relied on Decapods, Mountains, Mikados, and Consolidations as its primary freight haulers. So, despite the national trend, the railroad did not own any Berkshires or Northerns and never would, although later, against its better judgment, it would build 2-10-4 Texas types during World War II. Super-Power was not a concept PRR wished to investigate. The reasons for its motive power philosophy: a staunchly conservative outlook toward locomotives, an individualized approach toward

The Pennsylvania Railroad built an experimental Class Q1 freight Duplex in 1942, with an unorthodox 4-6-4-4 wheel arrangement. The locomotive was similar to B&O's *George H. Emerson,* with rear-facing cylinders powering the rear two driving axles. PRR encountered the same problems with dirt and grime buildup that plagued the B&O machine. Originally the Q1 was streamlined but its shrouds were later removed; it is seen in Chicago in its nonstreamlined state. *Jay Williams collection*

its operations, and the fact that during the previous 25 years it had focused its research and development on what it believed would be the future of railroad motive power in the United States—electrification.

The PRR started experimenting with electric power in the 1890s. Its first serious use of electrification was a direct current third rail system on its New York Pennsylvania Station project, which opened in 1910. In 1913 it began electrifying its Philadelphia suburban lines with a high-voltage, alternating current overhead system.

Beginning in the late 1920s, the PRR started to electrify its extremely heavily traveled main line between New York and Washington—the largest and most intensive railroad electrification undertaking in the United States. Furthermore, the railroad was looking toward eventual electrification of its main line to Harrisburg, Pittsburgh and, possibly someday, even Chicago. The costs of the New York-Washington electrification were substantial. The railroad spent $39 million on electric locomotives alone. The brunt of its locomotive research in the 1920s and early 1930s was toward electrics, not

steam. It appeared electrification was the motive power solution of the future.

As a secondary consequence of PRR's main-line electrification, hundreds of steam locomotives were freed up for use elsewhere in the system, thus precluding the need for new steam power. The onset of the Great Depression lowered PRR's traffic levels, thus reducing the need for new locomotives. The last M1a Mountain type arrived on the property in 1930, and the railroad would not receive another new steam locomotive for nine years. While the PRR's electrification helped ease its need for new power, the trend was indicative of the motive power situation nationwide. Few locomotives were ordered by any American railroads, and some were already wondering if the reciprocating steam locomotive had reached the end of the line.

DIESELS DEMONSTRATE ON BROADWAY

In the late 1920s and early 1930s other lines had sampled diesel-electric switch engines, but the PRR paid them no mind. Despite PRR's earlier fascination with electric lines, the company was not as

A PRR Q2 Duplex at Crestline, Ohio, on May 8, 1946. These large freight Duplexes were primarily used on Pennsylvania Railroad's Lines West (its routes west of Pittsburgh), lines west of Pittsburgh. One Q2 was built in 1944, followed by 25 more in 1945. They were among the most powerful nonarticulated steam locomotives ever built. On the Altoona test plant, a Q2 generated 8,000 horsepower—more power than even the most modern diesel-electric locomotive can produce today. *Jay Williams Collection*

receptive to diesel-electrics. In 1935, however, PRR allowed novice locomotive builder Electro-Motive to demonstrate one of its new passenger diesels. For a month or so, the diesel-electric—an unremarkable looking boxcab—hauled Pennsy varnish through the most demanding territory.

Contrary to the expectations of the railroad's motive power department, the diesel excelled at every task. To the railroad's surprise, its performance equaled that of its K4s Pacifics, the pride of PRR's passenger fleet. Furthermore, the diesel-electric rarely paused for fuel and had little need for repairs.

While other railroads had been pleasantly surprised at the boxcab's remarkable performance, PRR did not view the diesel's performance as cause for celebration. The Electro-Motive diesel threatened the way PRR acquired locomotives and its relationship with its best suppliers. It felt it was not in a position to turn its back on steam, and in the mid-1930s it chose to pursue a radical divergence in its motive power policy by devel-

oping the next generation of steam locomotives instead of embracing diesel technology. The railroad felt that with some research and development it could match the performance of the diesel by advancing steam technology, and it set out to do just that.

By the 1930s, the Pennsylvania was one of just a few American railroads still building its own locomotives. Even as it entered the electric age, a considerable amount of work was delegated to Altoona. Where other lines often relied on locomotive builders to come up with suitable designs, PRR usually performed this work itself. The scientific approach toward locomotive design flourished at Altoona with the development of the steam locomotive test plant. The railroad took great pride in its ability to work through engineering problems.

Pennsylvania was not alone in its loyalty to steam—the feeling was shared by the New York Central, Chesapeake & Ohio, Nickel Plate Road, and Norfolk & Western. Each of these lines made concerted efforts to improve steam locomotive efficiency.

AN ASSEMBLY LINE *26,000 miles long*

That's *one* way to look at the Pennsylvania Railroad system —as a vast assembly line, now principally devoted to war transportation—26,000 miles of railroad facilities, crossing and criss-crossing a territory in which live half the people of the United States.

Over it flow coal to make power, light and heat...ore to produce steel...steel parts of a thousand different shapes and weights...rubber and textiles to manufacture tires... tanks, trucks, weapons, war materiel in abundance — in fact, most anything you can name, tiny or large. Add your food, too—for this mammoth assembly line handles what you eat, from field, cannery, packing plant to market.

Lump all these materials, parts, commodities together— call them *freight*—and here's what this Pennsylvania Railroad assembly system moved in the region bounded on the west by Chicago and St. Louis and on the east by New York and Norfolk in a single year, ending Nov. 1, 1944 . . . 287,000,000 tons! An amount equal to more than four tons for each of the 65,000,000 persons living in the 13 states and the District of Columbia, served by the Pennsylvania Railroad.

BUY UNITED STATES
WAR BONDS AND STAMPS

PENNSYLVANIA RAILROAD

Serving the Nation

★ *50,840 entered the Armed Forces*   ★ *538 have given their lives for their Country*

SEEKING GREATER EFFICIENCY

The Pennsylvania gathered together the big three steam builders, Alco, Baldwin, and Lima, and organized a task force that included the railroad's own designers. Their mission was to explore the best ideas for boosting steam efficiency and build an improved reciprocating steam locomotive, one that could outperform the Electro-Motive diesel. It would burn coal and be capable of hauling a 14-car train at 100 miles per hour between Harrisburg and Chicago with only a single stop for fuel. They hoped that a more efficient steam locomotive would save the steam locomotive industry.

Thus, in 1939, they introduced the latest generation in steam locomotive design, the Duplex. Pennsylvania Railroad Class S1 No. 6100, was unlike anything ever witnessed before. It was a streamlined monster with a 6-4-4-6 wheel arrangement. Like the *George H. Emerson*, it had two complete sets of cylinders and running gear, but all faced forward. Its drivers were enormous—84 inches in diameter. The locomotive with tender was 140 feet long wrapped in futuristic streamlined shrouds designed by Raymond Loewy. The S1 6-4-4-6 weighed 608,170 pounds and cost more than a dollar per pound. Total cost for the S1 was $670,000—a lot of money for one locomotive in 1939.

The locomotive had impressive characteristics: a vast Belpaire firebox with 132 feet of grate area, and a boiler that operated at 300 psi, which gave it tremendous steam potential. It could develop more than 71,000 pounds tractive effort. At speed its potential was never fully tested, but it could easily haul a heavy passenger train at 100 miles per hour. Despite its awesome appearance and formidable power potential, the colossal S1 Duplex was an enormous flop.

The railroad and the builders experienced a serious lapse in judgment in its construction and operation. No doubt it suffered from one of the same faults as other "must do" committee projects—too many cooks. Among its more serious flaws was its size. In designing the S1, the builders disregarded a basic premise of successful locomotive design: the locomotive must be able to operate over existing tracks. The S1 was restricted from operation on the PRR east of Pittsburgh because of curvature and it was ultimately limited to service between Crestline, Ohio, and Chicago. It appears that no one in the design department bothered to discuss the S1 with anyone in the operating department until after the locomotive was ready to roll. Another flaw with the S1 Duplex was that it required an inordinate amount of maintenance. Perhaps PRR had been so awed by the

In 1937 the Baltimore & Ohio built the first American Duplex type, a 4-4-4-4 experimental locomotive named *George H. Emerson* after its designer. As with other B&O experimentals, the Duplex featured a water-tube firebox and distinctly British styling. The rear two sets of drivers are powered by rear-facing cylinders located below the firebox, a design that proved troublesome. The unique locomotive is seen in Baltimore on October 10, 1937. *Bruce Fales, Jay Williams collection*

For a few years, Pennsylvania Railroad's T1 Duplexes hauled long-distance passenger trains—as they were intended—between Harrisburg and points west, including Chicago and St. Louis, Missouri. Unfortunately for the T1, Electro-Motive E7 passenger diesels proved to be more reliable and economical to operate and quickly took the premier runs. On October 15, 1947, T1 5517 leads train No. 11 past Olentangy Tower in Columbus, Ohio. *R. D. Acton, Sr, courtesy of Dave Oroszi*

Baldwin built a single turbine for the Pennsylvania Railroad in 1944. While this machine resembles a conventional reciprocating locomotive, it does not have cylinders or valve gear and was powered by a direct turbine drive. Two turbines were used, one for each direction—the forward turbine is seen above the second and third drive wheels. The sole S2 turbine, No. 6200, is seen in a heavily retouched photo, climbing around Horseshoe Curve, near Altoona, Pennsylvania. *Kaufmann & Farber, California State Railroad Museum collection*

diesel's ability to charge up Horseshoe Curve that it forgot to take notice that the diesel locomotive spent very little time in the shop.

Initially, instead of spending much time on the road, the S1 rolled away imaginary miles for two years on a test plant-style treadmill at the 1939-1940 New York World's Fair. It was advertised as the locomotive of the future and impressed millions of visitors with its gargantuan boiler and Flash Gordon styling. Meanwhile, Electro-Motive had developed its FT

freight diesel, which it barnstormed around the nation, impressing those who purchased new locomotives, and proving its merit in road service.

When the S1 finally entered regular service following the World's Fair, its flaws were revealed. What made matters worse for its sponsor, PRR, was that at the very time they should have been bolstering their roster with new practical locomotives, they had wasted time on the S1. When the surge of wartime traffic hit following the Japanese bombing of Pearl

Harbor, the PRR was caught short, as were the rest of the nation's railroads. Shortly after the United States became involved in the global conflict, its railroads were breaking new traffic records. Compounding the traffic problems were severe wartime restrictions on civilian use of rubber and gasoline, making highway travel prohibitive. Passenger travel skyrocketed, and passengers who had stopped riding trains over the past 20 years suddenly came back. As the nation's leading passenger carrier, the PRR felt the brunt of this surge.

Fortunately for Pennsy, its intensive investment in electrification had paid off and relieved some of the pressure, but the rest of the railroad was pushed to the edge of capacity. When the surge of traffic hit, the PRR needed new locomotives immediately. While it had plans on the drawing board for both freight and passenger Duplex types, none was proven and ready for service.

The War Production Board authorized the railroad to acquire 104 locomotives of an established design. This was how PRR came to own its first Superpower. It settled on the 2-10-4 design operated by the C&O and built 125 near copies of the C&O engine at its Juniata Shops between 1942 and 1944. These were conventional steam locomotives that did not employ any of the new design elements that went into the S1, yet they were exactly what the railroad needed. Pennsylvania's Texas types, Class J1 and J1a, featured 29x34-inch cylinders, 69-inch drivers, and a 122-inch firebox grate; operated at 270 psi boiler pressure; and could deliver 95,100 pounds tractive effort with their trailing truck booster (another concept PRR had generally shunned). Rather than PRR's preferred Belpaire firebox, the J Class had traditional radial-stayed fireboxes, making them peculiar among the ranks of PRR steam. Their performance was outstanding, and some locomotive historians have argued they were the best steamers PRR had ever owned. They certainly were among the last PRR steam locomotives in regular service.

BACK TO THE DRAWING BOARD

Baldwin still had faith in the Duplex concept and was prepared to build one of its own design. It could do better than the S1. And the Pennsylvania Railroad had not given up its efforts to design a more efficient steam locomotive. Even during the height of the war it pushed the concept forward. By 1942 it had learned from the mistakes of the S1 and

designed a better Duplex. The War Production Board permitted Pennsy to construct two passenger Duplex prototypes. These were Class T1, which featured a 4-4-4-4 wheel arrangement. The T1s were more digestible Duplexes, with dimensions the railroad could handle, and they quickly proved to be a vast improvement over the S1.

The T1 weighed 497,000 pounds, featured a Belpaire firebox with a 92 square foot grate, and like the S1, the boiler operated at 300 psi. Rather than conventional valves, the T1 employed rotary cam poppet valves—new valve technology still in its formative stages. Its four cylinders were 19.75x26 inches, and wheels were more conventional dimensions, just 80 inches (as opposed to 84 inches on the S1). It could produce 64,650 pounds tractive effort and was among the fastest steam locomotives ever built.

As with the S1, PRR looked to Loewy to provide the T1 with distinctive styling, and the result was a streamlined steam locomotive like no other. Loewy drafted several different designs, and the railroad ultimately settled on a "shark nose" design that embraced the Art Deco themes of the period. Three decorative portholes lined the sides near the pilot. Locomotive and tender were both painted PRR's "Brunswick Green"—a dark olive color. A large crimson keystone was set in the pilot, and the tender was decorated with smaller keystones and gold stripes that ran its length. The T1 was designed for speed and its unorthodox appearance conveyed this.

The Pennsylvania thoroughly tested the two prototypes, and reports indicate their performance was satisfactory. A single T1 was intended to replace two K4s Pacifics on PRR's long distance passenger trains west of Pittsburgh. They were designed for continuous 100 miles per hour operation with an 880 ton train. At 62 miles per hour a T1 could produce 6,000 drawbar horsepower. It was capable of evaporating 105,475 pounds of water every hour. Speed was the T1's forte; it could easily reach an astounding 120 miles per hour with a heavy passenger consist and on at least one occasion, one even reached 125 miles per hour. The steam locomotive had come a long way from Trevithick's *Pen-y-Darran* engine. Surely the Stephensons would have been amazed, and old Watt would have been outright horrified.

The Altoona test plant gave the prototypes glowing praise and the railroad seemed happy with the locomotive. When the war was over the railroad ordered 50 production locomotives. Half were built by Baldwin, half

A Norfolk & Western Y6 Class Mallet shoves on the rear of a coal train at Blue Ridge, Virginia, on July 31, 1958. The N&W was the last great steam show in the east and used big steam in heavy freight service through the 1950s. *Richard J. Solomon*

by Juniata Shops. In these later locomotives the styling was minimized, and the production locomotives did not have the visual finesse of the prototypes. This would have been easy to forgive if it had been the locomotive's only failing, but aesthetic difficulties were the least concern.

It is not clear whether something changed between the T1 prototypes and the production engines or if the initial assessment of locomotives had been overly optimistic, but something had clearly gone wrong. Several problems marred the T1's performance, and despite the locomotive's promise, the design is not highly regarded by critics and historians. This is unfortunate, because although the T1 is viewed by some as a failure, it could have been an exemplary locomotive if conditions surrounding its design and construction had been different.

Author Vernon Smith, in his August 1967 *Trains Magazine* article, highlighted the principle failings of the T1, all of which could have been corrected if time had permitted. The locomotive suffered from insufficient steaming capacity, attributable to its comparatively small firebox grate. Smith suggests this could have been corrected with a substantially larger firebox.

Probably the two greatest criticisms of the T1 were its poppet valves and flawed suspension, both of which were readily correctable. The poppet valves were prone to breakdowns and resulted in an inordinate amount of maintenance that severely affected the locomotive's availability. This was a particularly sensitive issue, because the T1 was competing with Electro-Motive diesel locomotives noted for comparatively low maintenance and especially high availability. Other more conventional modern steam locomotives, such as New York Central's J-3a Hudsons received high marks in availability, making the curious Duplexes particularly subject to criticism. The suspension problem caused an unequal weight distribution between the two sets of drivers, which resulted in more weight on the front set when starting up and accelerating, and caused the rear drivers to lose adhesion and slip. The effect was especially unnerving when it occurred at speed and resulted in rough train handling—a particularly unacceptable practice in the passenger business. The T1's distinctive streamlining presented a minor flaw as well; it had the propensity to direct exhaust from the stack back across the locomotive and often into the cab. This made the locomotives look abnormally dirty, and did not endear them to crews—diesels were noted for their comparative cleanliness.

The Pennsylvania also experimented with Duplexes in freight service. In 1942 PRR built a single freight duplex prototype, Class Q1. This semi-streamlined, nonconventional locomotive featured an unorthodox 4-6-4-4 wheel arrangement, where the rear engine was driven by backward-facing cylinders (in a similar arrangement to B&O's *George H. Emerson*). Although the very powerful Q1 was not successful, it led to the development of a more practical freight Duplex, the Q2. As World War II was winding to a close, the War Production Board permitted the PRR to build 26 Q2 duplexes with a 4-4-6-4 wheel arrangement. Unlike the prototype, all the cylinders on this engine faced forward. The locomotive also had

more reasonable proportions than the Q1 and provided an enormous amount of pulling power, some 115,000 pounds tractive effort with a trailing truck booster. Like the T1, however, its divided drive design and unorthodox technology led to more problems than the railroad was ultimately willing to solve.

DOOMED, THE DUPLEX DIES

The Duplex's performance capabilities were more than offset by its flaws, and in the face of growing diesel competition it did not fare well. Despite Pennsylvania's devotion to steam power, a change in management philosophy and its mounting economic woes following World War II left the railroad desperate. When the steam locomotives that were promised as the power of the future failed to live up to their expectations, the railroad took another look at the diesel-electric. The economics of diesel operation were very compelling and the PRR was no longer in a position to experiment with radical concepts to improve steam locomotive efficiency. Even as the duplexes were being delivered their fate was sealed. They were the last new steam locomotives ever delivered to the railroad, and their careers were very short.

While Pennsylvania continued to operate steam locomotives until 1957, the Q2 freight Duplexes were all out of service by 1949, and the T1s by 1953. The Duplex affair was an unusual adventure and a costly one, but ultimately a dead end. No other railroads ever adopted the Duplex and some lines remained loyal to steam longer than the PRR, notably the Norfolk & Western, which found ways to improve the efficiency of more conventional steam locomotives. Yet, by 1954, improvements in diesel-electric technology convinced N&W to make the switch, so by 1960 they too had run their last revenue steam locomotive.

Although doomed by the efficiency of diesel-electric technology, the thought of streamlined Duplexes regularly racing across the Midwest at 120 miles per hour is intriguing. One wonders how the Duplex might have developed if the diesel had never come to dominate the railroad industry.

TURBINES

Looking back at the end of the steam era, the superiority of the diesel-electric seems unquestionable, yet, at the time it was not universally accepted that the diesel-electric was the ultimate motive power solution. Historian John P. Hankey points out that in the 1930s and 1940s the motive power equation was still in flux, and those in the steam industry were desperately searching for a means to keep steam technology viable. It was this philosophy that led the PRR to develop the Duplex and to make a stab at the steam turbine.

Over a 16-year period several serious attempts were made to develop steam-turbine locomotive technology in America. The economy and efficiency offered by the diesel-electric precluded the successful application of the steam turbine on American railroads, although the Union Pacific did successfully employ a fleet of gas-turbine-electrics for more than a decade. Eventually, these too were replaced by diesels.

In 1938, General Electric built a two-unit oil-fired steam-turbine-electric for Union Pacific. Externally, this streamlined locomotive resembled diesel-electrics and straight electrics of the period. Technologically, however, it was a unique experiment that Alfred Bruce considers one of the most exceptional steam locomotives ever built. It certainly was an impressive piece of railroad equipment. Its water-tube boiler operated at extremely high temperature and pressure, an unprecedented 920 degrees F, and 1,500 psi—James Watt would have been apoplectic. The locomotive generated 5,000 horsepower and was used primarily in freight service. Although it appears to have been reasonably successful, it was never replicated and was scrapped during World War II. The wartime economy and government restrictions were unfriendly toward experimental designs and may have contributed to the locomotive's demise.

While the PRR was promoting its ill-fated Duplexes, it also experimented with a turbine. In 1944, Baldwin and Westinghouse built a geared-drive steam-turbine, PRR class S2, the only such machine ever built in North America. Except for its obvious lack of cylinders and valve gear, and a few extra pipes and boxes, this unique machine resembled a conventional reciprocating steam locomotive, complete with connecting rods. With 68-inch drivers configured in a 6-8-6 wheel arrangement, it featured a gigantic Belpaire firebox with a 120 square foot grate. The locomotive weighed 580,000 pounds and delivered 70,500 pounds tractive effort and an estimated 6,000 horsepower.

Although it was intended as dual service locomotive, it primarily operated in passenger service between Crestline, Ohio, and Chicago. It ran for only a few years and was withdrawn from service because of its high maintenance and fuel costs.

PRR never replicated the S2, but its form became familiar to thousands of children who received O-gauge and O-27 S2 turbine "third-rail electrics" from Lionel. The Pennsylvania had plans to build a steam-turbine-electric, but rising costs of coal combined with poor performance of the railroad's other radical steam locomotives and a new diesel-friendly management killed the project before it was built. The machine would have been a Loewy streamliner and classed V1.

In 1947, Appalachian coal hauler Chesapeake & Ohio picked up where the Pennsylvania Railroad had left off and ordered a coal-fired streamlined steam-turbine-electric, built by Baldwin and Westinghouse. This locomotive, C&O class M-1, weighed an unsurpassed 617 tons, and to date was the heaviest locomotive ever built. It was intended for both high-horsepower fast-passenger service and high tractive effort freight applications. It could deliver 6,000 horsepower and 98,000 pounds starting tractive effort. Chesapeake & Ohio received two more turbines in 1948, and the locomotives enjoyed a very brief stint in passenger service on the new streamlined *Chessie*, which ran between Washington and

Two Pennsylvania Railroad GG1 electrics meet at Penn Station, New York, in March 1966. The PRR was an ardent supporter of electrification. It electrified a number of its eastern routes including its heavily traveled New York to Washington line. Electrification resulted in steam surplus during the 1920s and 1930s, contributing to PRR's lack of new steam locomotives during that period. *Richard Jay Solomon*

Cincinnati. The locomotives did not perform well and all three were scrapped in 1950.

Norfolk & Western had taken an interest in turbines just as neighbor C&O abandoned the concept. In 1949, the N&W began designing a steam-turbine-electric for slow speed heavy freight service. The locomotive was built by Baldwin and Westinghouse and featured a Babock & Wilcox water-tube boiler. It was not completed until 1954, long after all the other turbines had been cut up. This lone engine was named the *Jawn Henry* after the legendary black laborer who boasted he could work faster than a steam drill and died trying to prove his strength. An apt name for the steam behemoth, which like the other turbines was retired after only a few years of service. The N&W considered buying a fleet of turbines but the cost per unit was too high.

The steam-turbine was a valid concept, but it simply could not compete with the economy of the diesel-electric and was never successfully refined into a practical locomotive. It is entirely possible that someday the steam turbine may have another chance, but until that time it remains just a strange, late era derivation of the steam locomotive.

AMERICAN STEAM TODAY

The day of the productive revenue steam locomotive in North America has long since passed. Technologically, the steam locomotive was dead by the beginning of World War II. Even the most modern, efficient steam locomotives could not match the thermal efficiency and reliability offered by the first diesel-electric road engines. Despite the loyalty of a few carriers, most railroads began ordering diesels in earnest when wartime procurement regulations eased at the end of the war.

The last commercial steam locomotives were constructed in the late 1940s, and the last railroad built locomotives in early 1950s. By the mid-1950s, most reciprocating steam locomotives were working off their final revenue miles. As shiny new diesel-electrics began hauling passengers and tonnage, many railroads stored their steam locomotives in anticipation of power shortages, largely due to Defense Department fears of a resurgence of hostilities. Long lines of dead locomotives—sans main rods and with stacks capped—were a common sight in the 1950s. The memory of locomotive power shortages in World War II, when all locomotives, including every serviceable antique and rusting relic available, were shopped and made to run again, was still on managers' minds. Many locomotives in the dead lines had not yet completed their first decade of service. It seemed wasteful to scrap something that was potentially useful and not yet paid for. In some cases, steam had one last blast. Traffic surges in the mid-1950s brought out big steam on railroads across the country before it was retired for good.

While many of the steam engines were scrapped, some conscientious railroads set aside locomotives for preservation. The Pennsylvania Railroad saved examples of the significant locomotive classes except for the most recent and most modern (they didn't save any J1s or Duplexes). For years, these historical relics were housed in the roundhouse at Northumberland, Pennsylvania. The Santa Fe likewise set aside a number of locomotives for

The morning sun glints of the builders plate for Valley Railroad's Mikado No. 40. This locomotive is serviceable in the 1990s. Today there are still many places where one can enjoy the sights and sounds of the reciprocating steam locomotive.

Southern Pacific GS-4 4449 climbs west of Worden, Oregon, at 8:20 a.m. on April 28, 1991. It is heading for Sacramento, California, to participate in Railfair 1991. This streamlined Northern is among the most popular locomotives operating today. When it runs it almost always draws a large crowd.

C hicago & North Western Ten Wheeler No. 1385 leads an excursion train past Ulrich road in North Freedom, Wisconsin, on February 17, 1996. The Mid-Continent Railway Museum is one of the best places to experience steam locomotives in the Midwest.

A view from inside the cross-tender's shack at North Freedom reveals Chicago & North Western 1385 pulling up to the water tank to take on water. Although this photograph was taken in February 1996 during Mid-Continent's annual "Snowtrain" event, it is reminiscent of railroading 70 or 80 years ago.

future display, but unlike the PRR it included several of its largest, most advanced locomotives.

Other railroads donated locomotives, large and small, to communities along their lines. This practice was more common in the Midwest and West than it was in the East, probably because most eastern towns were established before the arrival of the railroad, where in the West the arrival of the railroad brought prosperity and settlement. All along the routes of the Southern Pacific, Union Pacific, Burlington, and Soo Line are steam locomotives displayed in public parks.

Sadly, other railroads had little appreciation of history and cut up their entire steam legacy, forever depriving future generations the opportunity to see their engines. There are no surviving examples of New Haven

On a crisp, clear February 17 in 1996, C&NW No. 1385 waits at the North Freedom station for Saginaw Timber Mikado No. 2. The Mid-Continent Railway Museum is a virtual time machine; its destination, 1920.

steam locomotives—all were scrapped. Other locomotives survived the scrapper by being sold to shortlines, railroads in other countries, private individuals, or museums.

On the whole, the steam locomotive is alive and well. Hundreds of sites around the United States that have steam exhibits of one kind or another. Kalmbach publishes a 400-page book on precisely this, the *Steam Passenger Service Directory*, in which enthusiasts can find a nearly endless list of places to visit.

Throughout the 1960s, isolated steam sanctuaries kept the spirit alive. Some shortline railroads maintained steam for more than a decade after the last fires were dumped by the large lines. Into the early 1980s, Northwestern Steel & Wire at Sterling, Illinois, maintained a fleet of former Grand Trunk Western 0-8-0 switchers at its plant. The Union Pacific

never retired one of its finest engines, 4-8-4 Northern No. 844, and over the years this locomotive has continued to grace the high iron.

Surviving steam locomotives made their way to museums and tourist railroads around the nation, and through the efforts of dedicated individuals, an estimated 150 serviceable steam locomotives operate in North America today. Over 1,700 more are preserved, although often in poor condition. Reciprocating steam locomotives from virtually every stage of development can be found in operating condition. And while certain unusual types are missing—notably Duplexes and steam turbines—extant examples of most types of steam locomotives are on public display.

It's true, one can no longer witness a New York Central Niagara race along the shores of the Hudson with a part of the Great Steel Fleet in tow; experience multiple Southern Pacific cab-forward articulateds spotted at

Union Pacific regularly operates its last Northern type No. 844 in excursion service around its vast railroad system. On June 22, 1997, 844 and the railroad's historic Electro-Motive E8s lead a sold-out excursion over Tennessee Pass, near Leadville, Colorado. This scenic line was scheduled for closure as a through route by the end of 1997. The last through freight operated in mid-August. *John Gruber*

Occasionally, when it is not being used in excursion service and the railroad needs to move the locomotive, Union Pacific will operate its 844 Northern type in freight service. In September 1989, 844 hauls a westbound freight over Archer Hill in eastern Wyoming.

several places in a heavy eastbound fruit block thundering over Donner Pass; or listen to a Norfolk & Western Y6b Mallet bring a loaded coal train up to Blue Ridge.

These magnificent sights and sounds are gone, but steam still lives in many forms and places, and the experience it lends is part of our American heritage. We can still enjoy the sights, sounds, and smells of the American steam locomotive in action. It's just a matter of where and when to look!

NORTH FREEDOM WISCONSIN: TURN-OF-THE-CENTURY WONDERLAND

Located near the village of North Freedom, in south central Wisconsin, is the Mid-Continent Railway Museum. Here one can enjoy a turn-of-the-century railroad experience—Midwestern style!

On a warm summer afternoon at the rural Ulrich Road grade crossing, amid stalks of budding corn, a distant whistle sounds. It's Chicago & North Western 1385, an Alco-built Ten Wheeler, with a short passenger train. The locomotive whistles off, two long blasts; the engineer puts the reverse lever in forward motion, releases the brakes, and opens the throttle. With a hiss the train begins to move and march out of the depot. Soon it is climbing the short grade up to the crossing of Ulrich road. As it approaches, the sound becomes more intense.

The sound of 1385's exhausts reverberates as it approaches the crossing, and before the train itself can be seen, a tell-tale sign of steam and smoke gives its location away. Then the locomotive rounds the curve and whistles for the crossing, two long blasts, a short, and then another long. The bell rings, the drivers pound, and the locomotive rolls across the coun-

On December 27, 1991, Santa Fe 3751 rolls through Pico Rivera, California. A steam locomotive surrounded by modern freeways is a seemingly incongruous scene. Yet, in the 40 years since the demise of the steam locomotive, America has changed considerably, and the places where this locomotive once ran would now be nearly unrecognizable to the crews who ran it years ago. *James A. Speaker*

On a frigid July 6 in 1996, Duluth & Northern Minnesota No. 14, a Baldwin-built Mikado, backs out of the station in Duluth for its run up to Two Harbors. The North Shore Scenic Railroad regularly operates summer trips along the north shore of Lake Superior with this Mikado.

try road followed by four vintage steel cars. Soon all that remains are cinders from the stack, as the sound of the handsome Ten Wheeler fades away.

This scene was repeated thousands of times each day all across the Midwest in the early part of the century, and it is still repeated again and again today.

PURITY IN PENNSYLVANIA

On a misty autumn morning in Rockhill Furnace, Pennsylvania, the engine crew prepares Baldwin Mikado number 15 for its daily chores. In the eight-stall stone roundhouse are five more similar locomotives, two of which have not turned a wheel in 40 years. It may as well be the stage set for an Appalachian *Brigadoon*.

As the pressure rises in No. 15's boiler, the familiar smell of high-sulfur bituminous coal permeates the fog. This coal was once the life blood of the line, but today it's little more than fuel for the engine. Outside the roundhouse is a string of wooden passenger cars; nearby is a handsome two-story depot. Except for a few minor details, this scene could be 1955, or even 1935.

It's the three-foot gauge East Broad Top, a little railroad built primarily to haul coal and iron ore out of the Broad Top mountains in central Pennsylvania. It operated as a freight hauler until 1956, but today it is a tourist railroad. All around the yard are the rusting hulks of coal hoppers that once carried coal from the mountains to the connection with the Pennsylvania Railroad at Mount Union, just a few miles north of Rockhill Furnace.

While most of the East Broad Top is in place, only a few miles of track are still used. To the south of the Rockhill Furnace yard the tracks disappear into the trees. Yet the rails are there; they continue up the mountain toward the mines. Up in the hills, two tunnels lie abandoned, and between the rails 40-foot-tall trees sun their leaves. Forty years have passed since East Broad Top's faithful Mikados hauled loads of coal from the mines at Robertsdale.

At Rockhill Furnace, the Iron Horse still lives and breathes, although for no other purpose than to entertain the public. It's a tenuous situation that probably cannot continue unaided forever—East Broad Top is a privately owned railroad and not a museum. The family that owns the line has limited resources.

One of East Broad Top's greatest attractions is its historical purity. It is among the most definitive steam experiences in the United States. Around the roundhouse are East Broad Top's shop buildings, much the way they were in 1956 when the railroad closed. In the yard are three-foot gauge stub switches of the sort used in the nineteenth century.

This morning there is a minor problem with No. 15. The engine crew confer with the shop forces, and after a little work the problem is solved. Soon the pressure is up and the little Mikado ready to go. As the sun burns away the last of the mist, the engine crew releases steam into No. 15's cylinders; it rolls out of the roundhouse and onto the turntable. This turntable is of the "Armstrong" variety, meaning that manpower is required to turn it. Several able-bodied individuals grip the sweeps and rotate No. 15 clockwise. Then with a cloud of steam she rolls off the table, past the shops and into the morning sun. Soon she is watered and tied onto her train.

On weekends, between Memorial Day and mid-October, East Broad Top runs three round trips for the benefit of passengers. While lots of railroads offer train rides, few can match the authentic experience of East Broad Top. The scenery is pristine and uncluttered, and few modern edifices taint the scene. Almost everything looks as it has for decades. The locomotive and passenger cars are the same that East Broad Top used to run on its passenger train years ago. East Broad Top's Autumn Spectacular is the annual season finale where, for two days, the railroad brings out all of its active locomotives and runs a full schedule of freight and passenger trains. It happens only once a year, but it's a bit of the past rarely seen in the modern world.

ROCKY MOUNTAIN REFUGE

Portions of Rio Grande's once vast three-foot gauge empire in Colorado and New Mexico were among the last regular steam operations in the United States. Here steam survived into the late 1960s, and unlike other places in the United States, it was not the diesel locomotive that ultimately ended the last of the narrow gauge steam, but the paved highway that doomed the existence of the railroad itself. After Rio Grande discontinued its revenue freight in 1968, two long segments of track were preserved. Today the especially scenic Chama to Antonito line, over the 10,015-foot Cumbres Pass, is jointly owned by Colorado and New Mexico and operated by the Cumbres & Toltec Scenic Railway. It is a national historic site. (The other segment, the Silverton Line, is documented below.)

Chama, New Mexico, is the western counterpart of Rockhill Furnace. It is an old-time railroad town that retains more charm than most railroad museums could ever hope to recreate. Today it is the base of the Cumbres & Toltec Scenic Railroad, which operates the 64-mile narrow gauge line over the Cumbres Pass to Antonito, Colorado.

The engine house, servicing facilities, railroad yard, and depot at Chama look much the way they did 50 years ago, yet it is not a museum but part of a real working railroad. Granted it is a railroad with the sole purpose of carrying tourists and railfans over Cumbres Pass, but it is authentic and unspoiled. Six former Denver & Rio Grande Western 2-8-2 Mikados are maintained here. All were built by Baldwin. Four are Class K36, one is a K37 that was converted to narrow gauge from a standard gauge locomotive, and one is a diminutive K27 known as a "Mudhen."

Only two or three locomotives are required to haul the normal summer excursion schedule; however, the railroad also runs charter excursions and "photo freight trains" for the benefit of enthusiasts. As a result one might find as many as five of C&TS's vintage Mikados under steam simultaneously.

In addition to the locomotives, Cumbres & Toltec also hosts a steam-powered Leslie Rotary Snow Plow for the explicit purpose of clearing Cumbres Pass in the spring. Most years around the first week of May the railroad fires up the rotary and clears the pass from the heavy winter snow in preparation for the summer season. The extreme elevation of Cumbres Pass can result in very deep snow, and the rotary's performance can be spectacular. The clearing of the pass has become a real event for which the railroad sells tickets.

There may be no better time warp than to stand at Chama on a clear summer morning. As the dew burns off the grass and rails, the locomotives are prepared for the morning run. Fires are built, the pressure is brought up, ashes are dumped in the ash pit and the grates shaken down, the boilers are blown down to rid them of mineral impurities; then finally, one at a time, the engines steam up to the water tank and "take on" water. This is the sort of ritual that once took place at hundreds of small town engine terminals all across America, and between May and October it is still a daily event at Chama, New Mexico.

Once the engines are ready to go, the real show begins. The railroad to Antonito is a 64-mile, steep, tortuous path, without peer in the United States. The climb from Chama to Cumbres Pass encompasses a long, grueling, 4 percent grade that extracts every bit of tractive effort the three-foot gauge Mikados can muster. To reach the summit, the trains work, and they work hard. This ensures lots of steam and smoke. Barring the once a year rotary trip, the only trains more impressive than the Cumbres & Toltec daily passenger run are the chartered freights, which are often double-headed up the pass. This is a show not to be missed. The ride over the pass is fantastic: once the train crests Cumbres it begins a long, winding, downhill journey into the Toltec Gorge. At Osier the train from Chama meets the train from Antonito.

urango & Silverton Narrow Gauge Railroad No. 478, a former Denver & Rio Grande Western three-foot gauge Class K28 Mikado built by Alco in 1923, brings a passenger excursion up the Animus River Canyon toward Silverton, Colorado, in August 1991. The D&S operates as many as five daily trips along the former Rio Grande narrow gauge line between its namesake points.

On May 17, 1991, Southern Pacific 4449 with its *Daylight* consist rolls east along San Pablo Bay toward Sacramento at Pinole, California. Southern Pacific operated a fleet of streamlined Lima-built Northerns painted in its distinctive red, orange, silver, and black scheme on its *Daylight* passenger trains. As a result the paint scheme and the locomotives have both come to be known as *Daylights*.

The California Western Railroad operates passenger excursions in northern California between Fort Bragg and Willits. Some excursions are steam powered, while others use diesels or gas-electric cars. On May 13, 1990, CWR Mikado No. 45 leads Alco RS-11 No. 62 on a railfan excursion near the railroad's summit. No. 45 was built by Baldwin in 1924 for the Owen-Oregon lumber company. *James A. Speaker*

The locomotives continue on, but the train consists return to their respective terminals, allowing passengers a variety of trip options and ensuring both locomotives will receive proper servicing.

The Cumbres & Toltec is a national treasure, and without a doubt one of the best places to experience steam locomotives in North America. The six Mikados and rotary plow are indigenous to the Rio Grande and belong on the rails they work. Unlike other tourist lines and museums, which must make do with less, the Cumbres & Toltec offers an aura of authenticity and class without comparison.

STEAM ALONG THE ANIMAS CANYON

Only a couple of hours from Chama is another scenic remnant of the Rio Grande three-foot gauge empire, the Durango & Silverton Narrow Gauge Railroad. While not as pristine an experience as the Cumbres & Toltec, the

Durango & Silverton offers one the opportunity to see steam locomotives in action in a splendid mountain setting. The ride through the Animus Canyon (in Spanish it is Rio de Las Animas Perdidos, meaning the "River of Lost Souls") to Silverton is among the most spectacular in Colorado, and the steam trains that operate here are representative of the sort Rio Grande once employed on the route. The D&S has nine locomotives, three each of Classes K28, K36, and K37. The K28s are 1923 products of Alco's Schenectady works. Unlike the C&TS, which runs only one round trip daily, the D&S operates as many as five trips a day.

STEAM IN CONNECTICUT

Along the Connecticut River in southeastern Connecticut, the Valley Railroad operates a steam tourist train that captures the flavor of passenger railroading in the 1920s. The railroad operates two locomotives: No. 40, a handsome

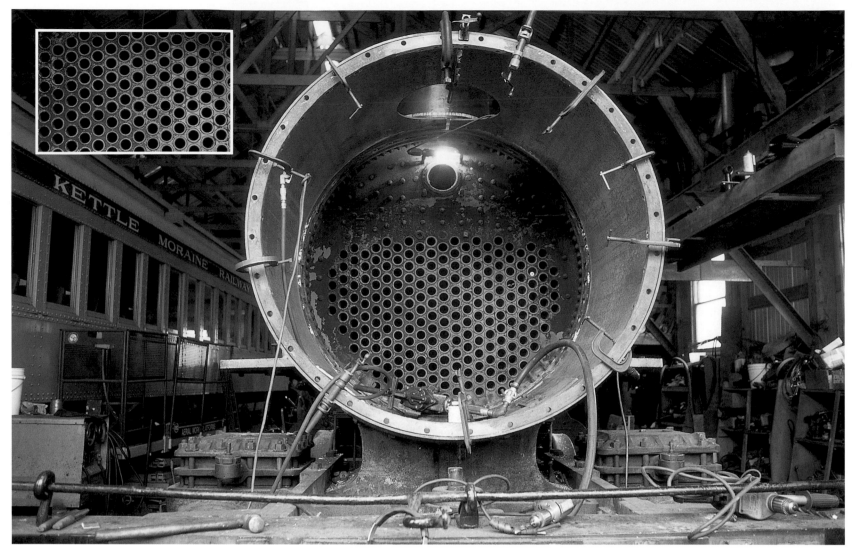

In the winter of 1995-1996, the Kettle Moraine Railway located at North Lake, Wisconsin, worked on its 2-6-2 Prairie type No. 9. The smokebox has been opened to reveal the fire tubes in the boiler. Steam locomotives require a great deal of heavy maintenance to operate safely. It's no wonder railroads abandoned steam engines for locomotives that required less heavy work.

Mikado built in 1920 by Alco's Brooks Works for the Portland, Astoria & Pacific Railroad in Oregon (later worked for the Aberdine & Rockfish as its No. 40), and No. 97, a Consolidation type built in 1923 by Alco's Cooke Works on speculation as a stock locomotive and purchased by the Birmingham & Southeastern Railroad in Alabama where it served as No. 200. Several other locomotives are displayed.

The center of operations on the Valley is the depot at Essex—an old New Haven Railroad freight station dressed up as passenger depot—where, in season, several scheduled trains a day begin their journey up the Connecticut Valley. Riding the steam-powered train as it ambles along the west shore of the river, one gets the sensation of branch-line train travel before the advent of modern equipment and diesel locomotives. The syncopated sound of the steam exhaust, long lonesome whistles, a clatter of steel wheels on jointed rail, and the gentle rocking of the steel coaches from side to side are all elements

of travel from a more relaxed time. Valley's steamers deserve more than a passing glance. These are not wheezing teakettles but immaculately maintained machines—truly gems of another age.

CHINESE MIKADO AMONG THE CORNFIELDS

Observing steam locomotives today we think of them as romantic antiques, technological remnants, and just outright old. In most cases the assessment is on target. However, in central Iowa we can find a handsome Mikado that is just now approaching its tenth birthday.

The Boone and Scenic Valley operates a steam-powered passenger train, not with an old restored steam locomotive, but with one they bought brand new in 1989. While Baldwin, Lima, and Alco had all stopped building steam locomotives nearly 50 years ago, China's Datong works continued to build new steam locomotives until the late 1980s. Today China is one of the last places in the world where one can still find big-time steam operations. While steam locomotives in China still run in regular service, they, too, run on borrowed time. The economies of diesel operation have finally caught up with Chinese railway practice, and the last production steam locomotive from Datong was locomotive JS8419 built in 1988 and sold to the Boone & Scenic Valley.

On inspecting JS8419 one will find that it is indeed new; while much of the equipment follows traditional designs, it does not have the scars exhibited by locomotives with many years of service. This locomotive never sat in scrap line or in a park, and it shows. There is no doubt of the locomotive's heritage either; Boone makes no effort to disguise the Mikado, but chooses to show it off for what it is. The locomotive is highly decorated with red and yellow trappings, displaying distinctive Chinese characters. Its driver centers are painted red, its smoke stack, clearly of a Chinese design, proudly displays two flags, one Chinese and one American. In the cab, the engineer sits where one expects to find the fireman and vice versa; the locomotive is set up for left-hand running. The arrangement of the steam valves in the cab may seem unorthodox compared to traditional American practice. Rather than a nearly random scattering of knobs there is a more orderly arrangement of equipment, all properly labeled, in Chinese. The locomotive is capable of moving heavy freight trains at speeds up to 40 miles per hour and is equipped with an mechanical stoker. Boone rarely needs to operate its relatively light passenger trains faster than 15 miles per hour, and it does not traverse any substantial grades, so it rarely uses the stoker. The valve gear is basically a standard Walschaerts arrangement, but the valves are a Russian design.

Regardless of its international peculiarities, Boone's Chinese Mikado is a sight to behold and it makes all the right sounds. The most spectacular aspect of the railroad's modern steam operation is the boiler blow down procedure. Water in central Iowa is not of the purest variety. So, in the morning after the fire has been kindled, the boiler pressure brought up, and the rods and valve gear lubricated, the crew backs the locomotive a mile up the line west of Boone to a tall trestle. Here the crew blows down the boiler to remove sediment and mineral deposits. This is done by directing boiler water through special valves that angle outward to send the water away from the engine. The visually gripping procedure lasts for several minutes.

With this accomplished, the locomotive rolls into Boone to begin the day's trips. On summer weekends, the railroad will operate three 14-mile round trips on its scenic line along the Des Moines River Valley. While Boone's Mikado is not the only new Chinese steam locomotive in the United States, it is the largest and most impressive. It is also probably the last locomotive ever to roll off a regular assembly line.

Northern Parade

Steam is not just relegated to museums and tourist lines. In recent years a number of steam locomotives have ventured out on North American main lines in various capacities, and thankfully, we still have the opportunity to watch late era steam locomotives in action. Most museum locomotives are relatively small as a matter of practicality. Museums do not have the need or facilities to operate anything much bigger than a Mikado type. Large loco-

motives require more substantial track and structures, and greater amounts of fuel. Also "big" modern steam was built to operate at high speeds with heavy tonnage, and museum and tourist lines today rarely operate heavy trains and usually plod along at only 15 to 20 miles per hour.

While the main line has changed greatly since the days of steam, it is still one of the best places to experience "big steam" at work. In recent years a number of modern super-powered locomotives have graced the American high iron. Several 2-8-4 Berkshires have seen main-line service in last decade, including Nickel Plate 765, one of Lima's best and last locomotives. Two articulateds have run: Norfolk & Western A Class 1218, and Union Pacific Challenger 3985. (While 1218 has been retired from active service, Union Pacific 3985 is slated for an expensive rehabilitation and may run again.) However, the most common type of modern steam locomotive on the main line today is appropriately the 4-8-4 Northern type. Several Northerns are serviceable in the United States today, and they make appearances from time to time, usually in excursion service.

Union Pacific 844

Union Pacific 844 was built by Alco in 1944. It was the last Northern built for the railroad, and today it is the railroad's last operating 4-8-4. It was *never* retired from the roster—giving it a rare distinction among the legions of American steam locomotives—and has been serviceable nearly every year since it rolled out of the plant at Schenectady more than 50 years ago. This fine locomotive is owned and operated by the railroad for which it was built, and it has roamed far and wide on the ever-growing Union Pacific system. It is often assigned to seasonal excursion runs, where it hauls a matched train of Union Pacific's streamlined passenger cars, creating a scene right out of the late 1940s or early 1950s.

The locomotive has participated in a number of well-publicized runs. It ran over the former Western Pacific in 1991 on the way to the California State Railroad Museum's Railfare '91. In 1984 it went to the New Orleans World's Fair where it crossed the colossal Huey P. Long bridge over the Mississippi River. In 1989 the 844 went to Los Angeles to participate in the 50th Anniversary of Los Angeles Union Passenger Terminal.

Recent years have seen a great consolidation of the American railroad network as different companies have merged to form new, large systems. Union Pacific is one of the few traditional surviving names. In 1995, Union Pacific purchased its long-time affiliate, Chicago & North Western, and in 1996, 844 rolled triumphantly into Chicago over the old C&NW main line.

While 844 is normally used in passenger excursion service, on rare occasion it has had the opportunity to haul freight, too. Main-line steam-powered freight in the 1980s and 1990s? Yes indeed. Periodically between passenger assignments, Union Pacific will put its last Northern type to work hauling freight. This is usually done when the locomotive needs to be moved, and it is not with an excursion consist. It's a flash out of the past to see old UP 844 under steam, racing along the Union Pacific main line adjacent to US Highway 30 in central Nebraska with 15 or 20 freight cars in tow.

Milwaukee Road 4-8-4 No. 261 is owned by National Railroad Museum in Green Bay, Wisconsin, and operated by the North Star Rail Corporation. It is one of several serviceable Northern types in the United States today and usually operates on several main-line excursions every year.

Boone & Scenic Valley No. JS8419 undergoing its morning blow down procedure on the high trestle west of Boone, Iowa. This Chinese Mikado type was the last steam locomotive in the world to roll off a regular assembly line. It was sold to the Boone & Scenic Valley in 1988. In the summer the Boone & Scenic Valley runs weekend trips with the locomotive on its former interurban trackage along the Des Moines River in central Iowa.

Few sights are as compelling as a working steam locomotive. A child gets his first look at a real live steam locomotive; Boone & Scenic Valley JS8419.

SOUTHERN PACIFIC 4449

There was a time when Union Pacific's 844—then numbered 8444 to avoid conflict with an Electro-Motive diesel on the roster—was the only serviceable 4-8-4 in the nation. But today it has a number of kin. The city of Portland, Oregon, holds title to two magnificent Northern types; Spokane, Portland & Seattle Class E-1 No. 700 and Southern Pacific *Daylight* Class GS-4 No. 4449. Both locomotives make public appearances from time to time.

For 20 years 4449 was displayed in a Portland park in sad shape. But it was restored to service in the mid-1970s and steamed around the nation in a red, white, and blue paint scheme hauling the American Freedom Train. It was restored to its proper appearance, a stunning red, orange, black, and silver—which it wore in Southern Pacific's *Daylight* service—in time for the 1981 Sacramento Railfair.

While the GS-4 does not run often, when it steams it is one of the most awesome sights in all of railroadom. It normally hauls a set of matched *Daylight* passenger cars, and save for a few minor details, looks the way a Southern Pacific passenger train of the mid-1940s would have looked. To see 4449 sail across the tall curved trestle at Redding, California, or race along California's San Pablo Bay at Pinole, with its matched train in tow, is candy to the eyes. It does not get much better than that.

NORTHERNS WEST AND EAST

One of the very first 4-8-4s, and *the* first of that type built by Baldwin, is Santa Fe 3751. The locomotive had been displayed in San Bernardino, California, for many years. In the early 1990s it was restored to service and since then has made a few trips out on the main line; however, it has not had the opportunity to run in recent years.

The West does not have an exclusive monopoly on 4-8-4s. The Minneapolis-based North Star Rail Corporation in cooperation with The Friends of the 261 regularly operates former Milwaukee Road Class S-3 No. 261 in excursion service. This modern locomotive was built by Alco in 1944 as part of an order of 10, designed to help the railroad carry a growing volume of wartime traffic. It was a static display for many years at the National Railroad Museum in Green Bay, Wisconsin. In the early 1990s it was leased and restored by North Star. Since its restoration it has made a number of trips in the Midwest and eastern United States It has recently been an attraction at Galesburg, Illinois, for the town's Railroad Days festival. Between 1994 and 1996 No. 261 entertained thousands at Steamtown in Scranton, Pennsylvania.

A fireman's job is to maintain the fire aboard the locomotive. which can require shoveling a fair quantity of coal on a coal burning locomotive. Although Boone & Scenic Valley's Chinese Mikado has a mechanical stoker, it is rarely used because the trains it hauls are relatively light, and there are no challenging grades on the line.

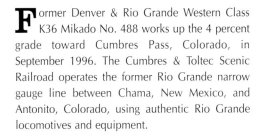

Former Denver & Rio Grande Western Class K36 Mikado No. 488 works up the 4 percent grade toward Cumbres Pass, Colorado, in September 1996. The Cumbres & Toltec Scenic Railroad operates the former Rio Grande narrow gauge line between Chama, New Mexico, and Antonito, Colorado, using authentic Rio Grande locomotives and equipment.

Other serviceable 4-8-4s in the east are several Reading Class T-1s , and a C&O 614 (properly known as a Greenbrier rather than a Northern). These locomotives are serviceable and make trips from time to time. Chesapeake & Ohio 614 makes periodic excursion trips, usually on New Jersey Transit lines in suburban New York City. In recent years the 614 has run seasonal scheduled round trips, often in the spring and fall, between Hoboken Terminal and Port Jervis, New York. The locomotive can haul a 22-car passenger train without straining, and it puts on a tremendous show. At Port Jervis the whole town comes out to the see the big engine, which is paraded through on high-speed "run bys" for the sole benefit of onlookers. However, the highlight of 614's run is the crossing of the gargantuan Moodna Viaduct—a tall steel trestle 3/4 of a mile long. The huge locomotive is dwarfed by the vastness of the bridge. Watching this Lima-built Greenbriar roll across Moodna or marching through Port Jervis with a full head of steam will make believers out of the most ardent supporters of internal combustion power.

On the evening of September 6, 1996, Cumbres & Toltec No. 487 rolls into Chama, New Mexico, with the passenger train from Antonito, Colorado. Save for a few minor details, Chama, New Mexico, retains the flavor and character of a railroad town in steam days. From the smell of coal smoke, to the sights and sounds of traditional railroading, Chama is worth experiencing.

Chama, New Mexico, is the base of operations for the Cumbres & Toltec Scenic Railroad and one of the best places to experience steam locomotives in action. In the 1990s it is one of the few places one can witness four or five live steam locomotives. On September 7, 1996, Baldwin-built K36 No. 488 is prepared for its daily run over Cumbres Pass.

LET THE GOOD TIMES ROLL!

So, while steam may have faded from the rails 50 years ago as a choice prime mover, we still have the opportunity to witness steam in action. Where once it was a common daily activity, today it is a privilege to watch a steam locomotive hard at work. It is a privilege that we should take advantage of because good things do not last forever. Steam locomotives require an extraordinary amount of maintenance, and even the best kept engines periodically require major repairs. The politics of steam are tricky and unpredictable as well. Despite the nearly universal appeal of the steam locomotive, for a variety of reasons there are people who would pre-

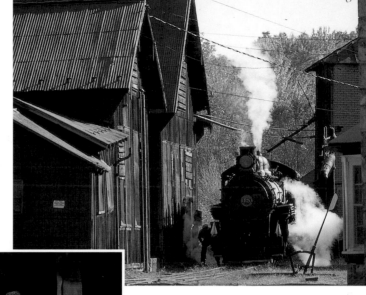

The East Broad Top is an unspoiled paradise for watching a working steam railroad. Although it now hauls only excursion trains, much of the East Broad Top is comparatively unchanged from the days of revenue freight more than 40 years ago. On a crisp September morning in 1996, East Broad Top No. 15, a three-foot gauge Baldwin Mikado built for the line in 1914, leads an excursion north of Orbisonia, Pennsylvania.

Fireman's shovel on East Broad Top No. 15. A tell-tale wisp of smoke reveals this locomotive is not a static museum piece but an active locomotive. Indeed, the East Broad Top is not a museum but a privately owned tourist railroad.

One of the attractions to East Broad Top are its vintage shop buildings at Rockhill Furnace, Pennsylvania. This is one of the few examples of a small town steam-era shop facility remaining in America. East Broad Top No. 15 rolls past the shops on its way to the roundhouse after its run.

fer not to have them in their way on the railroad. More than one excursion engine has been returned to static display after hauling thousands of devoted enthusiasts. A few have even been cut up, long after their brethren met the scrapper's torch.

A FUTURE FOR STEAM?

The long-term dynamics of our fuel oil supply are uncertain. Although internal combustion engines currently provide the most cost-efficient solution for America's transportation needs—and the high efficiency of the diesel-electric locomotive is proven technology—if the cost of oil were to rise dramatically because of serious change in supply, the economies of internal combustion may no longer be cost effective. The United States has enormous coal reserves, reportedly enough coal to satisfy our energy needs for hundreds of years. If the cost of oil were to rise to a point where it was no longer cost competitive with coal, it is conceivable, albeit a remote possibility, that the steam locomotive could again become practical in one form or another.

If the steam locomotive were once again to become a practical railroad prime mover it would most likely be in the form of a steam-turbine-electric, such as those C&O and Norfolk & Western experimented with at the end of the steam era. Yet it is possible, however improbable, that the reciprocating steam locomotive may again roll the rails. This may seem far-fetched, but in the early 1980s concerns about the rising cost of crude oil spurred renewed interest and research on conventional reciprocating steam locomotives. For about a month, a Chesapeake & Ohio 4-8-4 614 was tested in coal service in West Virginia in preparation for further steam locomotive development. The cost of oil stabilized, and the research was discontinued, but the interest was there, and it may be again.

In the meantime, the internal combustion engine will rule the American railroad, and steam will remain just pure nostalgia.

Valley Railroad No. 40, a Mikado built by Alco in 1920 for Portland, Astoria & Pacific, hauls an excursion train up the Connecticut River Valley north of Essex, Connecticut, in October 1996.

East Broad Top No. 15 brings its train to the Orbisonia depot. In the background are East Broad Top's vintage steam era shop facilities. The railroad owns six three-foot gauge Baldwin Mikados. Four are serviceable, two have not turned a wheel in many years. A seventh locomotive, a standard gauge 0-6-0 switcher, is stored in a shed at Mount Union, Pennsylvania.

On a sunny October morning, Valley Railroad No. 40 runs around its train at Deep River, Connecticut, for its run back to Essex. The Valley's line was once part of the New Haven Railroad line between Middletown and Old Saybrook, Connecticut. While most of the line is intact, only a few miles are currently active.

BIBLIOGRAPHY

Alexander, Edwin P. *Iron Horses*. New York, NY: , 1941.

Alexander, Edwin P. *American Locomotives*. New York, NY: , 1950.

Ball, Don, Jr. *The Pennsylvania Railroad 1940s–1950s*. Chester, VT: , 1986.

Beebe, Lucius, and Charles Clegg. *Hear the Train Blow*. New York, NY: , 1952.

Best, Gerald M. *Snowplow: Clearing Mountain Rails*. Berkeley, CA: , 1966.

Bruce, Alfred W. *The Steam Locomotive in America*. New York, NY: , 1952.

Bush, Donald, J. *The Streamlined Decade*. New York, NY: , 1975.

Comstock, Henry B. *The Iron Horse*. New York, NY: , 1971.

Conrad, J. David. *The Steam Locomotive Directory of North America*. Vols. 1 & 2. Polo, IL: , 1988

Drury, George H. *Guide to North American Steam Locomotives*. Waukesha, WI: , 1993.

Dunscomb, Guy, L. *A Century of Southern Pacific Steam Locomotives*. Modesto, CA: , 1963.

Forney, M. N. *Catechism of the Locomotive*. New York, NY: , 1876.

Keilty, Edmund. *Interurbans without Wires*. Glendale, CA: , 1979.

Kratville, William, and Harold E. Ranks. *Motive Power of the Union Pacific*. Omaha, NB: , 1958.

Lewis, Oscar. *The Big Four*. New York: , 1938.

Morgan, David P. *Steam's Finest Hour*. Milwaukee, WI: , 1959.

Morgan, David P. *Locomotive 4501*. Milwaukee, WI: , 1968.

Pinkepank, Jerry A. *The Second Diesel Spotter's Guide*. Milwaukee, WI: , 1973.

Ransome-Wallis, P. *World Railway Locomotives*. New York, NY: , 1959.

Reagan, H. C., Jr. *Locomotive Mechanism and Engineering*. New York, NY: , 1894.

Signor, John R. *Rails in the Shadow of Mt. Shasta*. San Diego, CA: , 1982.

Sinclair, Angus. *Development of the Locomotive Engine*. New York, NY: , 1907.

Smith, Warren L. *Berkshire Days on the Boston & Albany*. New York, NY: , 1982.

Staufer, Alvin F. *Steam Power of the New York Central System*. Vol. 1. Medina, OH: , 1961.

Staufer, Alvin F., Philip A. Shuster, and Eugene L. Huddleston. *C&O Power*. Carrollton, OH: , 1965.

Staufer, Alvin F., William D. Edson, and E. Thomas Harley. *Pennsy Power*. 3 vols. Medina, OH: , 1962– 1993.

Swengel, Frank M. *The American Steam Locomotive. Vol. 1: Evolution*. Davenport, IA: , 1967.

Westcott, Linn H. *Model Railroader Cyclopedia*. Vol. 1: *Steam Locomotives*. Milwaukee, WI: , 1960.

Westing, Fredrick. *Apex of the Atlantics*. Milwaukee, WI: , 1963.

Westing, Fredrick. *The Locomotives that Baldwin Built*. Seattle, WA: , 1966.

White, John H., Jr. *A History of the American Locomotive*. Toronto, Ontario, Canada: , 1968.

White, John H., Jr. *Early American Locomotives*. Toronto, Ontario, Canada: , 1972.

Ziel, Ron. *American Locomotives in Historic Photographs*. New York, NY: , 1993.

PERIODICALS

Locomotive & Railway Preservation. Pentrex Publishing, P.O. Box 379, Waukesha, WI 53187. Phone 414-542-4900.

RailNews. Pentrex Publishing, P.O. Box 379, Waukesha, WI 53187. Phone 414-542-4900.

Railway and Locomotive Historical Society Bulletin. Boston, MA (Complete address not available at this time.)

Trains. Kalmbach Publishing, P.O. Box 1612, Waukesha, WI 53187. Phone 414-796-8776.

Vintage Rails. Pentrex Publishing, P.O. Box 379, Waukesha, WI 53187. Phone 414-542-4900.

Morning in Essex, Connecticut, is much like morning at small-town depots all over America more than 50 years ago. The train crew gets ready for its run, as locomotive No. 40 simmers away. The Valley Railroad operates scheduled passenger excursions using vintage railroad equipment most of the year.

INDEX